Penguin Special
Civil Liberties in Britain

Born in 1942, Barry Cox comes from London and was educated at a local grammar school and Magdalen College, Oxford, where he graduated in English. After he graduated, he taught English for a year in a Jamaican secondary school in the West Indies. Since 1965 he has worked as a journalist – as a general reporter on the *Scotsman* in Edinburgh and on the *Sunday Telegraph*. In 1970 he went to Granada Television's well-known *World in Action* programme, initially as a journalist, then as a producer. He now runs a new current affairs programme for London Weekend Television. Barry Cox is married with four children and lives in South London.

Barry Cox

Civil Liberties
in Britain

Penguin Books

Penguin Books Ltd,
Harmondsworth, Middlesex, England
Penguin Books Inc.,
7110 Ambassador Road, Baltimore, Maryland 21207, U.S.A.
Penguin Books Australia Ltd,
Ringwood, Victoria, Australia
Penguin Books Canada Ltd,
41 Steelcase Road West, Markham, Ontario, Canada
Penguin Books (N.Z.) Ltd,
182–190 Wairau Road, Auckland 10, New Zealand

First published by Penguin Books 1975
Copyright © Barry Cox, 1975

Made and printed in Great Britain by
C. Nicholls & Company Ltd, Manchester
Set in Monotype Times

To Pam

Acknowledgements

I would like to thank the following present and past members and staff of the N.C.C.L. for their help and advice in preparing this book: Christina Birch, Martin Ennals, Yvette Gibson, Larry Grant, Patricia Hewitt, Christine Jackson, Sylvia Scaffardi and Tony Smythe.

Contents

Introduction

The British consciousness of civil liberty can perhaps be best encapsulated in the two popular assertions, 'It's a free country', and, 'I know my rights'. It is of great value that this consciousness runs so deep, but it is very fuzzy, perhaps because our liberties are so imprecise. Nowhere are they defined in a constitution, though lawyers will claim they can put together the essence of the thing from a maze of common and statute law. But even these experts do not really 'know their rights', since rights subtly and constantly change in response to a curious political economy of supply and demand.

A free country? Freedom is to be able to gather together in a room above the public bar to promote a revolution. It is for several thousand people preaching that revolution to be able to march through a city without being shot at, beaten up or arrested without cause. It is for passport-holding citizens to be able to come and go at will. It is for magazine editors to be able to publish foul-mouthed political nonsense without risk of fine or imprisonment.

Our rights are to know that the police cannot come crashing through the door at six in the morning just because they are suspicious of our politics. To know that we cannot be picked up and detained indefinitely, without a lawyer being allowed to see us. To know that we will not go to prison without being heard, and that the judge, jury and prosecution will never be the same people.

Our rights extend equally to all of us, whether we are male or female, black or white, Protestant or Catholic. They cannot be taken away by men in white coats with syringes, or by soldiers with rifles. We cannot lose our jobs because of our religious or political beliefs.

That catechism is a reasonable, though not exclusive, characterization of civil liberty in Britain. Yet in the early 1970s, only the first of those dozen tenets was absolutely true (and then only if Ulster is not considered). In 1970, Cambridge students were arrested and gaoled merely for taking part in a demonstration (again, to ignore the infinitely more serious matter of the thirteen unarmed demonstrators killed by the paratroopers in Londonderry in 1972). In 1971 and 1972, British citizens from East Africa were shuttlecocked around the world to discourage them coming to the country which issued them with passports. In 1971 the three editors of *Oz* were sent to gaol. In 1972, after the Aldershot bombing, the homes of sixty people were raided simply because they were known to hold Left-wing views. In the same year, a police inspector admitted keeping a man in the cells for a week without charging him. In 1970, more than nine out of ten cases heard by the Bootle magistrates were dealt with without a defence lawyer. In 1969, there were more than 10,000 complaints against the police, all of them investigated and judged by the police themselves: in all but 235 of them, they decided they were innocent.

In the early 1970s, we were still devising legislation to make women and Ulster Catholics as free as the rest of us. We could still in certain circumstances be forcibly drugged or electrically shocked, even if we could no longer be put away in a mental institution for forty years, to work for sixpence a week, as we could in the 1950s. Some of us could still sign twelve years of our life away at 15 by joining the Royal Navy. And in 1971–2, at least four university teachers lost their jobs apparently because they were Marxists.

Looked at like this, the prospect for the National Council for Civil Liberties was as gloomy in 1974 as it was when it was founded forty years earlier. Started by a group of liberal and radical intellectuals, lawyers, journalists and politicians, the N.C.C.L. in 1934 saw itself as defending traditional freedoms against the encroachments of a repressive government. Forty years later, supported by the same kind of people, the N.C.C.L. was just as convinced that civil liberty was in danger.*

*We should not forget that the N.C.C.L. has a certain interest in keeping us thinking we need it even more this year than last.

Such a perspective concealed an essential difference between the two periods: since the 1930s, civil liberties have become more widely available and have been more widely used. It is the continuation of a fluctuating process that has been going on for hundreds of years. The Whig ideologists of the nineteenth century were very good at tracing the development of English freedom from Saxon times while simultaneously oppressing their factory workers. Some of our liberties are indeed ancient, but only in the twentieth century have they been taken up on any scale by ordinary people. Freedom of expression, for instance, was easy to maintain when most people could not read. When information is pouring from mass media like the press, the cinema and the broadcasting services, freedom of expression is substantially different in quality – and far more threatening to those running the country. Equally, the law developed a fine neutrality in settling property disputes between rival landowners. As that impartiality had to be extended to impoverished tenants, or the unemployed, it was transformed, but creaked badly in the process. The strains to which civil liberty was subjected in the 1960s and after were the inevitable concomitants of growth.

That growth is not always a conscious process. Many civil liberty issues develop incidentally out of actions or events with quite different primary political objectives.

Those who marched in protest against unemployment in the 1930s or nuclear arms in the 1960s were not doing so to demonstrate the right to free assembly. It was the methods adopted by the police and the courts in dealing with those protesters that affected civil liberty. (The improvement in civil rights has been a conscious achievement, however, in the attack on discrimination and the attempt to provide protections for harassed and under-privileged minorities.) But what has always been deliberate has been the response of those in power to this process, when they choose whether to repress or to tolerate.* In Britain there are institutions – Parliament, the courts, the press – which can hinder the exercise of repressive executive power. Whether those institutions will be part of the process of repression itself, or will

*Those who follow Herbert Marcuse's theory of repressive tolerance will presumably feel the 'choice' is unreal.

be organized to oppose it, depends not only on those inside the institutions but on the state of public concern outside.

It is truly political societies that have the greatest civil liberties: that is societies in which conflicts of interest are recognized and permitted genuine expression in an institutionalized way. Such societies are not necessarily democracies: they can be slave-based, or aristocratic, states, in which case the freedoms are available only to a small élite, as in Periclean Athens or parts of Renaissance Italy. This was the situation in seventeenth-and eighteenth-century Britain, when most of our civil liberties were created. But as Britain developed from an aristocratic oligarchy into a liberal democracy, as more people gained more control over more areas of their lives, so the old aristocratic freedoms had to be made increasingly available to the ordinary citizens. Clearly this was not (nor is now) a process of sweetness and light, which is why the strains as the changes are made are so great; and why periods like the late 1960s, when freedoms and rights are more widely used and more aggressively asserted, are the periods when the threats to those freedoms and rights increase.

The history of civil liberty between the early 1930s and the early 1970s records the largely frustrated attempts of those in authority to slow down or even reverse this process. That they were so often frustrated must in part be to the credit of the N.C.C.L., from whose files and publications the material for this book has largely been drawn. (Where I have relied on other authorities, these are noted.) I have organized this history into four sections. The basic freedoms are association, assembly, expression and movement. These are essentially, though not exclusively, political. Freedom of association is genuinely available without qualification in mainland Britain, and therefore makes almost no appearance in this book. The restrictions suffered by the other three are described in the first part, Civil Liberty and Freedom. The second is concerned with the workings of justice: two chapters deal with the impact of the police and the courts on our liberties. A crucial test of civil rights is the extent to which society makes these available to the minorities in its midst. Britain's record in this respect is described in Part Three, with chapters on racial discrimination and oppressed groups. In the final section there is a chapter on privacy – the right to be left alone and to preserve your personal life from all the differing intrusions of authority.

Part One

Civil Liberty and Freedom

1. Freedom of Assembly

Repression in Britain is a delicate instrument. Fingered lightly by authority, it can almost convince a half-asleep audience that it is not being played at all. A heavy-handed player at the other end of the keyboard can bang out a tune that even the South Africans might envy.* Such a range requires different performers, perhaps; but the important point is that the same instrument appears adequate for all authority's needs.

This versatility derives from the haphazard quality of English law. In the area of public order, there are major common-law offences such as riotous assembly, which can lie dormant so long that learned experts will pronounce them extinct at the very moment they are about to erupt into extremely damaging activity (as in the Cambridge hotel trial in 1970). There are statutory offences such as those under the Public Order Act. There are a large number of local by-laws permitting an action in Liverpool that would be illegal in Edinburgh. There is the discretionary power available at all levels – to the police, who decide, say, on even the likelihood (rather than the fact) of a breach of the peace; to the magistrates, who can grant or withhold legal aid, detain in custody or release on bail (both powers which can be used as punishments in political cases); to the D.P.P. and the Attorney-General, who can decide exactly what legal hammer should be used to nail a dissident, or even if he should be nailed at all. This wide-ranging discretion, and the opportunity to abuse it, is there constantly. What varies is the readiness to take advantage of it. Liberty fluctuates; there is no simple progression towards greater and greater freedom. The political muscle of the

* Mr Vorster once declared he would willingly swap his 'anti-communist' powers in their entirety for Northern Ireland's Special Powers Act.

liberal element in the population at any particular moment often determines where authority will draw the line.

Freedom of assembly is a classic freedom, a *sine qua non* of any society with pretensions to openness, and is duly enshrined in many contemporary constitutions. It is a hallmark of South Africa's tyranny that a meeting of three or more Africans is of itself unlawful. But even in more democratic countries, political gatherings have differing functions, methods and purposes. To assess the quality of political tolerance at any given moment, it is first necessary to distinguish the various kinds of meeting, and the intensity of the challenge to authority that they represent.

The simplest assembly is the indoor meeting in private premises (usually a hired hall). This is such a low-level activity it scarcely warrants official interest. Needless to say it sometimes gets it, and there have been occasions in the past forty years when even this elementary right has run into difficulties. Then there is the small open-air public meeting. It has no legal status. Indeed, given the laws relating to obstruction of the highway, it is often in legal danger, but where there is a local tradition for such meetings it does not normally run into problems.

Both of these are essentially inward-looking, in that they cater for a predictable (and, in many cases, invited) audience of the converted and any wider appeal comes from reports in press or broadcasting, if they can get them. They rarely have any demonstrative function, though in the unemployment struggles of the 1930s and the nuclear disarmament campaigns of the early 1960s the small open-air gathering assumed a more aggressive stance.

Marches and mass rallies are more outgoing. Since the target is public opinion in general, numbers are often crucial to success. Both in a narrow physical sense (the traffic jams, etc.) and the wider political one, demonstrations apply much greater pressure on the authorities, and are much likelier candidates for repression. Marches have a somewhat hazy common-law status – the 'right to pass and re-pass on the highway' – and statutory limitations under the Public Order Act. And there is a privilege – which can be withdrawn – to hold mass meetings in places like Hyde Park or Trafalgar Square. Though the large-scale demonstration has established itself as a basic British 'right', the logical dilemma implicit in a demo will never be satisfactorily resolved – i.e., that the demonstrators are trying to achieve by weight of numbers what they cannot immediately achieve by the ballot box.

This contradiction becomes much more glaring, and poses a much more destructive civil liberty problem, when the pressure inherent in any demonstration changes from the incidental or intangible (that is, the abstract idea of 'protest') to something decidedly tangible – in its extreme form, the riot or insurrection. Genuine insurrectionary violence has not occurred in Britain this century. Despite their surrounding rhetoric and publicity, the big Vietnam demos of the late 1960s were, at most, quasi-insurrectionary. The fighting that can occur during a demonstration is not usually regarded as constituting a riot, and those arrested have not normally been charged with taking part in a riot, but with individual offences relating to assault or breach of the peace. The recent exceptions, like the Cambridge Garden House affair (1970) and the trial of the Mangrove Nine (1972), are notorious, and mark a deliberately heightened response by the authorities. On the other side, the deliberately provocative behaviour of some of the demonstrators in the late 60s (based on the theory that in 'repressively tolerant' states it is necessary to force the police into violence and thus demonstrate the 'true' nature of the otherwise masked repression) also damaged the hard-won concepts of liberty.

Much more positive tactics developed in the 1960s around the idea of the assembly as occupation. A lawful gathering would turn itself into a group of trespassers by taking over a particular place, which usually had an intimate connection with the point of the protest, whether it was a Whitehall street, a university hall or an empty council house. The mass sit-down, conceived by the Committee of 100 and imitated by subsequent radical groups – most notably the anti-apartheid demonstrators during the South African rugby tour of 1969–70 – was not intended to hold permanently the place taken over, but to disrupt normal activity and, if possible and if pushed that far, the machinery of the law. The student sit-ins of 1968 and after took the idea of disruption much further, since the unlawful possession was maintained until the political demands were satisfied. Even more extreme was the squat, since this was normally the preface to long-term occupation, once the victim authority had been forced to concede possession. Widely and successfully used after the Second World War, the squat was revived in 1968 to dramatize the housing problem and to secure specific changes in the housing policies of local authorities. The squats were the best controlled and most successful of all the radical direct action techniques of the 1960s, and whatever their strict illegality furnished a valuable new democratic weapon.*

Not that the illegality went unremarked or unchallenged. A powerful refrain, 'taking the law into their own hands', was raised by conservative critics of the new protest methods. Though this viewpoint rightly pointed to the weakness of street politics – that basically they are a substitute for the electoral variety – it failed to see that some electoral issues start on the street; indeed, for people without access to the established media, it is sometimes the only place to initiate a public debate. Equally the law is not an absolute once and for all but, in healthy society anyway, something which changes to fit the needs of society. The argument continues unresolved. In 1972, the new Metropolitan Police Commissioner, Robert Mark, recognized direct action as an integral part of modern democracy, at the same time that Lord Hailsham, the Lord Chancellor, was repeatedly attacking demonstrations as anti-democratic.

There is one other important type of public assembly – the trade union picket. What constitutes a legal picket has been continuously disputed since the Second World War, and on occasions during particularly bitter strikes police pressure on pickets has led to considerable disturbances.

Thus there is a spectrum of public dissent, from the ordinary meeting on private premises to the quasi-insurrectionary crowd and the direct action occupation. The intensity of repression can be gauged by the point in this spectrum at which authority

---

*The wave of factory work-ins in the early 1970s was another, and arguably even more successful, form of occupation, but they raised no civil liberty issues and belong to the history of the labour movement.

chooses to clamp down. In the 1930s, small meetings were regularly broken up; in the late 1960s, potentially violent demonstrations and widespread squatting were often permitted to continue unmolested.

As well as the restrictions deliberately imposed by authority, the accidental workings of social change can effectively erode freedom of assembly – witness the effect of traffic and building developments on traditional open-air meeting places in old city centres in the 1950s and 1960s. The work of bodies like the N.C.C.L. in the area of public order has been essentially conservative, attempting to prevent any restriction on the existing rights to free assembly; but to the extent that the pressure from liberal forces in general compels those in authority to adopt more lenient attitudes, the N.C.C.L. and its allies have also had the rather more positive rôle of extending the area of tolerance.

When the council was founded in 1934, it could foresee no such positive task. Those who gathered in the crypt of St Martins-in-the-Fields on 22 February (they included Kingsley Martin, Edith Summerskill and Claud Cockburn) came specifically to arrange for respectable observers to check police conduct during the imminent arrival of a large Hunger March in London. But they were also brought together because they shared Ronald Kidd's assessment that the government of the day was more repressive than any of its predecessors since the Napoleonic Wars, and that in this desperate situation a permanent watchdog, capable of fighting back, was vital.*

Kidd, the first general secretary of the N.C.C.L., believed that the post-war government in 1918 had been extremely reluctant

---

*The formal statement of aims of the new council were 'to assist in the maintenance of hard-won rights, especially freedom of speech, the press and assembly, from all infringements by executive or judicial authority contrary to the due process of law, or infringement by the tendency of governmental or other agencies to use their powers at the expense of the precarious liberties for which citizens of this country have fought ... the Council shall aid in advancing measures for the recovery or enlargement of these liberties.' In addition to the above names, the new council immediately attracted the public support of Nye Bevan, Jimmy Maxton, Clement Attlee, Harold Laski, Ellen Wilkinson, Ivor Jennings, E. M. Forster and H. G. Wells.

to give up the repressive powers available under the Defence of the Realm Act, and that it and its inter-war successors had passed a series of statutes aimed at recovering as many of those powers as they could. Writing in 1940, he listed the Police Act (1919), the Emergency Powers Act (1920), the Official Secrets Act (1920), the Trade Disputes Act (1927), the Northern Ireland Special Powers Acts (1922 and 1933), the Incitement to Disaffection Act (1934), the Public Order Act (1936) and the Prevention of Violence Act (1939).

'Not,' he wrote later, 'that these acts are necessarily objectionable *in toto*. Certain of them contain perfectly reasonable sections – but they are reactionary in tendency and confer greatly increased power on the police.'[1] As well as this battery of statutes, authority between the wars appeared to be rather more tolerant of Fascist activities than of their Left-wing opponents. Consequently, the civil liberty record of the 1930s reads like a battle-roll of defeats – particularly for freedom of assembly.

In the repression of what I have described as low-level activity – the small open-air gathering or the technically private indoor meeting – 1934 was something of an *annus mirabilis*. Two incidents with major civil liberty implications occurred that summer – the arrest of Mrs Duncan at Deptford and the confrontation between the Glamorgan police and local Labour activists in a public library. These had an ironic and brutal preface in the circumstances surrounding Mosley's rally at Olympia on 7 June. Those who interrupted that meeting were thrown out with such vigour that even Conservative M.P.s who witnessed what happened protested in Parliament and the press at the methods of those whom the *Daily Mail* glossed cheerfully as a 'first-class Rugby team'. A week later, the Home Secretary, Sir John Gilmour, defended the police failure to go in and protect those under attack from the Blackshirt stewards: 'The law provides that, unless the promoters of a meeting ask the police to be present in the actual meeting, they cannot go in unless they have reason to believe an actual breach of the peace is being committed.' While this evaded the particular circumstances of Olympia, where the police outside the hall had plenty of evidence of actual breaches of the peace from the battered state of those emerging from it, Gilmour accurately restated the traditional restriction on police powers of entry.

Yet two months later this very same safeguard, so clearly propounded by the Home Secretary, was lost by a police action, and the loss made permanent by the subsequent decision of the Divisional Court in *Thomas v. Sawkins*. (Permanent in that no police case has ever occurred since which has led a court to overturn that precedent.) A meeting had been called at the library in Caerau, Glamorgan on 17 August to protest against the Incitement to Disaffection Bill and to demand the dismissal of the Glamorgan Chief Constable for his part in the prosecutions of Tom Mann and Harry Pollitt for sedition. Relations between the police and the Left in South Wales were tense: the week before the Caerau meeting, one of the speakers, Alun Thomas, had twice unsuccessfully objected to the police presence at similar meetings. At Caerau a police inspector, a sergeant (Sawkins) and a constable persisted in attending the meeting despite two requests from the organizers to leave. Thomas went down to the police station, lodged a complaint, gave an assurance that there would be no breach of the peace, returned and again asked the police to leave. On their refusal, a vote was taken which overwhelmingly supported Thomas's request. Thomas then laid a hand on the inspector, clearly intending to eject him (as he was in theory entitled to do as the law of trespass was then understood); Sawkins physically intervened, and thirty policemen burst into the hall with batons drawn. Thomas made no further attempt to remove the police, but subsequently brought an action for assault against Sawkins. This was dismissed by the magistrates who said that Sawkins had not been trespassing since he apprehended that a seditious speech, incitement to violence or breach of the peace might occur. The N.C.C.L. supported Thomas's appeal against this, and briefed Stafford Cripps and Dingle Foot (one of their own legal panel) to appear for him before the Lord Chief Justice, Lord Hewart, and two of his colleagues. Hewart ignored the lack of any evidence that could reasonably suggest there would be a breach of the peace – which by the standards of Olympia that June should have prevented the police from entering the Caerau library – and went on to assert that the police had a right to enter if they believed an, undefined, 'offence' was likely to be committed. The appeal was rejected, and the manner of the rejection considerably extended the discretionary powers of the police, particularly in their preventive aspect. The police, fortunately, have rarely used this extra power, but it has never been tested since in a court action.[2]

Two weeks before the Glamorgan meeting, another meeting in the campaign against the Incitement to Disaffection Bill had been due to take place in Deptford, South London. At lunch time on 30 July, Mrs Katharine Duncan, a leading member of the National Unemployed Workers Movement, was scheduled to speak with three others at an open air meeting in a cul-de-sac opposite an unemployed training centre. Fourteen months earlier, Mrs Duncan had addressed a meeting in the same place which had led to trouble inside the centre: and the centre's superintendent warned the police about this proposed second meeting. As Mrs Duncan was about to speak, the police stopped her and suggested she moved to a site 175 yards away. She persisted; was arrested; charged with obstructing the police; and fined £2 at the magistrate's court. The N.C.C.L. sponsored her appeal, which went via quarter sessions to Lord Hewart in the divisional court – at considerable cost to the slender resources of the Council. Two lawyer M.P.s, D. N. Pritt (Labour) and Dingle Foot (Liberal), appeared for Mrs Duncan. She lost: the judges failed to see any constitutional issue at all. That the police appeared to have few grounds for reasonably apprehending a breach of the peace – their only justification for acting as they had done – did not worry them. In a Commons debate on the issue, Pritt blamed the obscure state of the law and pointed out that it gave the police wide discretionary powers (made even wider by the judges' decision) to stop ordinary meetings. Kingsley Martin's *New Statesman* elaborated the tenuous nature of the criteria for banning meetings now available to the police: they were justified 'in prohibiting any meeting at which some speaker might in their view say something which might lead someone else to say something which might lead to a disturbance somewhere else.' And an article in the *Cambridge Law Journal* pointed out that there was no longer any guarantee that a public meeting could be held anywhere in a public place – the courts had provided the police with powers no Parliament would have granted through legislation.[3]

These total defeats in such bedrock causes demonstrated both the need for the N.C.C.L. and the difficulties it faced. After all, it could be argued that if the N.C.C.L. had not been such busybodies, if they had not gone around stirring up meetings to protest against the Sedition Bill, and then made major test cases out of minor incidents at some of those meetings, Lord Hewart could never have handed down his reactionary decisions. That would have meant acquiescing, even if only temporarily, in the diminution of liberty; and it would be just as easy to argue that although English law can be stretched to such repressive limits, the fuss made discourages such stretching thereafter.

More positive justification for the new-born nuisance came from its successes, even though these were small beer compared with *Thomas v. Sawkins* and *Duncan v. Jones*. Before the 1936 Public Order Act, there was no statutory power to regulate marches outside London. Nonetheless, in the tense atmosphere of 1934, the police made several attempts to frustrate legitimate Left-wing street activity. In Manchester, a Blackshirt rally was to take place at Bellevue on 29 September, and an anti-fascist counter-demonstration was planned for the same day. This was banned by the Chief Constable.

A formidable protest lobby was put together by the N.C.C.L. It included Wells and George Lansbury, who took a carefully argued brief exposing the illegality of the police action to the Home Secretary. The march was allowed after all. An attempt by the Blackburn police to ban an anti-Fascist march in the town on Armistice Day was similarly successfully challenged. Comparable action over a Liverpool ban in October failed, however, and the police vigorously broke up the march as it was about to start. This Lancashire hotch-potch illustrates both the strength and weakness of our unwritten rights: if the pressure is strong enough, they can be secured even in unfavourable times. But if it is not, there is no Supreme Court to which you can appeal.

The other point of course is that the pressure has to be

maintained. At moments of crisis throughout the 1930s, the authorities curtailed quite elementary rights. During the Munich episode in 1938 the owners of the Albert Hall closed it for all meetings, a decision which particularly affected the League of Nations Union which had just called a rally there to protest against the betrayal of League principles. And at the same time the Chief Constable of Hull banned political meetings 'because a state of emergency exists', though the Emergency Powers Act which would have empowered such action had not in fact been invoked by the Government.

Not all these infringements were aimed at the Left. The local councils in Birmingham, Bournemouth and Oxford at various times refused their halls to the Fascists for fear of public disturbance.[4] Since the Fascist stewards seemed constantly bent on repeating their Olympia successes, one can see why the town halls took this illiberal attitude. The Oxford council, for instance, found itself in an embarrassing situation following complaints about police inactivity during a Mosley meeting in the city on 25 May 1936. The usual violent ejection of opponents took place, and provoked a scuffle, during which Frank Pakenham, a fellow of Christchurch,* was beaten up when he tried to rescue a 'diminutive undergraduate'. For all his aristocratic status, Pakenham failed to get either the police or the authorities – he personally saw the Home Secretary – to do anything about it. Hugh Dalton raised the matter in Parliament, and a group of Labour M.P.s, including Attlee, returned to the subject during the Home Office Supply vote in July. In the debate, Pritt accused the police in general of attempting to crush the ordinary expression of political views, and commented tartly on the Government's behaviour: 'They do not need the Six Acts now; they have the Metropolitan Police.'[5]† At the time they seemed

*Now Lord Longford. When we come to his Lordship's rôle in the censorship battle in the 1970s, it will be only fair to remember he had once been on the right side, and bravely so.

†Pritt was overstating his case, as usual. There were the occasional signs even in mid-thirties Britain, that the law had not completely forgotten what the police were for. In 1935, the Cambridge police were successfully prosecuted by a pacifist whose leaflets had been confiscated during an R.A.F. display at Duxford aerodrome. The judge ruled that the police had

to make no impression on Simon, the Home Secretary – indeed one result of the debate was to suggest that Parliament had precious little sovereignty over the provincial police anyway[6] – but the accumulating evidence of police indifference to the behaviour of Fascist stewards at indoor meetings, and the increasing anger at the Fascists' ability to get away with it, finally forced Simon to act. In January 1937, after a Fascist meeting at Hornsey Town Hall in which the stewards had assaulted people in the audience, as usual without police redress, there was public pressure from the N.C.C.L. for an inquiry.

Simon gave way at last, and the police were ordered to take more positive action at indoor meetings. No further 'success' for the Blackshirt stewards was reported.[7] And so, nearly three years after Olympia, scores of injuries and one disastrous court decision, the law arrived at what should have been its starting point – that the police should intervene when there is physical violence at indoor meetings.

The contrast between police and judicial attitudes to Mosley and to the Left was even more marked in large outdoor demonstrations. Up to 1934, the activities of the militant unemployed, particularly the National Unemployed Workers' Movement, attracted their most energetic attention; but, between that year and the outbreak of war, the clash between the Fascists and the Left was the major concern of authority. Despite the mutual thuggery on the streets, the worst violence in fact developed from the actions of the police rather than through direct contact between the hostile factions. The bias – and anxiety – shown by the police was reflected in Parliament, when it passed the Public Order Act in 1936. The danger for the N.C.C.L. was that circumstances combined with the inclination of most of its members to make civil liberty a partisan issue. (Vyvyan Adams, their one active Conservative M.P., was forced by his own party to resign in 1935.) Repression was, in the view of many N.C.C.L. activists, inevitable in a class system, and curable only by revolution. Such an attitude precluded any genuine attempt to exploit

---

had no reasonable grounds for anticipating a breach of the peace. The pacifist was perhaps lucky that he did not have to take his case before Lord Hewart.[8]

the vulnerability of authority. It was an attitude shared by too
many of the N.C.C.L. – though not by its general secretary,
Kidd, or liberals like Dingle Foot and Forster. Politically, it
would have been an advantage to have identified at least some
of those in power with the good old causes (as the N.C.C.L. did
manage to do in the late 1960s). Instead, they fought virtuous
battles with an air of outraged indignation which implicitly
expected defeat. Not surprisingly, defeat was too often their diet.

In this respect the Hunger March of 1934 was something of a
false dawn. One of the factors contributing to the setting-up
of the N.C.C.L. had been Kidd's attempt in the *Weekend Review*
to expose the excessive violence of the police during the first
large unemployed demonstration in London two years earlier,
when the police had used *agents provocateurs*. On the second
occasion, Kidd collected a group of Establishment observers who
went to Hyde Park to keep an eye on the behaviour of the police.
Just as the great anti-Vietnam war demonstration in October
1968 was preceded by officially-inspired scare stories in some of
the press, so the then Home Secretary, Gilmour, issued warnings
a couple of days before the marchers were due in London
advising people to keep children off the streets, and to shutter
shops and offices in case of possible bloodshed. To what extent
the well publicized presence of intellectuals of the stature of
Wells, Julian Huxley and Laski affected the conduct of the police,
it is impossible to assess; but neither Gilmour's bloodshed nor the
1932-style beatings took place this time.*

The growth of Fascist activity after 1934, however, imposed

---

*The event was not without its lighter moments. Claud Cockburn has
several times recounted how he was detailed by Kidd to collect Wells from his
Sunday lunch. They joined the rest of the distinguished party – 'the flower
of cultural London' – and were crossing the space between the mounted
police and the marchers' platform when Wells dug his umbrella in the mud
and refused to continue, on the grounds that Cockburn was about to carry
out a Machiavellian plan. 'At any moment now, as the result of some pre-
arranged signal on your part, the situation will get out of hand, the police
will charge, a dozen prominent authors and legislators will be borne to the
ground, and you will have the incident you desire'. Cockburn says he was
only sorry he hadn't thought of that idea himself.

great strains on police good sense. The manner in which they exercised their discretionary powers when faced with the admittedly severe public order problems posed by Mosley and his anti-Fascist opponents definitely diminished liberty in Britain in the 1930s. The disparity between police behaviour at Olympia and the anti-Sedition Bill meetings in 1934 has already been examined. In March 1936, Mosley staged another vast rally, this time at the Albert Hall. Violent attacks on those in the audience brave – or foolhardy – enough to voice opposition occurred again, with a similar lack of effective police intervention. Outside the hall, the police showed much more energy. It was, however, directed at peaceable anti-Fascists. Some streets near the hall were closed, and no marches were allowed near the rally. In Thurloe Square, exactly half-a-mile away, a meeting was being held to protest at the partiality of the Albert Hall's owners towards the Fascists and their lack of it towards the Left. After an hour – when the meeting was being addressed by a clergyman – the waiting mounted police suddenly drew their batons and charged into the crowd, totally without warning and for no obvious reason. They caused a number of injuries, though there was no attempt to fight back.* The N.C.C.L. tried to get Simon to conduct a public inquiry, but although they had impressive and wide-ranging support – an all-party group of M.P.s went to see Simon – the Home Secretary maintained his customary refusal to act. The N.C.C.L. therefore set up its own commission of inquiry.† It found that the meeting had been entirely peaceful and orderly; that the police had not asked the speaker to stop

---

*Cockburn describes how he, Palme Dutt and John Strachey sang *Rule Britannia* during this meeting on the grounds that it was anti-Hitler and therefore appropriately anti-Fascist. This would hardly seem sufficient provocation for a police attack.

†Such commissions were fashionable among the European Left of the Thirties. The model was the Reichstag Fire inquiry, which Neil Lawson, one of the N.C.C.L. founders, worked on. He was secretary to the N.C.C.L.'s most ambitious and successful commission, into the Northern Ireland Special Powers Acts in 1936 (see below, p. 260). The Thurloe Square commission included J. B. Priestley and Eleanor Rathbone among its members. According to Pritt, the N.C.C.L. had to keep him well away from it to maintain its respectability.

the meeting; and that the charge, itself unnecessary, had been even more unnecessarily brutal. Simon ignored all this, too.

The following year, the police again employed harsh tactics against an orderly anti-Fascist crowd. A small group of the British Union of Fascists, well protected by the police, who even silenced ordinary heckling, held a meeting – with a largely hostile audience – in Jewish Stepney Green on 14 July. As it was about to disperse peacefully, the police were ordered to draw their batons: the crowd panicked, and the police waded in, pursuing people into doorways as they fled. Several people were taken to hospital; one such victim was discharged when he was later brought to court, on the grounds that there was no evidence to convict him of any crime. On this occasion the police largely failed to get the usual benefit of the magistrates' doubt. One man was arrested for whistling during the meeting, and charged under the 'insulting words and behaviour' clause of the newly-minted Public Order Act. Discharging him, the magistrate commented, 'I think it would be a sad state of affairs if it were a criminal offence for some irresponsible young man to put his fingers in his mouth and whistle. I do not regard that as conduct which ought to fall within the scope . . . of the Act.'

The same magistrate also dismissed the case against a man, out looking for his ten-year-old daughter, who had been arrested for blowing his nose in what the inspector regarded as a provocative manner.[9]

Occasionally the N.C.C.L. was able to assist individual victories in cases like these. In the summer of 1938, a mounted policeman struck a young woman in a crowd at a Fascist meeting in Battersea. He was sued on her behalf by the N.C.C.L. chairman, W. H. Thompson, the tough solicitor who was famous for his handling of trade union cases. The case was settled out of court with a payment of £100 to the woman. But up to the outbreak of war the police failed to keep a consistent attitude to Fascist and Left demonstrations, with the inconsistency savagely unfavourable to the Left. Within a fortnight in January 1939, there were two demonstrations in Piccadilly Circus. The first was a Fascist protest at special ten per cent donations by West End theatres and cinemas from their 14 January takings towards a refugee fund. Traffic was dislocated for an hour, and there were several incidents when Fascists assaulted people in the street, with little police interference. Eventually, four Fascists were arrested and fined 7s. 6d. each. On 31 January there was an 'Arms for Spain' lobby at the Houses of Parliament. This was first frustrated by the police, then batoned by a mounted charge, and finally, when the rump of the lobby was holding a small protest demonstration in Piccadilly Circus late in the evening, violently dispersed again. By the end of the day, fifty-six people had been arrested. An N.C.C.L. dossier on the affair was sent to the Home Secretary, and three Labour M.P.s – Cripps, Strauss and Silverman – raised the matter in the House. They got little response, (Hoare promised to look into the case, but soon ruled out any need for an inquiry.) Silverman commented in the Commons: 'Large numbers of people believe that the demonstrators were unlawfully and violently prevented by the police from demonstrating in a cause which did not happen to be pleasing to the Government of the day.'

The police record in the 1930s reveals the price we pay for the advantages of a flexible law on public order. In a country divided as bitterly as Britain was in that decade most policemen were bound to align themselves with the more respectable side, emotionally and practically. W. H. Thompson said in 1938 that 'nowhere in pre-war times does one find such a readiness to baton and arrest demonstrators ... the prevention, banning and stopping of meetings in the history of the working-class movement before the (First) war.'[10] Yet the police only reflected the prejudices of the authorities in general, as the courts and Parliament showed in most cases when they had to deal with public order matters.

The passing of the Public Order Act in November 1936 is the clearest example of this. The act was the one major Parliamentary attempt this century to lend some shape to the inchoate law on assembly.* Far from being the reflective, detached and sane article that a vital constitutional statute ought to be, the tone of

*The 1908 Public Meeting Act, and the 1963 Public Order Act, were minor statutes, the one overtaken and enlarged enormously by the 1936 Act, the other merely an amplification of just one part of its predecessor.

niggling repressiveness throughout stamps it for what it was –
an ill-considered response to the street battles of the times. Its
most imaginative feature was the deft enlargement of discretionary and summary powers for police and magistrates – the easiest
and least troublesome way to intensify control without producing
a major political fuss. Nowhere is there a major, positive statement of the simple democratic right to assemble in public.

The immediate occasion of the act was the battle of Cable
Street, on Sunday 4 October, when the police tried to force a
passage for a Mosleyite march through the East End, and were
totally frustrated by the scale and vigour of the opposition.
In Parliament, Labour M.P.s had been pressing for some time
for action to curb the provocative behaviour of the Fascists*,
and the Government took the chance to satisfy this demand, but
also – and more significantly – used the opportunity to realize the
plans for adding to the powers of the police which it had been
formulating for some two years.[11]

The act did strictly circumscribe the wearing of political
uniforms (and effectively so, too, as the test cases brought by
the Fascists in 1937 showed).[12] And it outlawed private armies,
though Colin Jordan's 'Spearhead' fascist élite have so far been
the only victims.† But it also gave the police power to ask for
the names and addresses of hecklers; extended the 'insulting
behaviour' powers of the Metropolitan Police to the whole
country; and created stringent new weapons for controlling
marches and demonstrations, from fixing the route to a complete
ban.‡ It is the arbitrary and discretionary quality of these
latter provisions that have caused the damage to civil liberty. The
chief police officer may take such measures 'as appear to him
necessary for the preservation of public order' – a subjective
test that, as David Williams points out, is unchallengeable in a

*See below, p. 227

†In 1962.[13] This section deliberately exempted the use of stewards at
private meetings.

‡Meetings and marches in London had previously been banned under the
1839 Metropolitan Police Act. Lord Trenchard, when police commissioner
in the early 30s, forbade meetings in the vicinity of labour exchanges.
Naturally, this caused resentment on the Left at a time when high unemployment was the major political issue.

court.[14] The untrammelled nature of this power is the greater outside London, since Parliamentary supervision of the police is limited to the Metropolitan force, who alone are directly responsible to the Home Secretary. Local authorities have been notoriously unable to exercise any meaningful control over their chief constables.

Another reactionary feature of the act was its allocation of most offences to the summary jurisdiction of the magistrates' courts. Public order has traditionally been enforced at this level, and the authorities have recognized the value to themselves in doing so – Williams quotes the Commission who inquired into the 1886 Belfast riots: 'There can be no doubt that one of the best methods of checking riots is sharp punishment inflicted in the early time of the troubles.'[15] But such judicial methods reinforce the political nature of most public order prosecutions. Magistrates are inevitably less independent of their ruling-class background than judges (sometimes) manage to be. And, most important of all, indictable offences ensure trial by jury. Despite Lord Devlin's delineation of juries as middle-aged, middle-class and middle-brow, their value in giving some protection to the right of free assembly has been most recently shown in the spate of riot prosecutions since 1969.[16]

In 1934, a Worthing jury acquitted Mosley and some of his followers of a riotous assembly charge without hearing the defence, but juries did not help the Welsh miners involved in the two major political riot cases that took place in the thirties.

The resort to an indictment for the common law offences of affray, riot, riotous or unlawful assembly in a political case is the most distinctive mark of a period of repression in modern British history (coinciding, not unnaturally, with a period of political tension). In the past forty years, there have been two such periods – 1935–6 and post–1969. The first period starred the Welsh miners; the second Left-wing students, the blacks and the Irish. In each instance, the victims belonged to the contemporary stereotype of militant 'anti' figure. The established powers at least had the grace to select their cast with reference to popular myths.

On 21 March 1935 an unemployment demonstration took

place in Blaina, Monmouthshire. In the course of it, eighteen miners were arrested and charged with riot and unlawful assembly. Eleven of them were sent to prison for periods of four to nine months.[17] (The bitterness this prosecution left behind in the valleys of South Wales was partially responsible for the Thomas v. Sawkins confrontation described earlier.) In the following year, there were disturbances at a Fascist meeting in, of all places, Tonypandy, and thirty-six Rhondda miners were charged with similar offences. The majority were convicted at Glamorgan Assizes in December 1936, and sentences of up to a year were imposed. Even the judge had deplored the fact that the Fascists had been permitted to behave provocatively in an area where 'they know (their views) are not accepted'. The most depressing feature of the case was the quality of the police evidence, which relied on the nature of the defendants' politics and their involvement in working-class agitation to buttress the argument for the prosecution.[18]

A similar political discrimination was evident in the Harworth Colliery trial in the following year. This Nottinghamshire pit was the centre of a bitter dispute between the miners' union and the company union, and during the strike and lock-out which climaxed the dispute early in 1937 a number of miners were arrested for rioting around the pit and in the village. It does not appear to have been a serious riot, yet twelve men were given prison sentences, one for as long as two years. The N.C.C.L. sent Geoffrey Bing, Pritt and Cripps to defend them, and subsequently to fight a partially successful appeal which reduced the sentences. The attitudes of the judge, in sentencing, and of the police, in giving evidence (the local superintendent appeared to regard picketing as a criminal offence) would justify a Marxist analysis of the class nature of British justice.[19]

The 1930s showed what the authorities could do with our liberties if they really wanted to be repressive, without giving themselves much in the way of special power – simply by stretching that they already had. Ironically enough, the war immediately demonstrated the reverse; that authority could give itself very special powers indeed, and then largely feel constrained not to use them. It is difficult not to ascribe this turnabout to the complete change in public mood. The divided thirties became the united forties, with that celebrated wartime consensus we have sometimes looked back at with admiration.*

Not that the introduction of emergency powers legislation in 1939 passed totally unchallenged. Radicals like Kidd of the N.C.C.L. could scarcely be blamed for looking askance at the sweeping powers the Government that had cheerfully inspired the repressive measures of the previous six years was now arrogating to itself. The act was passed in one afternoon on 24 August; it enabled the Government to introduce its new powers whenever it wished. As Kidd put it, 'All constitutional safeguards of the liberty of the subject built up through hundreds of years of struggle may be modified or entirely scrapped to suit the whim of the Government.'[20] The first two batches of regulations, brought in almost immediately, tended to confirm his forebodings. Freedom of assembly was curtailed in three ways. The government could designate 'protected places' and penalize any activity in the vicinity of these which it felt was prejudicial to public safety. This precaution was pushed rather hard on a few occasions in the first two years of the war: two Communists were fined under Regulation 15 for addressing a political meeting outside a Hampshire enginering factory; a worker who brought twelve copies of the *Daily Worker* into his factory was fined;† and another man was sacked and fined under this regulation for 'addressing an assembly in a protected place'. He had in fact been idly discussing politics with a mate in his factory lavatory.

Under 39(E), processions and marches could be banned. The traditional May Day March, which had taken place every year since 1889, was prohibited for the first time in 1940, even though it had been permitted in every year of the First World War. This power was supposed to belong solely to the Home Secretary, yet sometimes Chief Constables used it arbitrarily and without reference to the Home Office. An equally unsatisfactory procedure

*Most recently with reference to Ulster. The press and TV censorship argument in 1971 often used this analogy. See p. 110.

†Until Hitler attacked Russia in 1941, the Communists were of course hostile to the war, but that scarcely justified this kind of petty repression, which was inconsistently administered anyway. A Portsmouth worker similarly prosecuted was found guilty of only a technical offence.

obtained under Regulation 23, which banned public assemblies. It was a blunt instrument modified by a proviso that the local police could lift it at their discretion. This inevitably meant widespread inconsistencies. In Birmingham they even banned football matches.[21]

The N.C.C.L. led the attack on the regulations in 1939, and mobilized considerable press and public support for their policy. 800 delegates attended an October conference they called in London, and in Parliament Dingle Foot, the Liberal M.P. and N.C.C.L. lawyer, managed to secure some important modifications in November 1939. As it turned out, apart from the early small-mindedness already noted, Government and authority in general for the most part used their dictatorial powers very sensibly. Only on one further occasion did they arouse a storm of protest, early in 1944. After a series of shipyard and pit strikes, they introduced a regulation – I.A.A. – which laid down a five-year sentence for anyone inciting strikes in essential services. Bevan, Pritt and Silverman attacked this in Parliament (and Pritt wrote a special N.C.C.L. pamphlet). They concentrated on the constitutional implications of making such a major change by delegated legislation. No-one was ever prosecuted, however, and the regulation lapsed at the end of the war.[22]

Considering the real repression of the 1930s and early 1970s, and the aggressive protest movements of the 1960s, there is an almost phoney quality about the libertarian anxieties (what few there were) over freedom of assembly in the two intervening decades. Some hot air was expended over Fascist 'revivals' after the war, and authority's alleged support for them, but it was only an echo of the pre-war indignation. And with the exception of the 1955 anti-rearmament demonstration there were no major clashes with the police or magistrates. There are perhaps three reasons for this. Firstly, the 1940s and 1950s saw the flood tide of mainstream politics in Britain, when most meaningful political activity found its expression in the conflict between the equally matched Labour and Conservative Parties. (This was not true of the thirties, when the Tories had an undue predominance, and became increasingly untrue of the 1960s, as many radicals turned away from the Labour Party.) Taking to the streets is essentially the resort of those who feel they have no other satisfactory outlet for their politics. Secondly, and doubtless as a result of this first reason, authority appeared to have lost its pre-war enthusiasm for the big stick, though it would be too generous to say it had replaced this with an affection for liberal precepts. And, finally, the civil liberty activists found themselves on the fringe of politics, partly because the scarcity of issues deprived them of natural platforms, and partly because the N.C.C.L. was to some extent identified with the Communist Party.

Though this narrow connection damaged civil liberty, since genuine injustices could be too easily dismissed as Red propaganda, the Communists did happen to suffer more restrictions during this Cold War period than anyone else. Between 1947 and 1954, the N.C.C.L. fought a persistent campaign against the discrimination shown by some private hall owners and local councils against the Communists. (The attitude was inspired, according to its critics, by Attlee's purge of the Civil Service in 1948.) Successful tactics ranged from obtaining injunctions to suing for breach of contract, though the owners of the Liverpool Stadium resisted a major local campaign to get them to rescind their ban on a meeting planned by Bevan and Wilson – ex-Cabinet Ministers though they were – in 1952. To refuse a hall to a political organization is one of the easiest minor restrictions on freedom of assembly that authority can impose, particularly if it is glossed as a concern about possible damage from interruptions. In 1951, the Croydon Council tried to dissuade Left-wing groups from using their halls by asking them to pay for the hire of extra police, but since the undermanned Croydon police couldn't provide any men, anyway, they had to drop this discriminatory condition. As the Cold War anxieties declined after the early 1950s, this practice disappeared. It surfaced again in 1959, when the anti-apartheid movement were refused the use of Chelsea Town Hall; but this belongs to the new wave of politics of the 1960s.

Small open air meetings also felt the effects of the Cold War attitudes at their worst in 1949–51. In Grimsby, the local Communists were prosecuted for obstruction when they attempted to use a traditional street site, but prompt action by local Conservative and Labour councillors won a promise from the police not to interfere in normal political activity. In Leeds, however, several meetings on Korea were similarly broken up, and the N.C.C.L. failed to win redress in the courts. But, in London in 1952, police harassment of 'peace' petitioners and poster parades were successfully challenged in the magistrates' courts.

Between 1947 and 1950, there was a brief revival of Mosleyite activity in London, which led to considerable hysteria on the Left and an over-reaction which had more damaging consequences than anything the Fascists themselves achieved.* Apart from setting race legislation on a wrong track, the Fascist street meetings resulted in three civil liberty defeats. Their attempts to break up opponents' meetings (a tactic admittedly not exclusively their own) lent some colour to the fears expressed by hall owners about potential damage. More importantly, in 1947 the police interpreted their powers under the 1936 Public Order Act to obtain the names and addresses of hecklers to mean they should give such information to the meeting chairman. The Fascists exploited this cheerfully, to the dismay of their opponents, who accused the police of assisting in the formation of a Mosleyite black list. Pritt raised the matter in the Commons, but Chuter Ede, the Home Secretary, defended the practice because it enabled the chairmen of meetings to pursue private prosecutions, if they wished to, when the police did not undertake public ones. However, the fuss made by the Left may have had more effect behind closed doors: the police appear quietly to have dropped the practice, and no further complaints were made during the remaining three years of the Fascist campaigns.

Finally, the troubles provoked the Home Office to use their powers to ban demonstrations. Late in 1947, Chuter Ede met an N.C.C.L. delegation (which included Pritt, Labour M.P. Orbach and journalist Hannen Swaffer) and told them he was contemplating a ban on processions in London. The N.C.C.L. argued that it would be all right to restrict the Fascists, who were causing the trouble, but wrong to impose a blanket prohibition

*For effect on race relations legislation, see below (Chapter 6, p. 231).

which would affect innocent political groups. (They seem to have been oblivious to the dangers in such a double standard.) On May Day in 1948, Mosley marched through Hackney and the predictable disturbances occurred. Ironically enough, some sections of the Left called on the Government to use those powers of repression – to break up meetings as in *Duncan v. Jones*, and to bind over – which they had criticized before the war. Apparently, such measures were not repressive if used against Mosley. Chuter Ede's response was to invoke the Public Order Act and ban political marches in London for three months.

The ban was renewed until February 1949, being dropped a few days after Pritt had acidly pointed out that only two European capitals would be without the traditional May Day marches – London and Madrid. The Fascists immediately organized two marches, the first in February in East London (singing the *Horst Wessel* song) which largely escaped interference, the second a month later in North London, which did not. Chuter Ede immediately slapped another three months' ban on the city, refusing Left-wing pleas to allow the May Day trade union march. (The Communists tried to argue that it was not 'political' in character.) The bans were renewed every three months throughout 1949 and 1950, thus catching a second May Day. The Fascists, however, tried one ingenious way of getting round the ban. They assembled in the City (which was outside the scope of order) and marched to Temple Bar, where, breaking up into small groups, they proceeded to Knightsbridge and re-formed, to head back towards Piccadilly Circus, under the visible directions of an organizer. These directions proved, however, enough to convict the organizer under the 1936 Act.[23] Overall it is a sorry period, in which none of those involved emerge with much credit. The Fascists were deliberately provocative (and occasionally violent), the Communist-oriented Left were either naively or cynically outraged, and the police and the Home Office were rather too ban-happy. Possibly the experience made authority wiser, however; no subsequent Governments have used these extreme powers in such sustained manner again.

The post-war period also saw two new, though unrelated, threats to traditional freedoms, one arising accidentally from the re-development of city centres, the other a more deliberate attack on the trade union right to picket, which became increasingly circumscribed, despite occasional successful re-assertions such as the miners' flying pickets of 1972.

The demand for car parks and wider roads was an unexpected threat to freedom of assembly which suddenly emerged in the mid-1950s. Police pressure on a traditional open air speaker's site in Lincoln's Inn Fields* was first felt in 1956; the site was not secured until a compromise agreement was reached with the police in 1961. During 1957–8, the N.C.C.L. unsuccessfully campaigned to prevent the old Tower Hill site being cut in half by a car park. (The Ministry of Transport, unhappy at the site's use as an unofficial lorry park, had formally indicated their intention to change this in two transport union journals neither of which, as the N.C.C.L. pointed out, were normally read by the site's regular speakers.) The N.C.C.L. was successful, however, in winning specific protection for Speakers Corner in Hyde Park when the Park Lane Improvements Bill was debated in 1958, and they inspired amendments which allowed marchers to enter the park at street level instead of through a subway.

The problem was not of course confined to London. In Birmingham, the lack of any replacement for the speakers' site in the old Bull Ring was criticized when the re-development plan was published in 1957; by the time the new Bull Ring was built in 1967, the police had allocated a speakers' corner, but well away from the shops, which did not appeal to the audience-conscious speakers very much. There was a protest march the following year, and in May 1968 the council agreed to abandon a proposed new by-law which would have given the police additional powers to act against 'loitering' in the shopping area. Other campaigns were briefly, and with varying success, fought during this time in Brighton, Watford and Wolverhampton, but the biggest, and longest-lasting, struggle took place in Manchester.

With the re-building of the city centre, the old speaker's site in Deansgate disappeared. In 1961, the Town Clerk told local Labour M.P. Leslie Lever that the council had decided that a

*Like Tower Hill and Hyde Park (Tyburn as was), it owed its noble modern function to its less auspicious origin as a place of execution.

suitable replacement was not available, and that anyway 'the purpose for which the site was proposed was not an essential public need.' Fortunately, there were enough people in Manchester prepared to ignore this bureaucratic effrontery, and pressure to get a site was maintained. In 1965, the council felt they had to make a car park available for this purpose on Saturday afternoons, but this proved unsatisfactory, and the Free Speech Committee was formed to press for a permanent site in the city centre. In December 1969, the N.C.C.L. formally requested the Piccadilly garden and esplanade as this site. At first the council, though not agreeing to this specifically, indicated it would look for a suitable site; then, a few months later, it blandly announced it would take no further action. Another local Labour M.P., Frank Allaun, led a direct action campaign to challenge this and in January 1971 the police rather reluctantly prevented him from addressing a meeting in the gardens, making fifteen arrests as they did so.* The council leaders met the free speech campaigners in March, and the matter was resolved when the Crown Court ruled in April that there were no powers to stop meetings on a council directive (something of a 'discovery' as far as the local Press was concerned) and that if the police felt no obstruction was being caused, the meetings were perfectly legal. That it took ten years to reach this position – the law, of course, had always been thus – is a sad example of how easily authority can suppress a traditional freedom unless vigorously and tenaciously challenged.

Political will-power, and the public support opposing forces can muster, can often prove as important as the letter of the law. Obviously this is double-edged – repression can be intensified as well as liberties extended. Trade union pickets encountered both sets of circumstances in the post-war period. In the 1960s, when generally there was a movement towards enlarging traditional freedom of assembly, legal decisions and police attitudes came close to restricting the size of pickets to the absurd figure of two men. 'The only indisputably lawful pickets,' wrote

*The N.C.C.L. was understandably peeved that the council, while considering the gardens unsuitable for public speakers, had cheerfully tolerated a Milk Marketing Board exhibition cow there a few months earlier.

Professor Wedderburn at the time, 'are those who attend in small numbers near the chosen place and who keep out of everyone's way.'[24] Yet in 1972, when in every other area of public order and free expression a considerable repression was under way, the miners, with their 60,000 pickets deployed to blockade oil supplies to the power stations, and the dockers, with their defiance of the Industrial Relations Court, almost re-defined common and statute law on picketing. It is one of the strengths of British democracy, though not one recognized by those strict constitutionalists who shudder at the prospect of any group 'taking the law into its own hands', that the law bends, or hides its face, at moments like these.

Though police and trade unions generally work a sensible compromise in strikes, most cases that reached the courts after the war went against the unions. In 1947, the National Union of General and Municipal Workers called a strike of staff at several large West End hotels. Supplies to these were blacked by other unions, and the pickets tried particularly to dissuade tanker drivers from delivering oil. Arthur Lewis, the Labour M.P., lay down in the road on one occasion to achieve this end; and got away with it. A few days later, a large escort of police accompanied an oil tanker convoy into the Savoy Hotel, and those who lay down that time were arrested, and some roughly treated. The subsequent court action decided that section 2 of the 1906 Trade Disputes Act, which permitted peaceful picketing 'for the purpose of conveying information . . . or persuading any person to abstain from work,' did not extend to this kind of siege behaviour. This restriction was amplified thirteen years later when, following an incident in the 1959 printers' strike, the Divisional Court supported the action of a policeman who had ruled that two pickets were enough and had arrested a third picket.[25] Siege tactics were even more firmly ruled out of court in 1966, when the courts promoted the common-law concept of nuisance over the statutory rights laid down in the Trade Disputes Act, in the case of *Tynan v. Balmer*.[26] Striking draughtsmen organized a picket of forty men which kept circling their Liverpool factory; their leader was arrested and convicted of obstruction, even though the courts accepted there was no breach of the peace nor any question of intimidation. The Lord Chief Justice wondered aloud to the defence counsel 'whether, by pursuing this, you are not really finding at the end of the day that the activities of pickets will be more and more restricted.' The effect of the court attitudes was immediately reflected in police practice. In the bitter building industry disputes the following year, the police insisted that only two pickets would be allowed.

Even without court support, high-handed police behaviour was occasionally enough to restrict trade union liberty in this period. During the 1959 printing strike, the police sometimes quoted the Seditious Meetings Act even though this referred to gatherings of more than fifty people; and in 1965, during a dispute at Southall, local police warned one particular union official not to appear on the picket line. The vigour of police tactics during the Barbican dispute in October 1967 – they allocated four officers per picket at one point – was challenged by the N.C.C.L., who sent observers to witness what was happening. The council felt sufficiently disturbed to ask the Home Secretary whether the police had been ordered to take tough measures. They received no reply.

Perhaps the worst incidents at this time occurred during the protracted Roberts Arundel dispute in Stockport. Members of the Amalgamated Engineering Union at the factory struck in November 1966 when the new American management refused to recognize the union. Clashes between police and pickets, and demonstrators supporting them, took place several times during the eighteen months' strike, notably in February and November 1967 and January 1968. The violence used by the police led to a successful civil action by injured workmen in January 1969, when damages of £2,280 were awarded against the Cheshire police force. Considerable, though unavailing, public pressure to get the three officers particularly involved suspended from duty was applied by local Labour M.P.s Orbach and Gregory, the N.C.C.L. and the *News of the World*. Ironically enough, the police were also successfully sued by Roberts Arundel's management, who won £1,000 damages under the Riot Damages Act of 1886.

Despite this rather grim roll-call, most strikes were handled by the police in a more restrained manner, and it was in accordance with this more tolerant tradition that most local forces met the massive picketing during the miners' strike early in 1972. In Birmingham the siege tactics, so clearly outlawed by the court decisions of 1947, 1961 and 1966, were blatantly successful; 10,000 miners and supporting car workers forced the closure of a large coke depot. 'You don't pick a fight with 10,000 people,' and, 'You can't blame the miners. It's a gross provocation when long distance lorries that have never used the depot before start arriving' were among the sensible comments of the police on duty.[27] In the one major court case that arose from the strike, when thirteen pickets were charged with 'mobbing and rioting' after incidents at Longannet power station in Fife, all were found not guilty. Later in the year, when the new Industrial Relations Act – which basically restated the right to picket peacefully – was invoked against dockers blacking container traffic in Essex, and enforcing the blacking by picketing, the country was treated to the hilarious spectacle of the Official Solicitor stepping in to save three shop stewards from martyrdom. Lord Denning ruled that the new court did not have sufficient evidence to gaol the dockers for contempt.

The success of the miners and dockers in getting round the law in 1972 provoked agitated attempts by some Conservatives to redress the balance. As lawyers well knew, however, the machinery to do this was already there if the will to use it was as well. In 1973, that will was there. The new repression only partially succeeded: the flexibility of British justice not only thwarted it, but confused the state of the law on picketing still further.

In that year the fight by Left-wing building workers against the 'lump' (contract labour) system provided the Conservatives with an opportunity to strike back. Four important court cases were brought out of incidents involving pickets and other strikers. Two of them produced results which restated the position as understood in the mid-1960s, with a strictly limited right to peaceful picketing. In December 1973, the House of Lords ruled (in Broome v. Hunt) that strikers could not physically stop a lorry in order to persuade a driver not to cross a picket line. Two months later, in another case, the High Court decided that the police could cordon off pickets to prevent them getting anywhere near lorries approaching strike-bound sites. The right to picket meant little (the N.C.C.L. indeed felt it was 'non-existent', though this was overdoing it) when the relevant targets for peaceful persuasion were lorries thundering past at 30 m.p.h. and when the courts had decided that these could not be stopped, even temporarily, to hear the strikers' arguments.

The two other cases arising from the builders' strike were far more vindictive. In Birmingham five members of the building workers union, U.C.A.T.T., and three TV men who had gone with them to cover the story, peacefully occupied the offices of an agency employing lump workers. They were arrested and charged with conspiracy to trespass, a brave new concept successfully employed by the authorities against demonstrators a few months earlier. (See below, p. 94.) They were defended by N.C.C.L. lawyers. As the council's new general secretary, Martin Loney, put it, 'The N.C.C.L. chose to fight the case because fundamental issues of civil liberty were involved.' Loney was concerned not only about the general attack on pickets that year but with the extreme seriousness of the charge (carrying unlimited penalties) for such a minor incident. Fortunately, all the accused were acquitted. 'The D.P.P. may be a wiser man ... he will now understand that conspiracy to trespass in industrial disputes is perfectly lawful', commented the N.C.C.L.

A less satisfactory result emerged from the early stages of the trial of the 'Shrewsbury 24' at the same time. Six building workers (out of twenty-four charged altogether) were accused of conspiracy to intimidate under the 1875 Protection of Property Act – an act which many lawyers thought dead and buried, and which had been originally passed to protect trade unions from civil actions arising from disputes. It had never been used against strikers before, and is part of the general pattern of the early 1970s in which the prosecuting authorities resurrected dead laws and resorted to vague conspiracy and incitement charges in their attempts to push back the advances in the right to demonstrate achieved in the 1960s. The charges arose from an incident at Telford in Shropshire, when hundreds of strikers protesting at the use of lump labour arrived at a McAlpine's site to try and persuade workers there to stop work. There is no doubt that very real intimidation of these workers occurred. The response of the authorities, however, who could have chosen lesser and more appropriate charges, showed their desire to teach the 'militants' a political lesson. The Shrewsbury jury were clearly worried by these political implications: they were divided, and the foreman walked out in protest at the severity of the sentences. Three men were convicted of conspiracy and three acquitted, though all found guilty of the lesser unlawful assembly charges. The first three were sentenced for periods of up to three years in gaol.

In the 1970s, the most serious industrial unrest for fifty years took over from the essentially middle-class protest movements of the previous decade: the right to demonstrate was complicated by the confused state of the law on picketing, and the pickets' own confusion about exactly what they were trying to achieve. In a strict legal sense, though not necessarily a practical one, the right to picket was extremely limited, amounting to little more than a symbolic gesture. When strikers used pickets for other purposes – to strangle power supplies, or bring pressure on other workers – they were relying not on the law but on public sympathy for their success. The miners of 1972 had that support, the building workers of 1973 did not. If the authorities chose to respond in a repressive manner, as they did in 1973, they were gambling not only on the impact of such attitudes on industrial relations but on the dubious willingness of British juries to accept that extremely grave conspiracy charges were the correct answers to relatively minor public order offences.

By then juries had already shown considerable sophistication in judging cases arising from the unprecedented upsurge in street politics in the 1960s. Despite the occasional severity of the repression, which at moments was comparable to that of the 1930s, civil liberty – though not, oddly enough, the street politicians – emerged from ten years of struggle far stronger than it went in. Methods no-one would have dreamed of in 1960 had become commonplace in 1970. It is a mark of the depth of the change, rather than of any real threat to freedom, that in 1972 a private citizen, Francis Bennion, and the Lord Chancellor, Lord Hailsham, were in their different ways trying to test even the right to demonstrate. The demonstrators had hurt the conventional political process that much – their threat and achievement was real.

The street became such an important political arena because the older, hierarchical two-party politics had lost a lot of their meaning for an active minority. Whether or not the 'new politics' achieved many of their objectives, or whether in fact real change still ultimately needed the *imprimatur* of the old system, the wave of protest did open up new channels of dissent, of pressure on those in power. Harold Wilson has explained the effect of the Vietnam demonstrations on his foreign policy[28], and the squatters achieved a major change in local authority housing policies after 1968. The M.C.C. was forced by the Home Secretary, who in turn had been forced by the demonstrators, to cancel the proposed South African cricket tour in 1970.

The victories were not won easily.* During the 1960s, the authorities showed a great deal of ingenuity in exploiting the range of controls available to them. This was true even of quite humble, one is tempted to say harmless, events. In June 1964 an Oxford student who shouted 'Free Mandela' during the visit of the South African Ambassador was prosecuted (unsuccessfully) under the Public Order Act, a misuse of power as ludicrous as that tried on the man whistling at Stepney Green in 1937; and two years later a handful of Americans who were protesting against the Vietnam War on the steps of their Grosvenor Square embassy were, rather sinisterly, asked for their alien registration cards by the police. Three months later, after strong protests by Tony Smythe of the N.C.C.L. and Labour M.P. Dick Taverne, the Metropolitan Commissioner conceded that the inspector had been 'unwise' to use those powers in such circumstances.

Two movements, born in the late 1950s but reaching maturity in the 1960s, inaugurated the era of street politics – the 'Boycott South African Goods' campaign and the Campaign for Nuclear

*Brownlie argues that since 1870 there has been a general increase in legal restraints, since grass-roots pressure is distrusted by authority. The restraints have perhaps increased, but not nearly as much as the number of citizens now making use of their freedoms.

Disarmament. The anti-apartheid campaigns ran into difficulty getting halls, ostensibly because of the threat of Fascist counter-action. The problems posed by C.N.D. were much larger and more widespread, but even at a mundane level the support for the campaign meant that small outdoor meetings, which could hardly snarl up the Saturday shopping, became a regular feature of a suburban Britain whose police had rarely had to deal with their like before. Sometimes, the inexperience led to petty controls. In the first five years of the decade, the N.C.C.L. had to help C.N.D. and other young Left groups in places like Dartford, Maidstone, Richmond and Watford that had had difficulty in getting elementary rights of public assembly from their local police. In 1965, for instance, the Lewisham police were persuaded by the N.C.C.L. to drop their objections to the date of a local march, but in the same year and only a few miles away in Beckenham, the police could charge the veteran radical Jim Radford with obstruction at a street meeting on a site where Radford had spoken many times before. Although Radford produced several convincing witnesses to the fact that the police had deliberately broken the meeting up, he and all except one of his colleagues were convicted (the other got off on appeal on the grounds that he was there only as a member of the public). The hit-and-miss quality of the law of assembly became increasingly apparent as the decade wore on.

Similarly with hiring private halls; the traditional and arbitrary chariness of their owners affected both Left and Right at moments of particular tension. In 1968, the Moot Hall in Colchester was made readily available to the Anglo-Rhodesian Society but not the local Vietnam Committee. The size of the financial assurance demanded of the latter – £50,000 – forced them into a church hall instead. In the following year Birmingham Corporation, pressured by Conservative M.P. Tom Iremonger, refused their facilities to the Union Movement. Similar rejections came from London boroughs like Tower Hamlets, Hackney and Islington. The N.C.C.L., breaking with its partisanly anti-Fascist past, supported the Movement's right to a hall, though with some evident distaste for their objectives.

Other anti-Fascists allowed their understandable hostility to extreme Right-wing politics to turn them into threats to freedom themselves. In 1974 the National Union of Students adopted a policy of actively preventing 'fascists and racists' from speaking at universities. This formalized a practice that had intermittently been carried on by some Left-wing groups since the late 1960s. The policy was bitterly attacked by liberals on the Left (though not, unfortunately, by the N.C.C.L.); but twice within a month of the N.U.S. decision, Right-wing speakers were either banned (Martin Webster of the National Front at Newcastle) or physically threatened (Harold Soref of the Monday Club at Oxford).

In the streets, even handing out leaflets became a hazardous occupation in these years. In 1968 a young pacifist, Gwyneth Williams, was distributing a War Resisters International leaflet outside an American Army hostel in London which offered U.S. Servicemen various ideas on how they could help end the Vietnam War – one of which was by deserting. She was arrested and charged with distributing an insulting writing which could cause a breach of the peace. Though she had not caused any obstruction, nor indeed had any actual breach of the peace occurred, she was convicted: and the Divisional Court dismissed her appeal with the somewhat political judgment that it would be hard to imagine anything more likely to cause a breach of the peace than an invitation to soldiers to desert.

In the same year, five members of the Medway Vietnam campaign proposed to leaflet the crowd while the Queen visited the Royal School of Military Engineering in Gillingham. They were harassed – or felt they were harassed – by a large number of local police during the time the Queen was in the town, and sought the help of the N.C.C.L. Smythe asked the Chief Constable of Kent for an inquiry, which was refused, but consoled the protesters with the thought that 'the affair may have had more impact internally than was now obvious'. A more obvious success was achieved that autumn, when there was a minor police campaign against certain literature sellers at Speakers Corner. Again the N.C.C.L. badgered the police, who again publicly stood their ground – but the campaign stopped. An even more convincing defeat for authority came, however, in Edinburgh in 1970–71. It is a classic example of the virtuous flexibility of the British system – provided pressure is applied with enough tenacity from below. In October 1970, Peter Wallington, a member of the Scottish Council for Civil Liberties, was found guilty of illegally distributing leaflets (pointing out the 'gross disparity' between the corporation's spending on welfare and on the Commonwealth Games) outside the Meadowbank stadium during the games in July. He was prosecuted under a local act, designed to preserve the amenities of the city, which forbade the distribution of leaflets except of a political or trade union nature. This narrow definition of 'political' was challenged on appeal by two S.C.C.L. lawyers, and the Law Lords decreed that the local court 'had adopted the wrong approach and reached the wrong result'. Subsequently the Edinburgh council decided to re-phrase its legislation in a less oppressive manner.

Best of all perhaps was the decision of the Lambeth magistrate H. L. Beaumont (not always regarded as a friend of dissent) in a London case the following year. It went some way, at least as far as leafleting was concerned, to cut back the arbitrary police power to interpret the likelihood of a breach of the peace that had been so sadly extended by the *Duncan v. Jones* case in 1934. A young man, Shineld, had been handing out leaflets urging people to attend a demonstration outside the Marylebone Court during the trial of four people arrested after the Metro Club disturbances in 1971.* He was charged under the 1936 Public Order Act with distributing a leaflet which was abusive and insulting and liable to cause a breach of the peace. Beaumont accepted that it was abusive and insulting, but rejected any breach of the peace connotations in view of the time lapse – at least four days – between handing out the leaflet and any threatened events; 'I do not see how it can be said that words or behaviour can be likely to cause a breach of the peace at another place or at another date.' Which was exactly the premise on which the police had won their 1934 case against Mrs Duncan.

*The case itself – the 'Metro Four' – which arose out of fighting between police and young blacks at a Paddington youth club was another in the series of jury defeats for authority in the early '70s. The accused were acquitted on twenty-one charges, including affray.

This pattern of random but persistent petty harassment was the background for the three moments when really important attempts to limit the right to small-scale protest occurred – the Pat Arrowsmith case at Bootle in 1962, the Brighton Church Affair in 1966 and the Andrew Papworth case in 1967. Their significance lay not in the events themselves, two of which were so trivial as scarcely to justify a mention in the local paper, but in the manifestly political way the law operated. On 7 May 1962 Pat Arrowsmith, one of the most famous of the direct action pacifists, was addressing a lunchtime meeting outside Bootle docks, a spot which was almost a regular local Speakers Corner – both Harold Wilson and Bessie Braddock had spoken there. Briefly the crowd blocked the street, but the police cleared a way for the traffic, with Miss Arrowsmith's help. After the meeting she was asked for her name and address by a policeman. She refused to give it, was arrested and charged with obstruction, found guilty by the local magistrate and fined. On appeal the police argued that Arrowsmith had been told to stop speaking, and had failed to do so. She denied this; and though the judge confirmed her conviction, he indicated he thought the case against her should never have been brought. The implication of political discrimination – Pat Arrowsmith was particularly notorious for her C.N.D. agitation at the time – was considered beyond the scope of the High Court when the appeal went before Lord Parker, who further penalized Miss Arrowsmith by making her responsible for her own costs. A charge of obstruction, either technical (of the highway) or of the police themselves, provides the police with an absolute and arbitrary power: the highest courts of the land have shown themselves unable, or unwilling, to consider the test of fairness.[29] Though the Arrowsmith case does not extend police power in the way the famous 1934 cases did, it does show just how far it can be stretched in the absence of any constitutional safeguards.

The Brighton Church Affair in October 1966 stretched the law another way. No-one disputed the accuracy of the charge against Arrowsmith, given the almost unanswerable nature of an obstruction charge, but when eight men and women were arrested for interrupting the Labour Party leader's traditional church reading the Sunday before the Labour Party conference,* the accuracy of the eventual charge – of indecent behaviour under the Ecclesiastical Courts Jurisdiction Act of 1860 – was scarcely even technical. Even this was only arrived at after several attempts to find something that would fit, and the process would have been ludicrous had it not also been tyrannical. Equally alarming was the repressive treatment meted out during the ten months between arrest and the eventual imprisonment of two of the men, Nick Walter and Jim Radford. Bail was only obtained after the N.C.C.L. had interceded through a judge in chambers; defendants were handcuffed, fingerprinting was authorized (an unusual process for a public order offence), and the disparity between the £5 fines given six of the accused and the two month sentences handed out to Radford and Walter, was glaring and inexplicable – except that, like Pat Arrowsmith, they were victimized because their politics were notorious.[30]

Unlike the thirties, however, the mid-sixties possessed a large and influential liberal public opinion which disliked such restrictive manoeuvring. (The *Sunday Times* described the N.C.C.L. pressure to win bail as one of the council's greatest successes.) How much such attitudes affect the behaviour of the courts and the police is impossible to assess: but at the same time as Radford and Walter were being persecuted for their Vietnam protest, a Committee of 100 colleague, Andrew Papworth, was winning an important constitutional victory with his. In April 1966 the police banned a seven-strong anti-war vigil at the corner of Whitehall and Downing Street, using their 1839 'sessional orders' powers. These were traditionally the police weapon for preventing demonstrations within a one square mile area of Parliament while it was sitting. The origin of this order was a Commons directive to the police to ensure access for M.P.s and prevent disorder in the neighbourhood of the House. This had increasingly been interpreted by the police as giving them total control over any kind of outdoor political activity in a large area

---

*The demonstrators accused Mr Wilson of hypocrisy in taking part in a religious service while his Government were supporting U.S. policies in the war.

of central London; but Papworth's appeal against his £2 fine
for taking part in the vigil was upheld by Lord Justice Winn
with a beautiful judgment which ruled that an assembly was
unlawful in the terms of the sessional orders only when it was
capable of obstructing free passage for the M.P.s or of causing
disorder or annoyance. This drastically curtailed police powers
in the area of Westminster.[31]

A further extension of the right to small-scale protest came in
1972. Dennis Brutus, a persistent and successful campaigner
against apartheid in South African sport, had interrupted play
in a tennis match at Wimbledon the previous year. He had been
convicted of using insulting behaviour: but the House of Lords
decided that even if behaviour caused offence to others, as it did
in this case to the tennis spectators, it was not necessarily insulting in the eyes of the law.

This peculiarly British pattern, of authoritarian and liberal
precepts and practices marching cheek by jowl, was just as
evident in the treatment of the great wave of street demonstrations in this period. It has been argued that the police became
much tougher in their attitudes to demonstrators as these parted
more and more from official two-party politics and into a short-
lived attachment for 'extra-Parliamentary democracy'.[32] This is
not really true, since the police methods at the Commons in
January 1955 and in St Pancras in 1960 were as vigorous as
anything seen in Grosvenor Square. Police tolerance veered
about quite erratically. What did indeed get worse was the rush
to riot, incitement and conspiracy prosecutions after 1967.
The blame for this, however, lies with the Government's law
officers rather than the police.

It remained true, of course, that the less clout you carried the
more liable you were to suffer restrictions. Fringe groups for
instance were much more subject to wilful decisions by the
Ministry of Works (now part of the Department of the Environment) regarding the use of Trafalgar Square. This administrative
control is the first line of defence for authority, though it is so
clearly a bureaucratic denial of democratic rights that it is rarely
resorted to unless its use is unlikely to provoke a major row.
Before the 1960s the Ministry adopted – or could afford to adopt

– a very liberal position: after a brief mix-up over a C.N.D. application to use the square on Good Friday in 1958 (the 1892 regulations spoke only of week-ends and bank holidays) they declared that 'it was never the intention that these powers . . . should be used as some kind of censorship'. Three years later they did just that: a Committee of 100 demonstration in September 1961 was banned. Once tried, the practice grew on the ministry; the Committee of 100 was again refused the square in 1962, because they would not give assurances that there would be no advocacy of civil disobedience, and in the same year the first of many negatives were handed out to far Right-wing groups. (By 1966, the National Socialists had been turned down thirteen times.) A subtle variation on simple refusal was tried later in the year when, at Cuba crisis and anti-apartheid demonstrations, newly installed crush barriers severely limited the crowds.*

The increasing ingenuity of demonstrators in the later 1960s presented the Ministry with fresh opportunities to restrict the use of the square. Hornsey students got away with a ballet and a 'happening' in 1968 despite the prohibition of theatrical performances, but a pro-Biafra group who wanted to include a John Lennon play in a demonstration the following year were unable to get the necessary permission. The Women's Liberation movement was more fortunate in March 1971. Their initial request for the square had been turned down on the grounds that the preservation of the square as a 'major national setting for serious public meetings based on the making of speeches' would not be helped by their proposal to include miming to songs like *Thank Heaven For Little Girls*. However, a deputation, which included Smythe of the N.C.C.L., managed to reach a compromise with the Ministry. Paul Channon, one of the Department's ministers, subsequently wrote to Smythe that 'we are not trying to ignore (the novelty of including dramatic presentation)' and promised to consider future applications on merit.

Much more seriously, in 1972 the Department of the Environment (which had taken over responsibility for Trafalgar Square) announced that they would not allow the square to be

---

*Martin Ennals felt that the erection of the fountains after the war was a similar attempt to reduce the potential size of demonstrations.

used for any demonstrations on the Northern Ireland issue. Smythe attacked the dangerous precedent: 'Many prospective users of the square may feel their freedom will be inhibited if they choose an issue that is a matter of public controversy.' The ministry's action was the gravest use of arbitrary bureaucratic power to restrict free assembly since the war.

Authority was denied a further chance to exercise administrative control over demonstrations when the Night Assemblies Bill was defeated in the Commons despite Government support in 1972. The Bill, aimed at the two- or three-day rock festivals that had become a regular summer feature in the years after 1967, was sponsored by Conservative back-benchers, and demonstrated a characteristic insensitivity to liberty; it proposed a blanket power over any assembly of more than 1,000 people between the hours of midnight and 6 a.m., which would have affected far more occasions – like charities holding all-night walks or any all-night vigil – than just rock festivals. A splendid *ad hoc* alliance of young people (it included the music press, the Young Conservatives and the National Association of Youth Clubs), supported by N.C.C.L. briefings of M.P.s, found sufficient Parliamentary support to get the bill talked out. More limited threats remained in the attempts to pass local government bills (such as the Isle of Wight County Council Act) containing this kind of power.

Once an assembly was under way, the next line of control was formed by the police. Their physical handling of demonstrations became a major civil liberty issue in the 1960s. It is of course true that just as the police have a number of options available – to allow a demonstration to run its course, to seal off its objectives, or to break it up by whatever means are necessary – so demonstrators can either confine themselves to marching and speaking or deliberately march themselves into a confrontation with the police. And despite the major infringements by the police during the decade, there is no doubt their attitude had in general improved since the 1930s. This can be seen in the basic tactic at demonstrations – to shepherd a crowd at very close quarters rather than standing back and charging it. 'It's very important to stand right up close,' explained one senior police officer at the time of the Vietnam demonstrations. 'It's very difficult indeed to hurt a stranger badly when you're nose to nose – much easier at a distance.'[33] Ennals wrote in 1966 that the painstaking police inquiries into complaints about their behaviour at two London demonstrations the previous year showed that

while the police themselves may sometimes infringe the rights of demonstrators, they are concerned that these rights should be publicly upheld, which is a long way from the situation that obtained thirty years ago ... had (one student complainant) been a demonstrator in the 30s he might have expected a truncheon blow over the head as a part of the normal price of demonstrating.

Furthermore, the biggest assemblies of those years – the C.N.D. rallies in 1960 and 1961, the Vietnam demonstration of October 1968 and the T.U.C. protest against the Industrial Relations Bill in February 1971 – all passed off largely without incident. There remain, however, perhaps a dozen major occasions when police tactics were a clear breach of the right to assemble freely. The anti-rearmament lobby of January 1955 was an omen. The British Peace Committee had agreed arrangements with the police for a march after their Westminster lobby against German rearmament. Suddenly at 7.30 in the evening, after six hours of lobbying, the police broke up the queue outside the Commons, prevented people from seeing their M.P.s (quite without authorization), and interfered with pressmen present. Then a group of mounted officers charged without warning into the march, which was both peaceful and keeping to the agreed route, riding down an M.P. in the process. It was an unexpected throwback to the methods of twenty-five years earlier, and the refusal of the Home Secretary to set up an inquiry was just as characteristic of that period. Less so were the implications of the aftermath: the public row may well have had its desired effect, for an identical demonstration the following October went off without trouble.

The St Pancras 'riots' of 1960 set the style for an almost annual street crisis thereafter. A prolonged rent dispute between the council and some of its tenants (who were refusing to leave their flats after notices to quit) had been well handled by the police for several weeks when right at the end of the dispute a mounted force was used to break up a demonstration. The following night a march of about 2,000 people to the town hall was dispersed with a truncheon charge in the old style. As a result, a three-month ban (under the Public Order Act) was imposed on the area.* Exactly a year later came the infamous affair of the 'Police at Midnight'[34] – the Committee of 100 sit-down in Trafalgar Square. The Committee, a breakaway group from the C.N.D. movement which felt that the urgency of the nuclear crisis demanded more direct methods than conventional protest, had that year inaugurated a policy of civil disobedience which, if carried out on a large enough scale, was expected to embarrass the Government and overwhelm its law enforcement machinery. They carried out two large sit-downs earlier in the year, in Whitehall (no arrests) and in Parliament Square (800 arrests). The Government decided there would be no third such event, and delaying their reply to the Committee's request for the square from June until August – when Parliament and its awkward questions were in recess – eventually refused them permission to use it. Five days before the sit-down was due, Lord Russell and thirty-two of his colleagues on the Committee were imprisoned for between seven days and two months for refusing to be bound over.† The following day, the police banned any marches in central London on Sunday 17 September, the scheduled day of the demonstration, and ordered the closing of several streets. The issue sharpened into one of principle. Liberals not otherwise sympathetic to the Committee of 100 felt the Government had embarked on a policy of active suppression, and on the Sunday 50,000 people packed the square. There were sporadic speeches, sit-downs and arrests throughout the after-

---

*The newly appointed general secretary of the N.C.C.L., Martin Ennals, laid most of the blame on the poor crowd control of the local police chiefs. They deliberately created bottlenecks on this and a Lumumba demo in Chelsea, so that the crowd in front couldn't go on and those at the back didn't know this – and there was no escape route. His successor Tony Smythe – also present at St Pancras – however attributes some blame to those demonstrators who came equipped with milk bottle missiles and a clear intention to cause trouble.

†The most infamous example of preventive justice since it had been applied to Mann and Pollitt in 1932. The heaviest sentence was handed out to the man regarded as the most active of the Committee, Ralph Schoenman.

noon and evening, but it was at the very end of the day that a sudden wave of police violence occurred. People were beaten, thrown into the fountains and even hosed down at the police station. The violence may not even have had the mask of legality – the renewal of the 24-hour ban was made late in the day (to cover the post-midnight period) and was in the opinion of many lawyers *ultra vires*. The subsequent furore was enormous – again, a change from the 1930s. The Home Secretary made a hopelessly inadequate statement in Parliament* and the performance of the police in court was a glaring fabrication. Though no public apologies were made – and an inquiry was naturally refused – there is no doubt a great deal of fuss was made in the privacy of the police stations.[35]

The Queen Frederika demos in 1963, though marked with less physical violence, were handled with an even greater display of legal muscle. The Government, fearful of a repeat of the embarrassment it suffered in April when some anti-Royalist demonstrators pursued Queen Frederika of Greece up a West End mews, authorized a major clamp-down on demonstrations during the Greek royal visit in July. Every device was used; the City police banned all marches in their streets, the Ministry of Works denied Trafalgar Square to the 'Save Greece Now' group; vigils were banned outside Claridges (where the royals stayed) and Buckingham Palace; the Aldwych Theatre was heavily guarded during the royal performance – over 5,000 police were mobilized during the period of the visit – and there was even a warning that the wearing of black sashes would be interpreted as coming within the political uniform provisions of the 1936 Public Order Act. All this, despite Prime Minister Macmillan's pledge that peaceful demonstrations would be tolerated.

Such massive repression invited defiance. The most significant feature of the arrests and prosecutions that followed the three days of demonstrations† was the attempt to crush the leadership, again largely drawn from the Committee of 100. George Clark was arrested on 9 July and charged, on the evidence of two plain

*He (R. A. Butler) made quite inaccurate accusations against the Labour Mayors of Greenwich and Wandsworth.

†Apart, of course, from the famous planting of four half-bricks on demonstrators by Det. Sgt Challenor – see below, Chapter Four, p. 185.

was arrested on 9 July and charged, on the evidence of two plain clothes police who had joined the demonstration, with inciting people to commit a public nuisance by unlawfully obstructing the highway. (Clark had been active in trying to get people to evade police check posts in Whitehall.) He was given sixteen months at the London Quarter Sessions, a harsh sentence; the Appeal Court quashed the conviction, however, because it accepted the defence contention that an obstruction of the highway was not unlawful if it were caused by reasonable use of the highway, and that a demonstration was not an unreasonable use. Though this was hailed as a major constitutional victory, and does indeed make prosecutions of marches more difficult than of stationary meetings, the obstruction law is so tilted in favour of authority that it would be optimistic to suppose a similar prosecution could not succeed in future.[36] The courts continued their defence of the right to demonstrate when they dismissed the conspiracy charges against Terry Chandler and Peter Moule, who had been arrested on 10 July during the demonstration outside the Aldwych Theatre. (They were, however, convicted on lesser charges.) This was the first time since the 1930s that the authorities had resorted to the dangerously vague common-law charges to attack free assembly. Though unsuccessful, these anticipated the wave of such prosecutions after 1969. A further indication of the repressive atmosphere surrounding these demonstrations was the refusal of costs to two men who successfully appealed against a magistrate's conviction for obstructing the police when they were handing out leaflets during the Chandler-Moule trial – though the police were awarded costs for losing the case! It is another example of the way those in power can exploit the discretionary nature of British law to indulge their political sympathies.

In the second half of the 60s, the student Left and the various Marxist and anarchist groups succeeded the Committee of 100 as the most important radical agitators (though some people belonged to both phases). Just as the old anti-nuclear movement had found itself taking up wider foreign policy issues, so foreign issues (Vietnam, Rhodesia and South Africa, Ulster) provoked the most contentious demonstrations after 1964. The problem posed by the series of Vietnam demos of 1965–8 was that Grosvenor Square was too easily turned into a battleground. If the police chose to cordon off the area around the United States Embassy, as they usually did, and if the demonstrators chose to march up to the embassy, as they usually did, the result could only be the violent dispersal of the crowd. While the demonstrators must take much of the blame for this, the tactics of the police too often made their opponents appear the victims of injustice.

In 1965, the police imposed a ban on assemblies in the square without giving any prior warning to the three groups organizing demonstrations over one particular week-end. The police issued a verbal announcement which half the demonstrators didn't hear, and then harshly broke up the crowd. The subsequent court treatment (see below p. 68) reinforced the impression of vindictiveness. The following year saw a repeat performance – 'rough treatment and well-tried charges' as the N.C.C.L. put it – but the march on 22 October 1967 marked a change for the worse, on both sides. By now certain sections of the far Left regarded these occasions primarily as a chance to fight the police. On their side the police brought in mounted officers who, though easy targets for missiles, were brutally effective when they charged the crowd. The N.C.C.L.'s analysis, based on reports from its observers in the square, blamed the demonstrators for their provocativeness, but pointed out that the police could have allowed the march to pass in front of the embassy and out of the square on the other side. They also criticized the use of horses and dogs to control the marchers,* and of ambulances to break up a subsequent sit-down in Oxford Street. The council received an unprecedented number of individual complaints about police violence.

In March the following year, the whole thing was repeated on a grander scale – 25,000 people assembled in Trafalgar Square – and in front of television cameras. The N.C.C.L. had twenty-five observers in Grosvenor Square, and were able to send a detailed report to the Home Office, which had the grace to provide an equally detailed reply, though not surprisingly it conceded little. (The effect of some of these criticisms, particularly about the use

---

*In 1958 the N.C.C.L. had protested effectively about dogs used during a trade union dispute. This seems to be their first reappearance on the police side of a demonstration.

of mounted police to charge into the crowd, could perhaps be seen the following October, when very few horses were in evidence and none were used). Again the demonstrators were at fault, particularly the leadership whose objectives – apart from handing in protest letters at the embassy – were unclear, and who offered no guidance to their followers once the march reached the square. Equally the police allowed the confrontation to develop into a battle inside the square instead of forcing the marchers to move away and disperse of their own accord. The disturbing effect on ordinary policemen of finding themselves in this situation can be seen from the hundreds of reports sent into the N.C.C.L.

> I saw one young man, who was already on his knees, being trampled on by a horse which its rider was deliberately urging over his body. I saw a young woman, hemmed in by the crowd on all sides, kicked in the side of the face by another mounted policeman. I saw another young woman, with long hair, who had become isolated from the front line of demonstrators, seized savagely by her hair by a foot policeman and her neck twisted round while another policeman hit her body with a truncheon,

said one typical account. The N.C.C.L. report also described the deliberate discomfort those arrested were sometimes subjected to: by ten o'clock that Sunday night one Paddington police cell (measuring twelve feet by twenty) contained fifty-three people, some of them injured and bleeding, with no room to sit even on the floor and no ventilation – the one window was sealed. More than 280 people were arrested. The police suffered 117 casualties, the demonstrators forty-five – officially.

There was more trouble at the next demonstration in July (the Hilton Hotel was stoned) but the great event was the march of 27 October. The build-up of expectation was unprecedented, and a month beforehand two papers, the *Evening News* and *The Times*, carried scare stories about Molotov cocktails and plans to take over buildings that were almost certainly based on police leaks (though this was denied later). Similarly the advice to shutter buildings along the route increased public apprehension. And then it all passed off peacefully. Even the confrontation between the small breakaway march and the protective cordon around the U.S. embassy ended with both sides singing *Auld Lang Syne*. For all the rhetoric of street power from the quasi-insurrectionary Left groups, the tradition of peaceful protest inhibited any real attempt to lead 60,000 people in an uprising.* On the other side the police had publicly announced the week before that they would concede the streets to the demonstrators. Even the Grosvenor Square *fracas* with the militant minority was more a pushing match than anything else. In fact the worst violence seems to have come from neither the demonstrators nor the police but from young football gangs from South London attracted by the highly publicized anticipation of trouble.[37]

The widespread satisfaction about this 'success' for the British way of protest did not last very long – or never penetrated to the provinces. In 1969 an energetic and imaginative campaign to disrupt the tour of the South African rugby team as a protest against apartheid and its supporters here – and as a rehearsal for the proposed cricket tour the following year – deliberately set out to commit civil offences by occupying the pitches during games. This led to considerable and understandable resentment on the part of those more interested in sport than politics, which was generally handled well by the police. The major exception was in Swansea. What happened there on 15 November 1969 was described by the N.C.C.L. as 'the worst display of public violence outside London in many years'. A march of about 1,000 people outside the rugby ground was suddenly and brutally attacked by the police, with some of the chief officers behaving as roughly as their men. There was no apparent reason why the march, which was peaceful, could not have passed the ground and dispersed; nor does there seem to have been any warning, or any request to disperse immediately. Inside the ground the police allowed large numbers of 'stewards' to attack chanting demonstrators among the crowd; and when the brief invasion of the pitch occurred, both police and stewards ejected the demonstrators very roughly indeed.

*At least one section of the Left revised its revolutionary tactics thereafter. The series of 1 May and Angry Brigade bombings got into their swing in 1969, peaking in the first half of 1971 – and creating a new civil liberty crisis. See below p. 167.

Many of them were made to run a gauntlet of kicks and blows. A large number of complaints were made against the police, and 236 of them were considered serious enough to be the subject of an official inquiry. This was never published, however, and the terse summary of its findings – that there were no grounds for criminal or disciplinary proceedings – was not surprisingly regarded as a whitewash by the N.C.C.L. and many others. The council pointed out that much of the resentment felt against the police was caused, not by examples of corruption or violence, but by their failure to admit that transgressions ever happened. On this occasion, the chairman of the Police Federation did admit that mistakes had been made by a force not used to handling demonstrations.

Authority's third and final line of control over public assemblies is the courts; and the way magistrates (and to a lesser extent the judges) used their discretionary power parallels that of the police in reflecting prejudice against minority groups whose dissent was particularly irritating. In the 1960s, the magistrates' response to the new kind of aggressive street politics lapsed into three kinds of petty abuse: refusing bail, refusing costs and binding over, all three intended as additional punishment or a way of censoring unwelcome views.

The power to bind over – that is, obtain a promise to refrain from breaking the law (usually breaches of the peace) – derives from the ancient 1361 statute designed to cope with the bands of renegade soldiers returning from the French wars, and more recently from the 1952 Magistrates Court Act. A vital difference in these two authorities is that the 1952 act requires the courts to hear evidence before making the order, while the older one bestows almost unlimited power. From the time of the Direct Action Committee's first acts of civil disobedience in 1958, the courts have frequently resorted to the 1361 statute in an attempt to prevent dissenters dissenting.

In effect these have been asked to sign away their right to protest.* Russell and the Committee of 100 went to prison in 1961 for refusing to be bound over. The Vietnam protesters

*There were famous earlier victims – Lansbury in 1913 for advocating suffragette militancy, Tom Mann in 1932 for Hunger Marching.

arrested in Grosvenor Square in 1965 and 1966 were bound over for a year, which in effect meant not taking part in demonstrations, or doing so at the risk of imprisonment. One man who was bound over by magistrates was acquitted at his subsequent trial, but his request to be discharged of the binding-over order was refused; which is punishing the innocent. In 1969, Pat Arrowsmith went to prison for six months – an astonishing sentence – for refusing to be bound over after a peaceful demonstration outside the Elliott-Automation factory which was supplying material for the American war effort in Vietnam.*
But in the same year, after a decade of abuse, the power finally blew up in the users' hands with the uproar caused by the 'Sixpenny Protesters' affair. A proposal to increase admission charges to a Havant park was resisted by local people, and a group of them led by some Labour councillors, including a magistrate, Mrs Bell, forced their way into the park. They planned a second demonstration, with a possible sit-in, but the police arrested the six leaders and took them before the Petersfield magistrates to obtain a binding-over order, which would have either prevented the demonstration or, at the least, severely hampered it by removing its organizers. Because Mrs Bell and her colleagues refused to be bound over, they were sent to gaol. The press and public response was staggering. Appeals were prepared (an opportunity only available since 1967), but before they could be heard the six were brought before an assize judge – in handcuffs – who freed them on condition they proceeded with the appeals. These were successful, but only on the technicality that the original order had been worded incorrectly. As the N.C.C.L., which had briefed a watching counsel, pointed out, the decision 'may turn out to be less a pillar of civil liberty than a direction to magistrates' courts how safely to go about the exercise of their arbitrary powers.' The *New Law Journal* put the general case against these orders succinctly: 'Binding over is a punitive measure imposed in circumstances which usually render it contrary to principle on which the fairness of our

---

*She became the first British prisoner of conscience to be adopted by Amnesty International, to the delight of former N.C.C.L. general secretary (then director-general of Amnesty) Martin Ennals.

system of justice is said to be founded.' However, the fuss forced the Home Office to initiate an internal inquiry in the whole procedure. And at the same time as the Havant affair Lord Parker and Lord Justice Davies emphasized in a Divisional Court Case[38] that even under the 1361 act people must have a chance to argue against an order, and that under the 1952 act there had to be proof of a complaint.

The use of legal costs as a punishment has already been noted in one case brought as a result of the Greek demonstrations in 1963. The magistrate or judge can either use his discretion in this matter to impose an extra penalty or, where the prosecution has failed, make sure the accused suffers at least financial punishment. It is perhaps not as frequently abused as the other two discretionary powers but it is easily done, and is unchallengeable. In February 1970, for example, a young man, Condry, who succeeded in his appeal against a conviction for assaulting the police during the anti-Springbok demonstration at Twickenham in December 1969, was denied costs by Judge Cassels. The latter argued that it was not a social thing to demonstrate, and that being on a demonstration was by itself likely to cause a breach of the peace – which was tantamount to saying demonstrations were illegal.

The most abused power is that of granting bail. (And not just in political or public order cases either – see below, Chapter Six.) By refusing bail the courts put in prison for months at a time many people who, when eventually tried, were either found innocent or merely given a fine. Needless to say, the bail system worked much more harshly against the under-privileged, whose lack of respectability was reason enough in the eyes of the law for keeping them locked up. Though there had been criticism of this in the C.N.D. days, the real attack on the system only developed in the second half of the decade as it became used with increasing severity and discrimination. Refusing bail to teenagers involved in the 'mods and rockers' disturbances at Brighton during Easter 1965 – and the overnight gaoling of many others – had no discernible justification, and was seemingly used as an unofficial deterrent. (The Brighton magistrates proved just as vindictive when faced with the Vietnam protest in the Methodist

Church the following year – see above pp. 53-4.) After the 1965 Grosvenor Square demonstrations, the police refused to accept sureties from anyone with a previous conviction – and, as many demonstrators were using friends who had minor public order convictions from previous demonstrations, seventeen people spent the night in prison for an offence which carried the maximum fine of £2. Again it is difficult to interpret this as anything except a little piece of unofficial punitive action.

Much more serious was the length of time spent in gaol by three members of the Black Panther party (including Biafran playwright Obi Egbuna) who were tried for conspiring to kill after speeches in Hyde Park in 1968. All bail applications were refused and, after five months in Brixton, one man was acquitted and the others given suspended sentences. In the following year there were three major cases where the police and courts used the bail system to punish or control political dissent. In January 1969, after his arrest during a demonstration outside South Africa House, Ed Davoren was granted bail on condition he took no further part in similar demonstrations. Davoren chose to challenge this on principle, and although it was not fully tested in court – the Lord Chief Justice offered him unconditional bail if he applied through a judge in chambers – the Divisional Courts' handling of the application suggested a lack of sympathy with this kind of judicial restriction on the right to political activity.

The following September, the police raided a school in Covent Garden where a large number of young people were squatting. Fifty-nine of them were arrested, most on the charge of resisting the sheriff. Though bail was frequently granted the conditions were such as to prove insuperable – personal sureties of £100, hardly the kind of ready money available to young squatters, or guarantees from parents who could not be contacted. Many therefore had to spend a month in custody, though charges against all but nine were eventually dropped. The court's reluctance to help those whom the law chose not to punish formally would appear to derive more from dislike of unorthodoxy than concern for justice.

In another squatting case the following month the police indulged in a blatant example of political discrimination. A house in Fulham had been taken over by a group of anarchists, six of whom were charged, on 1 October, with 'conspiring to cause actual bodily harm to persons endeavouring to effect lawful entry' – i.e., the police.* Five of these were refused bail on police objections, though two of them had earlier been allowed bail, with no police objections, on assault charges. The most disturbing case was that of a nineteen-year-old from Cornwall, Dave Griffiths. He had no previous record, and a large number of his Cornish neighbours, all respectable, were prepared to stand surety for him. The police objection to him was based entirely on his political beliefs and associations – not on any fear that he would abscond or repeat the crime again, the normal justifications for refusing bail. The police maintained their objections even after his five companions had obtained bail. Eventually the N.C.C.L. secured his release by application to a judge in chambers, and personal intercession with the Home Office, but even then the police managed to delay his actual release for a further eight days, until 23 December.

Bail, costs and binding over are threats to freedom from a relatively low level of the legal pyramid, with at least some opportunity for redress. Much more serious, because the threat emanates from the top, is the final control over free assembly available to authority – the use of statutes and common law to bring grave charges against selected dissidents. Here again, the 1960s have for this century a record, if not for unprecedented attempts to bend the law against those exercising their right to free assembly, at least an unprecedentedly sustained attempt. This is particularly true of the period from 1967 when there was a clear policy of cracking down on certain kinds of demonstrators, notably the students, blacks and Irish. Fortunately, it had less than a fifty per cent success rate.

Though statutory legislation was not a very effective weapon at this stage, largely because its precision prevented much manipulation, the prosecuting authorities did abuse the purpose

*The circumlocutory charge was a symptom of authority's difficulty in getting to grips with squatters, who were actually protected by the law of trespass once in occupation.

of the law with their resort to the Official Secrets Act – passed in 1911 specifically to cope with German spies and with liberal disclaimers about any repressive potential – to punish the Committee of 100 demonstrators at Wethersfield in 1961. Six of its leading members, including Terry Chandler, were given sentences of twelve and eighteen months for conspiring to incite others to commit a breach of the act, in that they had declared their intention of entering the U.S. air base and immobilizing it. In a sad day for British justice, both the Divisional Court and the House of Lords accepted what has rightly been called the 'dangerous doctrine that what is Crown policy is therefore necessarily in the interests of the state.'[39] In a political trial – they are not supposed to exist, of course – the courts refused to hear two sides of a political argument. They accepted the prosecution's case for national security but would not listen to the defence on the danger of nuclear arms.[40]

The flexible nature of terms like 'incitement' – which need merely mean announcing an intention – and conspiracy, which simply means agreeing to do something, were an understandable temptation for the authorities, to which they readily succumbed during the C.N.D. troubles. In the same year as the Wethersfield case George Clark had an incitement conviction quashed, and the failure of the prosecution to pin similar charges on Clark, Chandler and Moule during the Greek demonstrations in 1963 has already been described. (See pp. 60-61.) These setbacks seemed to have discredited the concepts for a few years, but when Chandler and fifty other demonstrators occupied the Greek Embassy in London in the week after the Colonels' 1967 coup as a protest against the military takeover, the D.P.P. tried another helpfully fuzzy common-law offence – unlawful assembly. Forty-one of the demonstrators pleaded guilty (the prosecution conceded that the elements of force and violence, which would have raised the offence to the much graver one of riotous assembly, were absent from this case); and the court threw out the charges of forcible entry, made under a statute of 1381. But although the judge accepted there was no particular leadership in the demonstration, he singled out three men – Chandler, Foley and Randle – for imprisonment (fifteen, six and twelve months respectively) on the grounds that their record of civil disobedience in C.N.D. activities had made them 'persistent lawbreakers'.) (The others were either fined or discharged.) When their appeals against this were dismissed, the N.C.C.L. and several Labour M.P.s unsuccessfully tried to get the Government to intervene. Lord Gardiner, the Labour Lord Chancellor, correctly wrote to Smythe that 'we shall sometimes disagree with a particular sentence, but this is better than going back to the days when judges were controlled by the politicians. We cannot have it both ways.' To which one Labour M.P. rather forlornly replied, 'Is it too much to have judges who are both independent and liberal-minded?'

Thus heartened, the authorities moved on to riotous assembly, against the people arrested in July 1968 after the windows of the Hilton Hotel had been smashed during a Vietnam demonstration. As one lawyer has argued, the crucial features of these common-law prosecutions are the arbitrary (politically motivated) selection of a batch of people* on a demonstration who are then indicted for taking part in it (rather than for specific individual acts), and the one-sided political nature of the trial.[41] Exploiting the blanket nature of such charges, the prosecution is able to probe the politics of the accused in a hostile manner while the judges expressly forbid political replies from the defence on grounds like 'I am not going to allow the court to be used as a vehicle for political propaganda.'[42] In the Hilton Hotel trial, however, this crude repression failed – the jury, presaging what was going to be a general dislike on the part of juries for this development, acquitted the defendants. Similar lack of success attended the prosecution of nine people for riot after South Africa House was damaged during a demonstration in January 1969.†

*'They usually seem to be political activists, or children from politically active families.' – Stephen Sedley.

†A minor irony can be savoured in what appears to be a flaw in the selection process in this case. Two of the nine were National Front members, who were hardly likely to have harboured any window-breaking radicalism in their breasts.

However, in 1970, the authorities again made the charges stick. Three London University graduates were convicted of unlawful assembly for their part in a demonstration at the Senate House in October the previous year which had caused some damage. The singling out of the particular individuals, two of them American and all of them well known socialist activists, in itself a serious infringement of civil liberty, was compounded by police objections to bail made on the quite inaccurate grounds that the Americans' visas had expired together with the unsubstantiated suggestion that they would, if released, continue to disrupt the university. This successful victimization was followed by the even more notorious Cambridge 'Garden House Hotel' trial in July.* The previous February, a demonstration protesting at a 'Greek Week' being held in the hotel had led to an invasion of the building and some £2,000 worth of damage. Twenty people were arrested and initially charged with unlawful assembly. After several delays and havering around over charges, six people were sent to prison for between nine and eighteen months, and two received deportation orders. (On appeal the deportation orders and two convictions were quashed or set aside.) There was a great deal of concern over the outcome of the trial – as Professor Street wrote, when has a judge been so criticized without contempt proceedings following?[43] – not only because the jury had convicted four of the accused of riotous assembly (for the first time since the 1930s) but at a succession of apparent injustices during the case. These included the way the defendants were selected – against many of them there was no evidence of any act at all except that of taking part in the demonstration, certainly not of any violence; the delays both in charging those arrested and then holding the trial; the introduction of new and more serious charges after committal; Melford Stevenson's smear about the 'evil influence' of certain Cambridge dons; the deportation orders; and the severity of the sentences.

This seems to have been the nadir for civil liberty, however.

---

*It is odd how three of the big common-law public order trials in the decade – the Frederika demonstrations of 1963, the Greek Embassy occupation in 1967 and the Cambridge trial in 1970 – have this Greek connection.

In 1972, a London jury* refused to convict the Mangrove Nine of riotous assembly. The Mangrove was a restaurant in Notting Hill which had become something of a centre for black activists; between 1969 and 1971, it was persistently raided by the police and lost its all-night licence. On 19 August there was a march, mostly of blacks, protesting at this harassment, which ended in a battle when the police tried to break it up. Many months later, and after prevarications similar to those in the Cambridge Hotel trial, nine people were tried for riotous assembly and other lesser charges, even though the magistrate at the committal hearing had dismissed the riot charges. A vigorous defence, some of it self-conducted, persuaded the jury to follow the magistrate – they, too, acquitted the defendants of riot.

A minor case at Uxbridge in June 1971 showed just how pervasive this attempt to nail groups of people collectively had become, particularly when authority was frustrated in the legitimate task of establishing individual guilt. Seventeen youths were charged with threatening behaviour after an incident at a school dance in which they were alleged to have blocked the road. The prosecution maintained – and the magistrate initially accepted the argument – that they had no need to identify individual actions by particular defendants, but that membership of a group behaving criminally was sufficient in itself. Though the seventeen were eventually acquitted, the prosecution's argument and the court's apparent willingness to concede it was an alarming development.

If it were not bad enough that the ordinary authorities had shown themselves eager to try out new forms of repression, a private citizen, Francis Bennion, felt it necessary to step in where they had failed. In the summer of 1972 he at last succeeded in getting Peter Hain on a private prosecution at the Old Bailey on a conspiracy charge for his part in organizing the anti-Springbok campaigns of 1969–70. Not only had the D.P.P. refused to prosecute, but Bennion himself had twice been

---

*There was a belief in Left-wing circles that London juries – like those which tried Prescott and Purdie and the *Oz* trio around this time – were more sophisticated than provincial ones, such as the one which heard the Cambridge trial.

rebuffed by the courts before he finally succeeded. He was financed in his efforts by supporters in South Africa: but much the most sinister feature of his crusade was his perception of the potential of the conspiracy charge, which, while more serious than the specific crime, actually required far less in the way of direct evidence.

Indeed at first Bennion's counsel announced that he was out to prove 'there is no right to demonstrate in English law'. The N.C.C.L., which had actively supported Hain (their legal officer, Larry Grant, acted as Hain's solicitor) commented after he had been acquitted on all the major charges that the prosecution had been forced to concede after all that there was a right to protest. However, they also pointed out that the confusion over conspiracy in relation to public order offences did no good to civil liberty: nor did the payment of Bennion's costs out of public funds, which Labour M.P. Charles Loughlin attacked for offering any 'backwoodsman . . . an open-ended inducement to take into court any person who exercises his right to demonstrate.'

Though the Government did not choose themselves to attack this right in the frontal manner adopted by Bennion, they resorted to potentially far more serious back-door assaults in the next two years. The use of conspiracy charges against pickets has already been noted. There was even an attempt to charge three Irishmen with treason, for calling on their fellow-countrymen to fight the British, while addressing people in Hyde Park in February 1972. This was soon dropped, however. Much graver was the creation of a new offence, conspiracy to trespass, in the Kamara case. This arose from an incident in 1972, when a group of Sierra Leonese students had occupied their country's High Commission offices in London for a day. They were charged with conspiracy and unlawful assembly, and were convicted on all counts. The effect of this, as the N.C.C.L. pointed out, was to render the traditional distinction between criminal and civil law meaningless. Trespass is a civil offence: if committed by an individual it is not a crime, although the property owner can sue for damages in a civil action. As a result of the Kamara decision, two people trespassing could now be prosecuted by the police for a criminal offence: an absurd and potentially dangerous situation. The readiness of the authorities to exploit the new weapon was seen a few months after the Lords had confirmed the Kamara judgment, when similar prosecutions were brought against Birmingham strikers (see above, p. 47): fortunately, these prosecutions failed.

With the return of a Labour government in 1974, the prosecuting authorities seem to have abandoned these more extreme charges. Instead the police, on two occasions, suddenly reverted to old bad habits. In June they violently dispersed a Left-wing crowd that had gathered to harass a National Front march in London's Red Lion Square. The police seem to have been provoked by a militant section of the Left-wingers, but over-reacted, with tragic consequences: one demonstrator, Kevin Gately, died in the subsequent turmoil. Two months later, the Thames Valley police vigorously broke up a rock festival at Windsor, with little apparent justification. Although in both cases the police hierarchies predictably defended these actions, it is clear they were embarrassed by the criticisms – which gives some ground for hoping such incidents will remain the exception rather than the rule.

As British politics changed significantly after the late 1950s, the right to demonstrate had been aggressively and ingeniously used on a scale greater even than in the 1930s. The aggression and ingenuity on the one side had inevitably been met with repression (and ingenuity) on the other. The willingness of the prosecuting authorities to invent new offences, revive old and supposedly dead ones, and to resort on a wide scale to con-spiracy and incitement prosecutions after 1967, all marked an unusual intensification of traditional responses to public order issues. In some cases, only the jury stood between demonstrators and serious injustice and victimization. Thankfully, in most of them, the juries stood firm for justice.

The right to assemble freely in Britain is not disputed. The ability to make that right a powerful political weapon always will be disputed, since when demonstrators are effective – as they often were after 1960 – the authorities will naturally do their best to neutralize their effectiveness. The extent to which those who govern will be successful in this will always be determined by the willingness of the governed to resist.

2. Freedom of Expression

Freedom of expression exists, is increasing and ought not to be diminished. It is perhaps the classic British liberty – after personal privacy – with such traditional sanctity that no-one wants to be seen to be against it. As a democratic concept it has considerable antiquity: one of its noblest formulations, Milton's *Areopagitica*, was made over 300 years ago. This aura of respect is a highly valuable asset, and a major safeguard against the complex of forces that operate censorship.

In modern times this has largely been concerned with religion, sex and politics; mostly the latter two, which in fact came together in the mid-1960s with such assertiveness that they precipitated a minor frenzy of repression. Despite the obvious set-backs, like the trial of the magazine *Oz* in 1971, freedom of expression was much stronger, because it was much more widely and vigorously used, at the end of the 1960s than it was before the permissive decade began.

Since few people – except the film censor, who is nowadays almost obliged to mitigate his odious title by displaying extreme liberalism – want to be caught in the act of censorship, the various regulatory processes are spread around, shuffled about and generally disguised as far as possible. From the point of view of those in authority, the ideal form of censorship is that which is self-imposed: and this obsequious and subtle system obtains in the more modern media, such as film, broadcasting and the press. Normal legal control does provide some considerable powers of censorship, through statutes like the Obscene Publications Act and the Official Secrets Acts, and through civil and common-law concepts of defamation and the rather dubious conspiracy to corrupt. In addition there has for centuries been a tradition of administrative censorship, of regulating what people might express by a licensing system operated by statutory agencies – like the Lord Chamberlain and the Stationers' Company. This regrettable tradition is maintained in a sophisticated form by the broadcasting institutions, the B.B.C. and the I.B.A., whose theoretical independence of government can provide a decent screen for political manoeuvring.

The older media, print and the stage, have thrown off most of these statutory encumbrances, but like everyone else are subject to the general restrictions on obscenity and defamation. Pictorial art, particularly when offered for public viewing, is controlled by statute, as galleries learned the hard way in the mid-1960s. As important as any of these, particularly in the more democratically-oriented media like the press and broadcasting, is the censorship built into the economics of production. The capital and equipment required have restricted ownership to a few private enterprises and a state-financed corporation. Access to these is inevitably limited. In the early 1970s, there were increasing demands for a more widespread diffusion of ownership and for ways of providing greater access for non-professionals.

Two of the statutes which N.C.C.L. Secretary Ronald Kidd singled out as distinguishing the repressiveness of the inter-war Governments (see above p. 24) particularly threatened freedom of expression – the Official Secrets Acts and the Incitement to Disaffection Act. It was perhaps characteristic of the time that the latter legislation covered even conversation. Largely as a result of the Invergordon 'mutiny' in 1931 and a couple of ham-fisted prosecutions of Communists under the Incitement to Mutiny Act of 1797, the National Government introduced this bill to counter subversion of the armed forces in April 1934. Between this and the royal assent in November it was subjected to such sustained opposition, both inside and outside Parliament, that the Government was obliged to amend the most offensive sections. The N.C.C.L. organized two major Trafalgar Square demonstrations (in July and October) as well as a delegate conference, and many meetings throughout the country.* There

*Such was the anger on the Left that the N.C.C.L. campaign succeeded in briefly uniting some ill-assorted bedfellows. Nye Bevan cheekily exploited Attlee's support for the N.C.C.L. campaign in his attack on the

was even a famous satirical trial, in which the cartoonist Low was 'tried' for a subversive cartoon in a court which included Kingsley Martin, Aylmer Vallance and Miles Malleson. Because of the lack of lawyers on the Labour benches the N.C.C.L. legal briefings for M.P.s was a valuable new service, though the deficiency was to some extent remedied once even Conservatives like Sir William Holdsworth, the leading Oxford jurist, condemned the measure as the 'most daring encroachment upon the liberty of the subject which an executive Government has attempted in a time which is not a time of emergency.'*

Under this pressure, the Government made important changes. In their definition of what constituted an offence under the act they inserted the words 'maliciously and advisedly', the phrase used in the 1797 Mutiny Act, but deliberately dropped from the, original draft of this one – which if left unamended would have enabled the authorities to prosecute someone who did not even realize he was talking to a soldier. Similarly the Government had at first intended to penalize the simple possession of documents which could subvert a soldier – the onus would be on the accused to prove that such documents had a different, legitimate, purpose. This of course would have upset the normal bias of English law, where the burden of proof is on the prosecution, and it greatly alarmed the Quakers and the trade unions. This clause was re-drafted to shift the onus back to the prosecution. Search powers under the act remained wide; but, alarmed at the accusation that they were restoring general warrants (which had been illegal since 1765), the Government agreed that these warrants could only be authorized by a High Court judge and an inspector of police, rather than a magistrate and ordinary officers, as they had originally proposed. This was an important safeguard in view of the much more unrestrained exercise of political discrimination in the lower levels of the law. A clause

---

Labour Party's proscription policy, and the second Trafalgar Square demonstration was notable for its mix of Labour and Communist banners.[1]

*Kingsley Martin felt that the attitude of non-radicals like the *New Statesman* drama critic Desmond MacCarthy, who went personally to see Baldwin about the bill, carried far more weight than the opinions of predictable dissenters like himself.

which would have extended the offence to include even a pre-paratory act – Professor Street gives the nice example of the danger of boarding the Portsmouth train – was scrapped alto-gether. The Opposition also secured the valuable right for an accused to opt for jury trial. The Government, however, refused to change the alarming, if simple, phrase 'seducing a soldier from his duty *or* his allegiance.' Under the 1797 Act the prosecu-tion had to prove that a soldier had been seduced from both – a much harder task. Both Pritt and Kingsley Martin, who were active in opposition to the act, have argued that the furore deterred the government from using their new powers and left them unwilling to attempt further restrictive legislation for at least another two years.[2] There was one prosecution before the war, of a Leeds student whose conversation with an R.A.F. man in a café about the Spanish Civil War earned him a year in prison. He was alleged to have tried to persuade the pilot to help the Republicans, and the judge gave him a severe sentence as a public warning. It was however reduced to a few months after public protests, led by his local Conservative M.P. (and former N.C.C.L. member) Vyvyan Adams. The revived, and successful, use of the Act in the 1970s serves as a barometer of the repressive quality of both periods.

The other major statutory attempt at censorship before the war occurred four years later, when the Official Secrets Act was invoked against several journalists. Coming at a time when the Government was trying to moderate troublesome press comment, in accordance with its appeasement policy, this produced another storm of anger. Freedom of expression was, however, an easier freedom to defend in the 1930s than freedom of assembly. The act of 1909 had been strengthened in 1920, making it a felony to communicate any document the Government chose to classify as secret. Journalists like Lord Burnham of the *Daily Telegraph* argued at the time that this was a danger to the press, but received assurances from a shocked Government that this could never be. Governments in fact began to brandish the acts at journalists in the early 1930s, once over what proved to be a speculative story about the imminent arrest of Gandhi, and once to punish a Somerset House clerk who had been making the contents of wills known to a reporter. These had aroused comment at the time, but in 1937–8 a series of cases occurred which, since they had no connection at all with espionage, provoked a widespread campaign against the acts.

A Hull post office clerk was convicted for passing information from official telegrams to a freelance journalist; and in August a Stockport journalist called Lewis was fined £5 for refusing to divulge the source of a story he had written about a Manchester swindler. This had been very close in content to a confidential police circular, and although the prosecution never maintained there was any danger to the state in Lewis's story, they persisted with their 'technical' charges. When Lewis appealed, the Divisional Court had no choice but to rule that the offence came within the scope of the acts. As Kidd pointed out[3], it was indeed ironical that the Attorney-General in the 1920 government who had so resolutely denied that there was any danger to the press in his act was eighteen years later the Lord Chief Justice – Lord, formerly Sir Gordon, Hewart – who had to reject a journalist's appeal against conviction under that same act.

As a result of this, the N.C.C.L. and the National Union of Journalists began a joint campaign to get the Official Secrets Acts changed. Just as it was getting under way, another scandal erupted. Duncan Sandys, then a young Tory M.P. on the Churchill wing of the party, had indicated to Hore-Belisha, the Minister of Defence, that he proposed to ask a series of Parliamentary questions to expose what he regarded as deficiencies in the country's defences. He was for his pains summoned before the Attorney-General and, by his account, threatened with the Official Secrets Act unless he named the source of his information about a serious shortage of anti-aircraft guns. Sandys immediately made the matter public, and the Government found itself on the receiving end of a wave of Parliamentary anger. They gave in to Sandys' demand for an inquiry, and set up a select committee.* In November 1938 a special conference

---

*The blunders continued even thereafter; the Army Council tried to summons Sandys, a major, to appear before them in uniform to answer questions on the subject. Sandys pleaded Parliamentary privilege and refused.

organized by the N.C.C.L. and N.U.J. – and enlivened by Compton Mackenzie's account of his encounter with the act – appointed a delegation to see the Home Secretary. The combination of this, the select committee's report and the threat of a Dingle Foot bill which went much further than they wanted, induced the Government to make a minor change in the Act in 1939, which limited the powers of police interrogation. But as journalists were to re-discover in the 1960s, the Official Secrets Acts remained a permanent, if sometimes latent, threat to the freedom of the press.

The governments of the 1930s were able to impose a much more effective (and less resistance–provoking) censorship on the two other news media, the B.B.C. and the cinema newsreels. In 1935–6 the Foreign Office successfully brought pressure on the B.B.C. to drop Pollitt, the Communist leader, and Mosley from a talks series on 'citizenship'. The correspondence between the B.B.C. and the Foreign Office has some revealing moments; 'There must be a limit to the English tradition of free speech somewhere', wrote one F.O. functionary. The B.B.C. even agreed in the end to forego their earlier insistence that any cancellation would have to be laid publicly at the Government's door.⁴ The excuse given at that time was the Abyssinia crisis; two years later, they again intervened to silence public criticism of national policy during the Munich crisis. Of the five regular newsreels, four were easily persuaded to show only pro-Government material during Chamberlain's visit to Hitler. One, Paramount, which had intended to include criticism by former *Times* editor Wickham Steed, was brought into line after the Foreign Office had secured the good offices of U.S. Ambassador Joseph Kennedy in forcing the American film company into line*.⁵

The Government did not even have to exert itself this much to keep politically unwelcome material out of the features shown in British cinemas in the 1930s, thanks to the sympathetic attitude adopted by Lord Tyrrell, the film censor. The origins of the British Board of Film Censors reveal a textbook illustration of the sleight-of-hand system of censorship in Britain – it is extra-

*At least the American press savaged Kennedy for this.

ordinary they even gave themselves such a blatant title.[5a] Powers to license cinemas had been given to local authorities under the 1909 Cinematograph Act, in order to secure decent fire and safety precautions. Perverting the course of legislation from its intended purpose is unfortunately a habit with British authorities, and almost immediately local councils began abusing this power to vet films, a practice rather surprisingly sustained by the courts. To avoid a plague of varying local vetoes, the film industry and the Home Office got together to establish the Board, which has no legal authority whatsoever but whose classifications are in general followed by local councils.

Throughout the late 1930s Tyrrell, the Board's chairman, demonstrated a clear bias against anti-Fascist material.[6] In 1935, a pacifist film was banned in the interests of 'public order', and, the following year, another peace film, made under the auspices of the League of Nations Union, was held up until public indignation forced Tyrrell to give it a certificate. In the same way he demanded such drastic revisions and cuts in the script for *Love on the Dole* that he prevented the film being made at all – a manoeuvre that was not publicly exposed for another four years. Tyrrell also cut and banned particular episodes of an American documentary series, the *March of Time*, which presented an anti-Fascist account of contemporary European history. Attempts in Parliament in 1938 to expose this kind of discrimination did not deter Tyrrell from his work; in March of the following year he banned a Russian anti-Nazi film, *Professor Mamlock*, which had had tremendous success in America and which was considered suitable in Britain once war broke out six months later.[6a]

Though the 1909 Act could thus be successfully bent to impose a stringent political censorship, its origins as a fire measure – film was highly inflammable in the early days – provided the N.C.C.L. with a valuable loophole once technical advances led to the widespread use of non-flammable film in educational and propaganda projects in the 1930s. In 1934 the Home Office indicated that it intended to bring these films within the system of controls created under the 1909 Act, but the N.C.C.L. pointed out, with strong support from the *Manchester Guardian*, that this was impossible without new legislation. Despite this, various local police forces used the 1909 Act quite illegally to threaten 'non-flam' film shows, and the N.C.C.L. developed a vigorous campaign to contest these usurpations.*

In 1935 the Durham police issued a summons against a miner's hall which had shown some of these films, and the N.C.C.L.-sponsored defence won the action in the Jarrow court, including costs against the police. Some authorities, notably Surrey County Council, still persisted in harassing 'non-flam' film showings, and in 1938 the Home Office, which had no wish to go through the chore of getting legislation through Parliament, felt obliged to set up an advisory committee to sort out the unseemly situation. Their report finally forced the intransigent authorities to come into line and recognize that 'non-flam' films were outside their jurisdiction.[7]

Political anxieties motivated the defiance seen in all these cases; it is clear that in the 1930s freedom of expression was regarded largely as a political civil liberty, very little as an artistic one. The period witnessed some famous obscenity trials, yet few civil libertarians – authors Wells and Priestley were honourable exceptions – came forward to defend the cause when art rather than politics was in the firing line. These two writers, together with Eliot and de la Mare, helped finance the (unsuccessful) appeal of the flamboyant Polish poet de Montalk in 1932, when his translations of Rabelais and Verlaine proved too much for the susceptibilities of his printer, the police and the court, who gave him a harsh six months' sentence. In 1935, there were three important book trials: Boriswoode were fined £250 for publishing James Hanley's *Boy*, and Heinemann £100 for Wallace Smith's *Bessie Cotter*. The sex-instruction manual *The Sex Impulse*, despite a defence by Professors Huxley, Haldane and Malinowski, was sent to the flames. Despite these reactionary results, two steps of great future value were taken in these trials; the law finally

---

*The trade union solicitor W. H. Thompson became the N.C.C.L.'s specialist on 'non-flam' films; Pritt has recorded the pleasure Thompson took in going to remote magistrates' courts and watching the police witnesses trying for two minutes at a time to light the non-flammable film with matches.[8]

conceded that there was a possible defence in claiming publication for the public good, and expert evidence was for the first time allowed, though in these instances ignored when it came to a verdict. The Public Morality Council, a precursor of Longford, Whitehouse and Muggeridge, sent a copy of *To Beg I Am Ashamed* to the Home Secretary, Hoare, in 1938; the threat contained in this action was sufficient to secure immediate withdrawal of the book by the publishers.[9]

Politics and the arts did, however, come together successfully during the war, to fight a B.B.C. ban on certain musicians whose politics it regarded with disfavour. Perhaps inevitably, more people seemed to value the peacetime concept of free expression during the war than that of free assembly, and a much greater tension developed around free speech, particularly in broadcasting and the press. The B.B.C. ultimately earned an enormous international reputation for its wartime performance, but some of its early behaviour augured no such happy outcome. The Chamberlain Government sacked all the B.B.C. governors at the start of the war (including Oxford historian H. A. L. Fisher and Margery Fry) save two, Sir Allan Powell, a former Conservative Mayor of Kensington, and Capt. Mills, the managing director of Baring Brothers. Their suitability for the job was quickly questioned by E. M. Forster. In 1940, the B.B.C. banned any broadcasters who disapproved of the war; two notable early victims were the pacifist Sir Hugo Roberton, conductor of the Glasgow Orpheus choir, and the Communist composer Dr Alan Bush. (Not just the composer; his compositions, too.) When this action became known early in 1941 there was a furious protest, particularly from other B.B.C. performers like Beatrix Lehmann and Michael Redgrave. At a conference organized by the N.C.C.L. in March (preceded five days earlier by an announcement from Duff Cooper, the Minister of Information, that the Government had appointed two 'advisers' to the B.B.C., an action which he said 'would no doubt increase the control exercised by the Government') Forster, Rose Macaulay and Dr Vaughan Williams pledged themselves to boycott the B.B.C. until the ban was withdrawn. The B.B.C. decided the weight of opposition was too great. Three days after the conference

Churchill told the Commons that the connection between 'minority opinion and musical or dramatic performance is not apparent nor worthwhile establishing.' On 2 April Cooper announced a reconstituted B.B.C. board of governors. Sir Ian Fraser returned, and Lady Violet Bonham Carter was added, both appointments which gratified the critics. To complete the victory, Labour M.P. George Strauss, prompted by the N.C.C.L., persisted with Parliamentary questions until he won an un-qualified public withdrawal of the ban on Roberton, whom the B.B.C. had continued to exclude even after Churchill's first Commons announcement.

Press freedom required much greater vigilance; indeed it suffered severer defeats, from the publication of the first Defence Regulations in October 1939 to the trial of the anarchist *War Commentary* in May 1945. At first, censorship powers were derived from regulation 39B, which made it an offence 'to influence public opinion in a manner prejudicial to the defence of the realm or to efficient prosecution of the war.' In addition, widespread restrictions were liable on any publication of material affecting foreign relations, and the War Office was given the right to vet all outgoing mail. For the press the real threat lay in regulation 3 which made it an offence to publish information of use to the enemy; the Government, of course, could decide what fell under the heading of usefulness. To cope with this, the papers set up a system of voluntary censorship in co-operation with the Ministry of Information.

When the real crisis of the war came in May 1940, with the collapse of Western European allies and the threat of invasion, the Government felt these powers were not nearly enough. Three new decrees strengthened its arm. Under regulation 2 (C) the Home Secretary could, after one warning, prosecute anyone whose published comments he regarded as likely to foment opposition to the war. 2 (D) gave him power to suppress any newspaper systematically fomenting such opposition. 94 (A) enabled him to shut down offending printing presses. A month later 39 (B) was re-worded to catch anyone 'causing alarm and despondency', an amazing concept, which was not surprisingly laughed out of effective use within a few months. On 21 June

Duff Cooper, the Minister of Information, told the Fleet Street editors that in his opinion the voluntary system had broken down and that he proposed to institute compulsory censorship. He was even thinking of reviving the *British Gazette* (used for Government propaganda during the General Strike in 1926) and suppressing all the national newspapers.

All this proved too much even for *The Times*, and the N.C.C.L. found widespread support when it organized an emergency conference on press freedom in July. Churchill had already dropped the idea of compulsory censorship in the face of a Fleet Street united front, but Frank Owen, the editor of the London *Evening Standard*, delivered a scathing attack on Cooper and Ratcliffe, the chief censor. He drew attention to the way the *Daily Worker* (which in line with Communist policy at this stage was still opposed to the war) was being intimidated by Anderson, the Home Secretary, and was already effectively censored by the ban imposed by most bookstalls. As a result of the conference Sydney Silverman moved a prayer in the Commons against regulation 2 (D) which was only lost by the surprisingly narrow margin of 60–98. In the course of the debate, Anderson felt obliged to promise that the new measures would only be invoked during an invasion. Both he and Attlee refused to see an N.C.C.L. delegation appointed by the press freedom conference. Cooper did meet them in October, when he had the effrontery – or the open-mindedness – to congratulate the N.C.C.L. on its watchdog work on the defence regulations.

The threat of suppression, staved off in 1940, became a reality in January 1941, when Herbert Morrison, who had replaced Anderson as Home Secretary, moved against the *Daily Worker* and Cockburn's news-sheet *The Week*. Morrison admitted in Parliament that the suppression of these papers was a preventive action aimed at eliminating what the Government regarded as the harmful effects of the Communist Party's anti-war attitude on their factory readership – though, as Kingsley Martin pointed out, it was difficult to imagine what influence the élitist *The Week* had on the shop floor. The *Daily Worker* had since the outbreak of war been subjected to considerable harassment; sellers were prosecuted (see above,

Chapter 1) and two of its correspondents, Ivor Montagu and Frank Pitcairn (Cockburn) had been refused exit visas to cover the Russo-Finnish war*. (Cockburn met this problem again at the end of the war; the second ban was not lifted until September 1945.) What particularly incensed the liberal-minded was not only that Morrison had broken Anderson's pledge that the regulations would not be used except at a time of invasion, but that in choosing 2 (D) to suppress the papers he was able to avoid any judicial process at all (2 (C) at least required an application to the courts) and was thus both accuser and judge. The N.C.C.L. organized a second conference on press freedom in June 1941, which called for the repeal of the repressive regulations. Owen was again in the forefront of the attack on the Government, and he gave open publicity to the Fleet Street inside knowledge that the Government had considered suppressing the *Daily Mirror* and the *Sunday Pictorial* as well.†

The Government considered their suppression even more seriously in the spring of 1942, when the war was at its lowest ebb and the authorities were consequently at their most censorious. In March Morrison managed to thwart Churchill's suggestion that 2 (D) be used against the *Mirror* (whose vociferous criticism of the way the war was being badly run was of course the more irritating because it was so widely read), but he did issue the paper with a formal warning. The Liberals in the Commons forced a debate on the issue, which so clearly went against the Government that it had to prevent a division taking place. But the damage was already done; in the debate Morrison shrewdly justified his action by pointing out that the *Mirror* had been much more restrained since his warning, and Cecil King, one of the paper's executives, has confirmed his assessment.[10] Earlier in the year the Government had acted less

---

*An act of censorship justified by the infamous phrase 'not in the public interest', when Labour M.P. Col. Wedgwood protested in Parliament.

†The inferior quality of the B.B.C. war coverage was also lambasted at this conference. Relying exclusively on Ministry of Information bulletins about the campaign in Greece, the B.B.C. killed the German Army five times over.

directly, but just as effectively, against another paper whose popularity was its most dangerous quality – *Picture Post*. In January 1942, the Ministry of Information withdrew the subsidy which enabled the magazine to be exported at an economic rate to the Middle East, where it was widely read by the troops. Though Brendan Bracken, the Minister of Information, denied that this action was in any way motivated by a dislike of the paper's criticisms of the Government, his credibility was somewhat undermined when it was recalled that his ministry had felt it necessary to ban one issue of *Picture Post* in the Middle East the previous November. Bracken refused to see an N.C.C.L. deputation of M.P.s on the matter.*

And so, for the third year running, the N.C.C.L. found it necessary to put together a press freedom conference – this time in April 1942. The support they received from even the Conservative papers indicated the depth of feeling aroused by the events that spring. Frank Owen, whose sudden conscription into the armed forces – and the implications of this – were highlighted by his successor at the *Evening Standard*, Michael Foot, was again the hero of the conference, despite the presence of such substantial public figures as Bevan and Joad. But the *Mirror* affair proved to be the last major attempt by the wartime Government to censor the press. In September that year, they even withdrew the ban on the *Daily Worker*, though the Communist paper, like the Jehovah's Witnesses, continued to suffer from the abuse of regulation 11 – affecting the dispatch of material by post – which the Ministry of Information turned to when it wanted to prevent the export of undesirable material. The *Worker* was not sent to Russia.

On balance, Fleet Street and the B.B.C. suffered surprisingly little damage from the stress of wartime; partly, of course, because they, the authorities and the mass of the country were overwhelmingly at one on the major issues of the day. But it would be unduly cynical not to recognize also the extent to which Fleet Street and its allies like the N.C.C.L. protected liberty through their own vigorous efforts at two or three moments of real

---

*The Middle East seemed to inspire censorship at this time. Throughout 1941, the *Palestine Post*, a Jewish paper, was heavily blue-pencilled.

danger. At a humbler level, those victimized by the workings of censorship were lucky if they managed to attract the ear of bodies like the N.C.C.L. One London housewife was fortunate in this way. In June 1941, a Mrs Rycroft made some pungent criticism of the conduct of the war at the Wood Green House-wives Club; her frank speaking earned her a £50 fine for 'causing alarm and despondency'. However, the N.C.C.L. sponsored an appeal which overturned her conviction and won costs from the D.P.P.; the appeal court chairman commented that even if Mrs Rycroft had suggested Britain would lose the war the prosecution would have had to prove that she was a person of such authority that her audience would have been likely to believe her analysis to be true. In April 1942, the N.C.C.L. criticized the ban on the journal of the National Union of General and Municipal Workers at a particular factory, pointing out that the 'protected places' regulations (see above, p. 37) which the management were using to justify their ban did not apply to trade union literature. The trade union movement subsequently applied pressure to get official confirmation that their literature was excluded from this censorship; though they succeeded, other Left-wing publications were still liable to occasional harassment in this way.

The censor-reflex naturally weakened as the war went better, but it returned briefly, as a harbinger of the Cold War, in 1945. The dying kick of the defence regulations was a particularly vicious piece of repression. Three anarchists involved in the publication of *War Commentary* were sentenced to nine months' gaol by Mr Justice Birkett in May that year under regulation 39 (A) for causing disaffection among the armed services. One article had recommended people with rifles to hang on to them at the end of the war in view of what the authors regarded as the likely emergence of workers' councils in the post-war situation. The most disturbing feature of the case – apart from the fact that the Government felt it necessary to bring it at all – was the complete lack of any evidence from witnesses to suggest that the periodical had caused any disaffection whatsoever.

The post-war decade was a relatively calm period, certainly when compared with what went before and after; but there was the first push towards what the 1960s came to regard as 'permissiveness.' By the mid-1950s, television established itself as *the* mass medium – and its potency provoked the first of many attempts by the politicians to tame it. Unlike certain other civil liberties, freedom of expression suffered few casualties in the Cold War, perhaps because as a freedom it is so ingrained in British politics. The mood of the country had of course changed since the 1930s; the *Daily Worker* was no longer harassed as it had been before the war. Perhaps it was no longer a threat to authority.

One casualty, however, and a faintly bizarre one, was poster advertising. A side effect of the 1947 Town and Country Planning Act was a ban on fly-posting except for religious or educational events of a limited and temporary nature. After pressure from Labour M.P. Woodrow Wyatt and the N.C.C.L., the Government agreed to include trade union and political posters within the exempted categories. But the act also put the licensed hoarding owners in a monopoly position as far as orthodox poster advertising was concerned, and some of these used the privilege to discriminate against Communist and fellow-travelling organizations at the height of the Cold War. In 1948, London Transport refused posters from both the *Daily Worker* and the Peace Pledge Union because of their supposedly controversial nature. Two years later, they banned a harmless recruiting advertisement from the Hampstead branch of the Anglo-Soviet Friendship Society for the same reason, and indicated that any poster from the society would be similarly treated. In the same year British Railways ruled that a tenants' association recruiting poster which included the slogan 'Fight now for a square deal' raised matters of political controversy, and refused to accept it. At one point the British Transport Commission, the largest owner of poster sites in the country, laid down the quintessentially reactionary rule that it would not accept any poster whose object was to change any particular law. There were protests at this, but the spectre of trade censorship, mooted by the N.C.C.L. during the debate on the 1947 Act, became a reality. The poster industry set up its own censorship committee which formulated a code of practice. Not unnaturally, trade censorship is the most cautious kind of all. Although policy clashes became less frequent as the Cold War became less intense in the later 1950s, the poster censorship system is not well equipped to cope with fast-changing social attitudes, and posters again became an important battleground in the 1960s.

The press, of course, had always operated such a censorship over the advertisements it accepted in its columns, and indeed complaints about newspaper discrimination in this respect were made on the Left at this time. Though on one occasion in 1950 the N.C.C.L. was able to persuade a Twickenham paper to change its policy on this, it was generally, if reluctantly, accepted that freedom of the press carried this less attractive corollary. The Royal Commission on the Press in 1949 provided a major chance to improve the positive aspects of press freedom, and attempts were made to persuade the commission that the libel laws and statutes like the Official Secrets Acts and the Incitement to Disaffection Act were severe restrictions on the press; but without success. Less surprisingly, the N.C.C.L.'s rather woolly attempts to grapple with the perennial problem of the ownership of the national newspapers also fell on deaf ears. The council wanted a system of public trusts, in which the public, the newspaper workers and the management would all be represented. Twenty years later, similar ideas would become current within the industry itself, but with no greater impact.

If there was little apparent public anxiety about press freedom after the war, the broadcasting institutions were less well favoured. In its evidence to the Beveridge Committee on broadcasting in 1949, the N.C.C.L. was among a tiny minority of witnesses who called for a greater democratic control over the B.B.C.* and attacked the internal censorship carried on by the corporation. They offered as examples the truncation of an Alastair Cooke *Letter from America* which appeared to be about to attack a Southern senator in 1946 when it was cut off, and the blacklisting of the 'Red' Dean of Canterbury, Hewlett Johnson. The demand for public declarations of such censorship (rather than the discreet and hopefully unnoticed system then operated) was

---

*As Beveridge rather drily pointed out, the N.C.C.L. wanted Government intervention in the B.B.C. to secure greater freedom of speech, while the Listeners' Association wanted Government intervention to prevent Left-wing programmes.

ignored, as was the more widely held view (at least in the Labour Party and T.U.C.) that certain news stories had carried an anti-Labour bias.

The independence from formal Parliamentary control so lamented by the N.C.C.L. at this time did not of course mean that the politicians could not put considerable pressure on the B.B.C. – and, after 1954, the I.T.A. – when they really wanted to. One instance of the pressure at a very formal level became a *cause célèbre* – the '14-day rule' affair of 1955. To protect itself from the threat of ministerial interference, the B.B.C. had devised a rule (and then got the rule incorporated in the 1947 *aide mémoire* agreement with the political parties) that there should be no broadcasts in anticipation of Parliamentary debates. The B.B.C. soon came to realize that far from providing any protection the rule was an unnecessary restriction on political discussion. The Beveridge Committee recommended that it be repealed in 1952, but the Conservative Government would not implement this suggestion. The B.B.C. then refused to renew this condition, which forced the Government to impose it directly itself. This it did, to a tremendous public uproar, in 1955. A select committee set up in the wake of this protest similarly recommended the withdrawal of this rule, and though the Government felt it could not totally abandon it, it did agree in the following year to suspend it; and the '14-day rule' has remained suspended ever since.* In 1955 the B.B.C. also successfully resisted a different kind of pressure, when a series of talks on morality from a secular viewpoint by Mrs Knight ran into strong criticism from religious and other groups. The B.B.C. refused to scrap them. Mrs Knight was mild stuff compared with what was to come, but in the climate of the mid-50s the corporation's attitude was brave enough.

In the cinema there was a similar tussle over religious censorship when the L.C.C. banned the Fernandel film, *The Red Inn*, in 1952, on the grounds that it might offend Catholic susceptibilities. As the N.C.C.L. pointed out, when they criticized the

*It was a tense time for political broadcasting in other respects, too; during the Suez crisis in 1956, Eden, the Prime Minister, is supposed to have proposed taking over the B.B.C. completely.

dangerous practice of suppressing anything for purely sectarian reasons, Catholic France had not been bothered by the film; and after this and other public protests, the L.C.C. withdrew the ban the following year. But civil liberty concerns, in film as in other media, remained essentially political in the 1950s. In 1953 a Liverpool campaign succeeded (with the help of a change of party control on the council) in defeating a ban on the use of a local hall for Left-oriented Unity Theatre film shows. In 1958, the East German film *Operation Teutonic Sword* was banned by the censors because they felt it libelled a German general, General Speidel. When some local authorities ignored the board's ban and granted the film a licence, the general successfully sued the distributors for libel; but, as the N.C.C.L. argued at the time, it was not the job of the censors to anticipate court decisions.[12]

The cinema was the one area of free expression which attracted major Parliamentary legislation in this period, with the passing of the Cinematograph Act in 1952.[12a] This extended the licensing provisions for 35 mm. film to 16 mm. non-flammable film. Naturally, in view of its successful defence of non-profit making non-flammable film shows in the 1930s, the N.C.C.L. was anxious to see the old freedom maintained.* During the debate on the bill the N.C.C.L. mobilized a formidable array of interest groups, from the film technicians' union A.C.T. to mission societies, which persuaded the Home Office to amend proposals that would have brought church halls and similar venues under the safety regulations (and thus into the censorship system). The final form of the act preserved the traditional freedom for non-commercial 16 mm. film shows, but the N.C.C.L. had to fight one final battle to keep it so. The act did not come into force until 1956 and the vital regulations were published only six weeks before enactment. These failed to include non-profit making film shows among the exemptions, and it took a hastily organized lobby to persuade the Home Office of its bureaucratic error.

---

*Particularly as a Congregational minister had, in the previous year, been convicted under an 1890 act (which licensed musical performances) for showing a 16 mm. film with a musical soundtrack in his church crypt. An N.C.C.L.-assisted appeal overturned the magistrates' decision.

Parliamentary legislation was attempted in one other area – the theatre – when a private member's bill to abolish the Lord Chamberlain was debated in 1949. The M.P., E. P. Smith, who was also a successful West End playwright under the name Edward Percy, was twenty years ahead of his time, however, and his bill got no further than the committee stage. He received support from the N.C.C.L., which listed several occasions in the recent past when the Lord Chamberlain had exercised a political censorship over stage material. The Unity Theatre had had to drop references to Fascism and Japan from public performances of one play in 1939, and the International Brigade Association lost two scenes from a Scala Theatre performance in 1943. Left-wing drama, even in its supposedly legitimate club form, was harassed again in 1951, when the Unity Theatre was fined £281 (including costs) for admitting the public into a private performance – an offence traditionally punished with a £10 fine. The political motivation behind this prosecution was clear from the police interrogation when they made their raid; not only the management but the producer and the cast were asked detailed questions about their political beliefs and associations. In 1953, the Lord Chamberlain at first refused to license a Poplar play about George Lansbury; when it was discovered that, since the play was rate-aided, he could not prevent its performance, he still insisted on harsh cuts.

Thus in nearly every aspect, freedom of expression was defended on a narrowly political front in the post-war decade, much as it had been before the war. But in 1954 literature, which had almost alone fought the non-political case against censorship in the 1930s, was the victim of a famous purge. As the result of five major prosecutions in that year there was a vigorous campaign to reform the obscenity laws, which achieved a small kind of victory in 1959; and this itself heralded ten years of unprecedented cultural and political assertiveness which pushed freedom of expression to new limits. The most famous of the 1954 prosecutions, that of *The Philanderer*, was in fact a defeat for repression – the publishers were acquitted. But the erratic (and expensive) quality of the law in the other cases so alarmed the literary world that a serious campaign was organized to replace the 1857 Obscene Publications Act with something more precise and less capable of letting reactionary judges run amok.* Hutchinsons were convicted at the Old Bailey for publishing *September in Quinze* – an account of an Arab potentate's love life–and fined £1,000. Heinemann escaped conviction for their *The Image and the Search* (about a nymphomaniac) with the help of a tribute to the novel's qualities from E. M. Forster, but only because two juries could not agree and the third was therefore obliged to acquit them; and they could not recover the considerable costs of defending the book. Barker were acquitted for publishing *The Man in Control*, again without recovering costs. The publishers of *Julia* – not part of the original package – chose to plead guilty before the Clerkenwell magistrate to avoid the cost of a long trial, and were fined £30. Mr Justice Stable's well-known summing up in *The Philanderer* case (which like *Julia* was prosecuted in England after it had been condemned in the Isle of Man–where each book had been fined £1) was an eloquent addition to the tradition of free speech. He nailed the danger inherent in the 'obscenity test' formulated by Lord Chief Justice Cockburn in 1868 (namely – is the tendency of the book 'to deprave and corrupt those whose minds are open to such immoral influences and into whose hands a publication of this sort may fall?') by ridiculing the notion that adult reading matter was to be determined by reference to a modestly-educated 14-year-old schoolgirl. But other judges in 1954 were less broad-minded. The Recorder of London, Sir Gerald Dodson, felt that *September in Quinze* was repugnant 'to every decent emotion' and that 'the fount of our national blood would be polluted at source' if the book were freely available; while Mr Justice Lynskey came perilously close to suggesting that *The Image and the Search* was the kind of book which inspired the criminal cases he had to deal with at assizes.[13]

For the publishers, 1954 had not only been indecisive, it had

*The purge itself appears to have been inspired not by any puritanical conspiracy but by a defence tactic in a genuine pornography case, which attempted to save itself by showing that three reputable novels were 'worse' than it was. All that happened was these three were prosecuted as well.[14]

been very expensive. Accordingly, the Society of Authors and the Publishers' Association formed a committee under the chairmanship of Sir Alan Herbert to work out a private member's bill for Parliament. The key provision in their proposals was that the prosecution would in an obscenity case have to prove either that the accused intended to corrupt or that he had been indifferent to this as a possible effect. Between 1955 and 1957 there were three such attempts, by Roy Jenkins, Hugh Fraser and Lord Lambton, and as a result of their persistence the matter was put into the hands of a select committee. In 1958 this recommended that the effect of a book should be taken as a whole, that there should be a valid defence of literary merit against an obscenity charge (with the concomitant of expert evidence to show this) and that authors should have the right to be heard. Jenkins came back immediately with another bill to implement this, and the Government, after some tussles – it was initially against expert evidence and the merit defence – accepted the main proposals in the Obscene Publications Act of 1959. The reformers had failed, however, in their crucial attempt to inject the concept of the intention to corrupt into the law.

The passage of the act, and the acquittal of Penguin Books in the Lady Chatterley trial that immediately followed, inaugurated the movement towards greater and greater freedoms that characterized the culture of the 1960s. As with street demonstrations in the same period, there is the phenomenon of increasingly vigorous challenges to accepted ideas, challenges mounted by increasing numbers of people; of the contradictory responses from those challenged, concessions frequently mixed with tougher crackdowns; and by the end of the decade, an unsuccessful resort to repression. The challenges and the resistance took place in all the media, which for the first time came to see themselves as involved in the same battle. The old division between political and artistic freedom died. Just as the decade has a progressive line, from the Chatterley trial through the abolition of theatre censorship, pubic hair in photographs and stage nudity to the Arts Council call for the dropping of all censorship, so this provoked a reactionary chain, from Mrs Whitehouse through the private prosecution of *Last Exit to Brooklyn*, Lord Longford's anti-pornography crusade '14A' and the trials of *IT* and *Oz*. This second, repressive, tradition was fed by a separate but equally unpleasant stream at the end of the decade – Ulster, which managed to poison Britain as well as Ireland, achieving television censorship and the revival of the supposedly dormant Incitement to Disaffection Act. But at the end of it all, the artist, the journalist and the activist could say what they wanted to say with greater freedom than they could in 1959.

This is only partially to the credit of the law, however. The workings of justice since the passing of the 1959 Act have been so confusing and contradictory that some experts feel that a writer is as little protected as ever he was.[15] In 1960 liberalism triumphed: *Lady Chatterley's Lover* was acquitted at the Old Bailey. Thirty-five expert witnesses testified that the Lawrence novel had all kinds of excellent literary qualities and the jury believed them. But the failure of the reformers to include any clause about the author's intention to corrupt in the 1959 act immediately caused trouble. Mr Justice Byrne refused to allow Penguin's counsel, Gerald (later Lord) Gardiner, to introduce evidence as to such an intention. But he also ruled that the jury 'had to have regard to what the author was trying to do, what his message may have been, and what his general scope was'. This appears contradictory, though liberals like C. H. Rolph have optimistically argued that it *de facto* establishes the concept of intention as a legal one.[16]

In the following year the *Ladies' Directory* case seemed to wipe out some of the gains in the 1959 act; worse, it actually added to the armoury of repression. This small booklet, produced by a man called Shaw, was a guide to London prostitutes, complete with photos and telephone numbers. Shaw, who fought his case up to the Lords, argued that his intentions were honest and that his likely customers, the prostitutes' clients, were not corruptible. Both these contentions were rejected by the lower courts, with a firm bang on the head as far as intention went: 'The test for obscenity depends on the publication itself, the intention of the publisher is irrelevant.'[17] But Shaw had also been charged with the almost unheard-of offence of conspiring to corrupt public morals. In arguably what is the worst decision the Lords have made in a civil liberty case, they confirmed (though in a split judgment, Lord Reid to his credit dissenting) what had hitherto been very doubtful, that the offence existed; secondly, that the mere agreement between Shaw and the prostitutes was sufficient to prove conspiracy – even if no *Ladies' Directory* had subsequently been published. The political dangers in this decision were realized ten years later when the publishers of the underground magazine *IT* were given suspended sentences for committing a similar offence.

By 1964 it was clear that the Obscene Publications Act was full of holes; the Government therefore passed another one, to close some of these gaps – but only those unfavourable to authority. The most important change was making it an offence to possess an obscene article with the intent of making profit out of it, which got round two unfortunate previous legal defects. A bookseller had been acquitted because the court felt bound to agree that displaying books was not an offer for sale, and another man had escaped conviction in another case because the police who bought the obscene books were held to be incorruptible. As the N.C.C.L. pointed out, not only did the changes make the net wider for the police but the Government had failed to meet any of the liberal criticisms: that the intentions of author and publisher were not taken into account, that cases of forfeiture (as opposed to indictment for a criminal offence) did not carry the right to jury trial,* and that no-one knew just what obscenity was. This last defect immediately claimed another victim, Alex Trocchi's *Cain's Book*. In 1965, the appeal court upheld a Sheffield magistrate's decision that obscenity was not confined to sex – Trocchi's book was about drug-taking – and that the jury were entitled to ignore expert evidence about literary qualities if they felt the social damage outweighed these.[18]

This affair turned out to be typical of the second half of the

*This arose out of the *Fanny Hill* case that year, when the book had been seized from a shop used by children, which clearly affected the magistrate's attitude. Liberals were to get themselves into quite a tangle over jury trials; two years later some would argue *à propos Last Exit* that juries were incapable of deciding obscenity cases – a dangerous sentiment considering the pressure on juries in other areas of civil liberty where their value is immeasurable.

1960s. Parliament had temporarily exhausted its interest in obscenity, and whatever the consequent chaos showed little inclination to remedy it. This left the field open for a guerrilla war between local police and private do-gooders on the one side, and radical bookshops and the liberal literary establishment on the other. No-one on either side could be sure that what was good for London would be good in Yorkshire or Brighton. This uncertainty was compounded by the sheer variety of censorious instruments available to authority. The Post Office Act outlawed the sending of indecent material through the post; the Customs could seize indecent or obscene articles (and the defence available under the 1959 act – literary excellence – was not available under the 1876 Customs Act). The Indecent Advertisements Act was used against underground material in the late 60s, and some local councils had their own by-law powers for dealing with obscenity.

The funnier aspects of all this can be seen in another 1965 case – the prosecution of Dave Cunliffe for publishing *The Golden Convolvulus*, an anthology which Cunliffe felt included both good and bad pieces and which was deliberately designed to make sure the defence of literary merit would not be available. He was acquitted under the 1959 act at Blackburn, because he was not publishing with a view to making a profit out of it, but he was found guilty of sending indecent material through the post, and fined £50 under the 1953 Post Office Act. The absurdity of all this as a way of dealing with something as important as obscenity was apparent to many, but it made little difference to the law, which pursued its ludicrous path unabashed.

In this it was helped by the crusading zeal of a few individuals. In 1966 Sir Cyril Black, a Conservative M.P. with a rather narrow view of social and sexual morality, brought a private prosecution against Hubert Selby's *Last Exit to Brooklyn* before the Bow Street magistrate, since the Labour Attorney-General Sir Elwyn Jones had declined to begin a public prosecution. Sir Cyril won a destruction order: both sides had assembled teams of experts – the first time a prosecution side had done so – and the magistrate was convinced that the novel's depiction of homosexuality was obscene. It was a Pyrrhic victory for the M.P., since he had to pay his costs of £1,000.* When the publishers, Calder and Boyars, continued defiantly to publish the book – the Bow Street order in theory only applied to that part of London – the Attorney-General felt obliged to bring a criminal prosecution for publishing an obscene article for gain, and they were tried at the Old Bailey in November 1967. They were found guilty and fined £100, though their accumulated costs of £20,000 were a much greater penalty. John Calder bitterly attacked the educational standard of the jury, and argued that obscenity case juries should have at least A-levels[19], an élitist argument that does civil liberty little good. Supported by a wide-ranging defence group which organized various efforts to finance his case, Calder appealed; in 1968 he was acquitted and, more to the point, was awarded his costs. The appeal court's decision has been described as 'technical' in that it was based on flaws in the judge's summing-up – his various omissions had confused the jury as to the exact meaning of the 1959 act, a confusion shared probably by most people outside the appeal court, anyway; and while it is true that the appeal court decision said nothing about the obscenity or otherwise of *Last Exit*, the N.C.C.L.'s comment that it left the outcome of future cases unpredictable is a little unfair to the excellent judgment of Lord Justice Salmon, who firmly laid down the guidelines for juries, and thus indirectly everyone else, in considering obscenity and the public good.[20] If we are to have censorship at all, an arguable point, it is perhaps best that the standard of public taste should be left to twelve randomly-selected citizens.†

Leaving censorship to the prejudices of local police and

*The liberals were outraged that a private individual had been able to step in where the Government had chosen not to. Their protests persuaded Roy Jenkins to add an inappropriate amendment to the 1967 Criminal Justice Act depriving any future Sir Cyrils of their power to bring obscenity prosecutions. Yet in 1950 the N.C.C.L. itself had powerfully argued that the right to bring private prosecutions in criminal cases was 'one of the major safeguards against abuse of power' and that to remove it even for one kind of offence 'is to introduce a principle fraught with danger for the liberty of the subject'.

† For an excellently argued case against letting even juries set the standard of public taste see John Montgomerie, *The Obscenity Laws*, Arts Council Report, 1969, pp. 23–9.

magistrates certainly had several undesirable results in this period. In January 1968 the Brighton police, inspired presumably by the fate of *Last Exit* the previous month, seized over 3,000 books and magazines from the Unicorn Bookshop. Most of the seventy-two titles were freely on sale elsewhere in the country; most of the magazines were academic periodicals. Six months later Bill Butler, the owner, was prosecuted in respect of a handful of these. The lengthy detention of much of his stock caused considerable financial suffering to Butler before he was even tried, and he was denied legal aid on the grounds that though he was only taking £10 a week from his store, a defence fund existed on his behalf (which raised just one tenth of the £2,000 costs). He was eventually fined £250 with 180 guineas costs, a ferocious penalty considering the £100 fine for *Last Exit*. The magistrate was, not perhaps coincidentally, the same man who had penalized Radford and Walter in the Church trial two years earlier. Six years later, the Bath magistrates declared a number of magazines (including *Penthouse* and *Mayfair*) obscene, in an unprecedented case in which the town's wholesale newsagent was prosecuted after he had gone to the police for advice on what exactly in his stock of newspapers and magazines might cause him legal trouble. (He did this because a series of raids in Manchester and Birmingham had compounded the confusion of the law with an increasing regional discrepancy in its enforcement.) The case revealed that the D.P.P. kept a 'bluelist' of potentially offensive magazines.

In the face of these attacks, liberals had at last formally recognized the political nature of artistic censorship with the setting up of the Defence of Literature and the Arts Society in 1968. In 1969, they achieved their greatest advance when the Arts Council working party on censorship recommended its total abolition.[20a] But an important section of public opinion was moving against the liberal trend even at its moment of triumph. Within two years liberalism was thrust right back on the defensive, and the obscenity trials of 1971 were overtly political in a way that even *Last Exit* was not. At the same time that *Oz* came before the Old Bailey, Richard Handyside was being convicted at the Lambeth magistrate's court for publishing an English version of the Danish *Little Red Schoolbook*. A tedious, solemn and harmless hotchpotch of radicalism, it was presumably attacked because like the schoolkids' *Oz* it was directly aimed at the young. Smythe of the N.C.C.L. felt even angrier about the Lambeth result than the Old Bailey one: 'If they can get away with the conviction of the *Little Red Schoolbook* they could in theory get away with anything; he wrote soon afterwards.[21] Would a jury have saved it? *The Mouth*, a more erotic work by playwright Paul Ableman, was acquitted of obscenity after supporting testimony from novelist Margaret Drabble, at the Old Bailey later that year. In 1973 a jury acquitted the underground comic *Nasty Tales* on an obscenity charge.

Even if all prosecutions under the 1959 act were in front of juries, this would not prevent the authorities from evading unpredictable criminal indictments, because the range of censorious instruments is so great. On 17 November 1967, the American poet Clive Matson arrived in London to give a series of readings. Sixty copies of his book *Mainline to the Heart* and seven copies of a magazine were seized by the customs, using their powers under the 1876 Customs Consolidation Act, which prohibits the importation of obscene material. The customs blacklist is not disclosed. There were apparently 165 items on it in 1964; five years later, the excise men seized 1,000 different titles and two million volumes*. Action like this had been frequent even in the early 1960s; Birmingham University's reference library lost their copies of Genet (in French) even though Reading University and the British Museum already had some, while in 1964 Sir Dingle Foot bought a copy of Burton's translation of *The Perfumed Garden* at Heathrow on his way out of the country only to have it impounded on the way back.[22] In Matson's case the liberals fought back. The N.C.C.L. persuaded Labour M.P. Ben Whitaker to raise it in Parliament. After six weeks Matson's material was returned to him, but the delay had badly damaged his tour. Harold Lever, the Treasury minister responsible for the

---

*Professor Street has suggested that this secretiveness does the Customs themselves harm since the list is composed of hard core porn rather than anything of literary merit.[23]

customs, wrote to Whitaker that the customs, 'anxious to avoid setting themselves up as censors', went to great lengths to harmonize their practice with what they took to be the general law of obscenity in this country. Since that law is still essentially subjective, the customs men could hardly avoid setting themselves up as censors. A year later they gave a repeat performance when David Hockney arrived from America with eight male nudist magazines which the customs regarded with distaste. Hockney was slightly luckier than Matson; he got his stuff back within a month. The N.C.C.L. wrote to Roy Jenkins, by then Chancellor of the Exchequer, whose liberal outlook and personal record as a reformer hardly fitted him for a repressive rôle; and Jenkins got the magazines returned. In 1974 Paul Raymond, the strip club owner, was convicted in a customs prosecution for importing the magazine *Men Only*. This was the first time such a case had been heard by a jury rather than a judge sitting alone.

Matson and Hockney at least knew what they were bringing in with them, even if they were surprised by the customs attitude. Even this advantage is lost to those importing material unseen by post, and a series of prosecutions in this area in 1969 prompted the N.C.C.L. to step in – and find itself investigated as a result. A sculptor who ordered two books, including one on Chinese erotic art, from the American book club attached to the magazine *Evergreen Review* was fined. And a young English homosexual who had received, though he had not ordered, publications from an international organization based in Denmark which was campaigning for the rights of homosexuals, was similarly punished. The Danish group complained to the N.C.C.L. that, in addition, its correspondence was being intercepted by the British police and the contents removed. Half the mail going to their British members was not arriving. When the N.C.C.L. ordered some of their booklets to assess what policy it should adopt, the Obscene Publications Squad promptly turned up on Smythe's doorstep to ask what he was doing getting such material through the post. The N.C.C.L., of course, was able to mobilize some heavy support on its own behalf – two M.P.s tabled Parliamentary questions – and in February 1970 the police not surprisingly told Smythe there would be no proceedings against him. They did not apologize for opening his mail. Nor did they return it.

The activities of some publishers in sending unsolicited material by post at this time unfortunately gave the authorities a good case for preserving their power to intercept letters. Though Ableman was acquitted of obscenity in writing *The Mouth*, his publishers were convicted under the 1953 Post Office Act of sending indecent brochures publicizing it through the G.P.O., and a spate of this kind of publicity promotion in 1971 – criticized by the N.C.C.L. which saw the dangers for other people's civil liberty – led to a wave of complaints by the unwitting recipients. As a result the Unsolicited Goods and Services Act in that year made it an offence to send out unasked-for material describing or illustrating sexual techniques.

The visual arts became almost as important a battleground as books in the 1960s. The 1964 revision of the Obscene Publications Act had extended its scope to cover photographic negatives after the High Court had found it necessary the previous year to rule, in the case against Jean Straker's nudes, that these fell outside the 1959 definition of something that could be looked at. Of course the old British Transport tradition of censoring posters lived on – the Family Planning Association joined the list of victims in 1961 – but by the late 60s it was the artwork rather than the words that was more likely to run into problems. In 1968 an anti-censorship poster put out by the N.C.C.L. and D.L.A.S. was felt to have 'too much thigh and a suggestion of a nipple', as London Transport put it, though the poster was accepted without demur by hoarding owners.[23a] Much more serious principles were raised in cases brought against galleries in the previous two years, however. The authorities fairly quickly realized that if they used statutes which talked about indecency rather than obscenity alone – as the 1959 act did – they had a much better chance of bringing a successful prosecution, indecency having been defined by the law lords as being at the lesser end of the obscenity scale.[24] That these statutes carried lesser penalties than the 1959 act was usually irrelevant to the person censored. By an odd quirk of legal history, the visual arts were peculiarly vulnerable to attack by offbeat legislation. The Vagrancy Act of

1824 for example, which prohibits the 'exposure to view' of an indecent exhibition in a place where the public can see it, proved its value to the police in 1966, when they successfully prosecuted the Robert Fraser Gallery in London for displaying collages by the American artist Jim Dine. Dine's subjects – the phallic graffiti on lavatory walls – had been commended for their delicate and witty treatment by the *Listener*'s critic, but the evidence of a passing policeman, who had just been able to see them from the street through the gallery window (a necessary condition for a prosecution under the Vagrancy Act) was sufficient for conviction. The prosecution admitted that the paintings were not obscene.*
At the same time as the Dine case, the London police seized reproductions of Beardsley drawings from a Regent Street shop, even though the originals were on view at the Victoria and Albert Museum. The Edinburgh magistrates in February of the following year ruled that similar prints seized there were indecent. It was noticeable that in this case the prosecution was not brought under the 1959 act – perhaps because, as one critic argued, a jury trial was unpredictable[25] – but under a local by-law. Another damaging result of this surge of police activity was an increase in self-censorship. The Arts Council forced the withdrawal of certain paintings by a Swedish artist from an exhibition it had organized 'in view of recent police actions'.

As with literature, the visual arts were becoming increasingly political at this time, and perhaps not surprisingly they were sometimes met with a robust political response from authority. In July 1967 the Croydon council removed two paintings about the Vietnam War from the exhibition at the Fairfield Hall of work by Australian artist William Routledge. And in the following year the Doncaster pacifist Danny Rogan created a window display for his bookshop on the theme 'Make Love Not War'; his display of photos and words (including 'fuck') offended a passing nun. Rogan was remanded for medical reports, and eventually fined. In London, the Obscene Publica-

---

*In December that year, a Cypriot artist, Stass Paraskos, was convicted of obscenity under the 1959 act by Leeds magistrates, despite an assertion by the head of the local art school that his nudes were neither indecent nor obscene.

tions Squad seemed, under Inspector Luff, to be conducting a crusade against long-haired dissent; it over-reached itself, however, when it raided John Lennon's exhibition of lithographs in 1970. Bringing charges eventually under the 1839 Metropolitan Police Act rather than the 1959 act – which they had used at the time of the raid – the police again needed to prove only indecency rather than the much harder crime of obscenity; and, just as important, they again did away with need for a jury trial. These technical manoeuvres failed, however, for a nicely technical reason: the 1839 Act talks of 'to the annoyance of passengers' and the magistrate, accepting the defence argument that a gallery exhibition cannot annoy 'passengers', dismissed the charges.[26]

Oddly enough, particularly considering the more immediately potent force of sex and politics on stage and screen than in book or picture, the theatre and the cinema suffered far less at this time than the other media. *Oh Calcutta* and *A Clockwork Orange* came and went undisturbed. The N.C.C.L. attributed this tolerance to a willingness on the part of authority to permit commercially successful outrageousness but not 'the off-beat, the intellectually provocative or the Left-wing' – an attitude which it understandably regarded as a danger to civil liberty. Certainly, the few examples of controversial censorship in the theatre would fit the N.C.C.L. categories. In 1966, the Lord Chamberlain successfully prosecuted the English Stage Society for performing Edward Bond's *Saved* (in which a gang beat a baby in a pram to death) without a licence from his office. The magistrates ruled that there was no legal basis in the traditional understanding that theatre clubs were exempt from the Lord Chamberlain's censorship. The public uproar at this was placated by a Government promise to review the whole question of stage censorship; and in due course the Theatres Act of 1968 replaced the Lord Chamberlain with a strictly limited censorship system based entirely on criminal law. The court official had one last fling before he went; in 1967 he agreed to license Hochhuth's *Soldiers* if written permission were obtained from relatives of characters in the play. Since the National Theatre had refused it because they felt Churchill and Cherwell had been maligned in it, the Lord Chamberlain's conditions were hardly likely to have been fulfilled had any other theatre attempted it. This kind of power disappeared completely with the 1968 act. Theatres are licensed by local authorities, who can only impose safety conditions – the kind of sleight-of-hand political censorship that this created for the cinema was specifically forbidden in the act. The Attorney-General can prosecute any play if it is obscene,* defamatory, racially insulting or liable to cause a public disorder – categories well established in criminal law. Whether this will protect all kinds of drama against censorship has yet to be seen.

That it cannot do so completely is suggested by the conviction of Gustav Metzger in 1967–before the act became law, but in the kind of case that would fall within the act's definition of criminal offences. Metzger was fined £100 for organizing the *Destruction in Art Symposium*, or more specifically for one item in it, a 'happening' by some Austrian artists, who left the country long before Metzger was prosecuted for presenting a 'lewd and indecent exhibition'. The N.C.C.L. argued that since the happening was spontaneous, and was only one in a month-long series of items, Metzger could not be held to have intended to outrage public decency, and that in most areas of the law – except obscenity – the defendant's intentions are crucial to his guilt. They were not successful. It was another example of the unfortunate consequences of the failure of the literary reformers to include the concept of intention in the 1959 act.

The lack of much controversy over censorship in the cinema at this sensitive period was almost entirely due to the intelligence with which John Trevelyan exercised his function of censor, somehow seeming to keep in step with rapid changes in public taste. Inevitably he did not please everybody, and the local councils showed an increasing willingness to differ from the Board when their sensibilities were challenged. Usually they were more censorious than the Board.[27] Manchester, for instance, banned *The Killing of Sister George* and Warwick *Saturday Night and Sunday Morning*. On the other hand, Cambridge and Maesteg

---

*Basically, obscenity as this is understood, if that is the right word, in the 1959 act, though the valuable exemption that that act extends to books not published for profit is not available to similar theatrical performances.[27]

were the only towns to show *The Wild One* on its first release –
the Board had refused it a certificate altogether – and London
allowed *Ulysses* to be shown without the cuts demanded by the
Board.[28] The increase in geographical disparity naturally provided
good ammunition for the critics of censorship. The N.C.C.L.
sarcastically pointed to the fate of Godard's *Weekend* in 1968 –
seen peacefully by members of the I.C.A. in London, raided by
the police at the British Film Institute in Edinburgh. Not surprisingly, the one major outrage in this period was perpetuated
by the Obscene Publications Squad. Early in 1970, they raided
the Open Space Theatre Club in London which was showing
Warhol's *Flesh*, on a warrant of doubtful legality*, seized the
projection equipment, thus putting the club temporarily out of
business, a piece of vindictiveness without legal authority – and
then took the names and addresses of the entire audience.[28a] The
D.P.P. refused to proceed with the case (the police action had
been prompted by a complaint 'from a member of the public')
but the club got no compensation from the police for its losses.
The N.C.C.L., which had complained to the Home Office on
behalf of the club, regretfully told the Open Space that their one
recourse – a civil action against the police – was prohibitively
expensive.

Then, in 1974, came two developments which threatened the
whole sophisticated edifice of film censorship. Two private
initiatives attempted to by-pass the self-regulating system that
had protected the film industry for sixty years. The first was
unsuccessful: the film *Blow Out* was acquitted in a prosecution
brought by Mary Whitehouse under the Vagrancy Act. Much
more dangerously, in a private action brought by a former
Salvation Army worker, Edward Shackleton, the Lord Chief
Justice Lord Widgery ruled that the Obscene Publications Act
of 1959 did in part cover films, and that the distributors of *Last
Tango in Paris* had to stand trial. This decision opened the way
for all kinds of extremist action, and potentially reduced the
film industry to the chaos experienced by publishing in the
1950s.

*Made out under Section 3 of the 1959 act, which regulates search and
seizure, it is not at all clear that this section extends to films.

In general, both the press and broadcasting institutions responded well to the conflicts of the 1970s, both as censors and the
censored. The press, attacked by the Government at both ends
of the political spectrum in 1971 with the trials of the *Sunday
Telegraph*, *IT* and *Oz*, just about won more of the big battles
than it lost. Television, which became perhaps the most important
medium of all in this decade, successfully held off the morality
of Mrs Whitehouse in the artistic arena[29] but performed much
more feebly on the political front. And for both press and
broadcasting the existing structure of ownership and control
was frequently, though ineffectually, called in question.

For broadcasting, the decade opened with the Pilkington
Committee. In its evidence to this committee in 1961 the N.C.C.L.,
still pursuing the theme of democratic control that had been
propounded to Beveridge ten years earlier, argued for a national
broadcasting council reporting annually to Parliament. Presumably the N.C.C.L. thought such a council would prevent the
kind of political censorship on the part of the I.T.A. that it
attacked in the next few years – the banning of a *Daily Worker*
commercial and the dropping of a religious talks series that had
developed too uncomfortable a political content for the Authority's
tastes. 1963, the year of *That Was The Week That Was* and *The
Wednesday Play*, saw the birth of Mary Whitehouse's disgust
with the new freedom in television, particularly that enjoyed by
the B.B.C. But for liberals her crusade at first mattered less
than the B.B.C.'s own internal censorship in the case of Peter
Watkins' *The War Game*. The B.B.C. had commissioned this
programme about nuclear war, and then refused to show it,
on the grounds that it was too harrowing for television. Despite
strong protests from the Left, which naturally felt that it was
Watkins' anti-war sentiments that had scuppered the film, it was
never seen except in the art cinema circuit. To add to all this, the
B.B.C. found itself increasingly at odds with the politicians over
its coverage of politics. The Conservatives felt that certain
programmes (like *Twenty-Four Hours* and radio's *World At One*)
had a general leftish bias, while Harold Wilson's dislike of
the B.B.C. treatment of him endured several years, reaching
an all-time low with the programme *Yesterday's Men*, which

took an irreverent look at the Labour leadership a year after it fell from office. The frustrations created by these conflicting (indeed contradictory) pressures led to increased calls for a broadcasting council from groups in all parts of the political spectrum, in an attempt to make what occasionally seemed like the sheer arrogance of broadcasters answerable to something other than their own consciences. Such a body had little appeal to the journalists inside the industry, but they too shared some of the frustrations, and they mounted an increasing challenge of their own. The Free Communications Group, a body of fluctuating fortunes and influence, was set up by newspaper and television journalists in 1968, and intermittently exposed the inadequacies of their employers and their self-censorship they imposed. This group aligned itself with other young radicals in 1971 to protest against the proposed allocation of the fourth (and supposedly final) television channel to the I.T.A. They were successful, though their own ideas of providing greater access won little response.

As well as inhibiting a truly frank discussion of political issues, the party politicians successfully resisted attempts by both the B.B.C. and the independent companies to change the party broadcast structure; and the treatment of the 1970 election was determined more by the wishes of the party leaders than of the broadcasters[30]. But the most serious attempt at political censorship came during the Ulster crisis, which inspired repression in broadcasting as in other areas of civil liberty. In 1971, when the I.R.A. stepped up its campaign after internment had been introduced in August, there were demands from conservative politicians and commentators for restrictions on TV coverage of Northern Ireland, specifically a ban on interviews with members of the I.R.A. In fact the B.B.C. had already instituted an internal code of practice which effectively kept the I.R.A. off the screens except in news bulletins; and the I.T.A. refused to transmit a Granada *World in Action* film about the I.R.A. in the Republic, without even seeing it.* The protests at this, largely from the journalists themselves, may have had some effect: the formal demands for

*They had similarly vetoed a Tyne Tees programme about N.A.T.O. in 1969 when N.A.T.O. officials objected to its content.

censorship were dropped, and early in 1972 the B.B.C. successfully resisted the very strong pressure from the Home Office
and the Unionists in Stormont to abandon a major programme;
the I.R.A. even began to reappear on television.[31]

The contradictions in Britain's public service broadcasting
system had been sharply illuminated by the Ulster crisis. The
broadcasting authorities sometimes had a drastically different
view of 'responsibility' from the broadcasters who worked under
them. The B.B.C. and the I.B.A. saw the national interest in
terms not dissimilar to those used by the Government, while the
radio and TV journalists tended to feel that the national interest
was best served by a professional attention to objective reporting.
The contradictions persisted after the immediate Ulster crisis
had passed. Early in 1973, two quite different but equally em-
barassing problems assailed the I.B.A. simultaneously. An
officious private citizen, Ross McWhirter, objected to what he
read in press previews about the sexual offensiveness of an
A.T.V. documentary on Warhol, the American artist and
film-maker. He obtained a temporary injunction from the High
Court preventing transmission of the film, on the grounds that
the I.B.A. had not fulfilled its statutory duty to make sure that
indecent material was not shown on TV screens. Subsequently,
the I.B.A. satisfied the court that it had considered the film
properly and the injunction was lifted: the documentary was
later shown to a vastly increased and largely disappointed audience. Though McWhirter, like Bennion in his action against Hain
earlier, had undoubtedly been exercising a valuable civil liberty
in being able to challenge large institutions (a right the court
subsequently nullified by insisting that future injunctions would
only be obtained with the consent of the Attorney-General), the
danger in his action had been pinpointed by the N.C.C.L.:
Larry Grant wrote that 'the case could set dangerous precedents
for pre-censorship'.

Pre-censorship was a perennial problem in television. The
liberals inside the industry argued that controversial programmes
should be transmitted: if they were seen to need corrective action,
this could be taken afterwards. This had been the situation over
Yesterday's Men. Usually, however, the TV authorities took

corrective action before the event, before it was even seen
to be necessary. At the same time as the Warhol ban, the I.B.A.
got itself into even more serious difficulties over a Granada
documentary on the corrupt career of Yorkshire architect John
Poulson. Although lawyers had passed the film, the I.B.A.
banned it for undefined public policy reasons. The presence of
several former political, local government and civil notables on
the I.B.A. board, with connections with people named in the
film, did not help the I.B.A. convince critics of this decision that
it had been made without political interest. Members of the TV
technicians' union, A.C.T.T., blacked out the alternative programme imposed by the I.B.A. in protest at what they regarded
as political censorship. Martin Loney, the new general secretary
of the N.C.C.L., commenting on the Warhol and Poulson programme decisions, argued that the Poulson ban was much more
dangerous. 'It indicates', he said, 'that British television is
perilously close to becoming more like the French system which
is under Government control.' The public criticism of the I.B.A.,
particularly from respectable newspapers, had effect: two months
later, the programme was transmitted in substantially its original
form. The delay had, however, probably weakened its public
impact.

The outside council with which television was threatened in
the early 1970s had become a reality for the press ten years previously. The Royal Commission on the Press in 1962 warned
that unless a Press Council with lay membership was created –
the existing body, set up after the previous royal commission in
1949, was purely professional – it would recommend Government action. In 1964, Lord Devlin became the first chairman of
the revised council, and under his guidance some measure of
external responsibility was achieved, though it was not quite the
annual accountability to Parliament that some critics had asked
for.[32] Much of the public anger at press behaviour had been
aroused by invasions of privacy; and the permanent conflict
between two basic rights in a democratic society – the need of a
free press to obtain information and the individual's right to
privacy – became acute in the late 1960s as various groups,
led by the N.C.C.L., began to press for major improvements in

the privacy laws.* Though the N.C.C.L., unlike Justice, the lawyers' pressure group, proposed a defence for the press in their legislative recommendations (an idea accepted by Labour back-bencher Brian Walden in his private member's bill in 1969), they were nonetheless increasing the restrictions on one freedom in the interests of another.

There had been an earlier breach in the traditional alliance between civil libertarians and journalists, when two pressmen were gaoled for refusing to disclose in court the sources of stories they had written during the Vassall affair in 1962. Fleet Street generally condemned the imprisonment of its fellows as a threat to the freedom of the press, but the N.C.C.L., though sympathetic to their case, also pointed out that there was an obvious danger in providing special privileges for one particular group – neither doctors nor priests, who similarly received confidential information, were for that reason exempt from the law. In 1970 Bernard Falk, a B.B.C. television reporter, also spent a few days in gaol for keeping silent about people he had interviewed in an Ulster assignment; journalists have come to regard this as a, fortunately infrequent, occupational hazard. Both these confrontations occurred when the State felt its security threatened; in fact, nearly all the civil liberty crises between Fleet Street and authority in the 1960s revolved around security issues.

In 1967, Chapman Pincher of the *Daily Express* revealed that the security services operated a system of reading overseas telegrams; the Government accused him of breaking the informal D-Notice system (a discreet agreement between press and government, in force since 1912, to vet topics which might create security problems); when a select committee of Parliament failed to agree with them on this, the Government gave up issuing D-Notices and replaced them with a series of *adhoc* agreements.[33] This informal self-censorship has worked too much in authority's

---

*Television was equally involved; in 1966, the interviewing of the relatives of the dead after the Aberfan disaster was strongly criticized, and a *Twenty-four Hours* film, secretly taken, of a landlady discriminating between prospective black and white tenants was attacked by the N.C.C.L. on privacy grounds despite their liberal sympathy with the objectives of the film. (For the privacy campaign, see below, Chapter 8, p. 308.)

favour; press and television have too readily accepted the Government's definitions of what constitutes a state secret. Freedom of expression in Britain had not reached the point achieved in the United States when the *New York Times* and the *Washington Post* exposed governmental decision-making with the publication of the Pentagon Papers in 1971, in the face of intense Administration opposition. That year did, however, see an important step forward even in Britain. The prosecution of the *Sunday Telegraph* for publishing a secret military report on the Biafran war* was an unusually harsh step for a government to take and, as it turned out, a badly miscalculated one. The acquittal of the paper was marked by an aggressively liberal summing-up by Mr Justice Caulfield. 'There is no duty in law for any editor of any newspaper to go running to Whitehall to get permission to run an article or print news.' He went on to point out that simply because a document was stamped 'confidential', it did not mean anyone handling it was breaking any law; and he recommended pithily that this section of the Official Secrets Act (under which the *Telegraph* had been charged) be 'pensioned off' forthwith. As a result, the Government set up a formal inquiry under Lord Franks.[33a] This recommended that the section so scathingly criticized by Mr Justice Caulfield should be replaced by an Official Information Act, with precise categories of information to be protected by the law. (These included foreign and defence matters, currency and Cabinet secrets.) The Franks Report argued against creating a 'right to know' similar to that existing in Sweden and the U.S.A., which the N.C.C.L. described as 'a serious missed opportunity'. Overall, the report sadly disappointed those in the press and elsewhere who had expected a genuine liberalization of the law to follow the *Telegraph* fiasco. Even the report's limited reforms were not implemented by the Government, which entered the 1974 election making the same promises about official secrets that it had offered four years earlier.

Even while the suggested Franks reforms were under consideration, the Conservative Government showed just how much it disliked unofficial leaking of information, even when it had no

*Unfortunately for the *Sunday Telegraph*, the 'scoop' which put it to so much subsequent legal bother appeared the day Biafra collapsed.

security content whatsoever. In October 1972, the *Sunday Times* published a report of drastic plans to reduce the railway network. The police were ordered to find out how they got this information. The *Sunday Times* was threatened with prosecution under the Official Secrets Act, and the humble *Railway Gazette*, which had passed them the documents, was subject to heavy police harassment, including tapping the editor's phone. Though no prosecutions followed this ponderous response, it scarcely encouraged hopes of the change of style promised by Heath. Smythe located the danger for civil liberty in this situation: 'If the government remains free to reveal just what is convenient ... it is clear that we do not have the system of open government promised by Mr Heath. Decisions are taken, policies developed, administrative rules imposed and monumental scandals covered up without public discussion or awareness.'

The *Sunday Times* was also in the front line of the battle to extend press freedom when it sustained an expensive court action over the restrictions imposed by the laws of contempt. This arose out of its desire to publish articles critical of the Distillers' Company's years of delay in settling compensation for the thalidomide victims. English law has always bent over backwards to prevent publicity giving an unfair advantage to either side in a legal action. This legitimate objective has meant that the unscrupulous have always been able to suppress critical comment by starting (or delaying) litigation, even when they have no real intention of pursuing a genuine court case. In the *Sunday Times* case, a limited step forward was achieved when the courts held that legal action should not inhibit discussion of matters of public interest. Nonetheless the contempt laws remained, as the N.C.C.L. said, essentially little different from direct censorship. Harold Evans, editor of the *Sunday Times*, and Katharine Graham, owner of the *Washington Post*, both publicly pointed out in 1974 that the press investigation of Watergate would have been impossible in Britain because of the *sub judice* effect of the contempt law.

Prosecutions designed to put the magazines out of business were brought against *IT* and *Oz* for conspiring to corrupt public morals. There may have been some narrow party political animosity between the Tory *Sunday Telegraph* and the Labour Government which inspired that prosecution; there clearly was a profound loathing between authority and the underground papers which affected the way they were treated. The two major prosecutions were preceded by a history of lesser harassment. The underground press had been characterized since its flowering in 1967 by a radical attention to sex, dope and rock music – which it regarded as the vital elements of social revolution. The mix was too much for the Obscene Publications Squad, which raided the two biggest underground papers several times, seizing subscription lists, correspondence and office equipment; which visited printers to deter them from producing the magazines; and which eventually successfully put *IT* and *Oz* in the dock. (It was not just these two publications that merited this treatment: the editor of *Student* was convicted under the Indecent Advertisements Act of 1889 for discussing the treatment of venereal disease, and the same act was used against the Marxist paper *Black Dwarf*.[34])

The attack on *IT* was peculiarly sinister. Homosexuals who had placed or were intending to place ads in the magazine's personal column were questioned after a raid in 1969. The N.C.C.L. complained to the Home Secretary, Callaghan, that the police could only have got their names from the magazine's private correspondence and that the only legal powers available were to prosecute for publishing for gain, not for material contained in private letters. The Home Office refused to see the point behind the anxiety, evading the issue by reference to the blanket search powers granted by the 1959 act. These enable the police to take anything relating to the trade or business carried on at the office raided. Late in 1969, some of these ads were the basis of a prosecution of the magazine for conspiring to corrupt public morals; the owners were given suspended sentences. The convictions were sustained by the Court of Appeal in 1971 and the House of Lords in 1972; it was decided that advertisements which encouraged homosexual activity were illegal even if the practice itself was not. The disastrous Shaw decision of 1961 was reaping a bumper harvest ten years later, for in July 1971 the editors of *Oz* were prosecuted under the same charge, as well as on others under the 1959 act and the Post Office Act. The basis of the prosecution was *Oz* 28, the 'schoolkids' issue, written by a group of teenagers under the supervision of the editors, and containing some feeble obscenities. The five-week trial elevated this unpromising material into the major confrontation between orthodoxy and the new culture of dissent – the Establishment v. the Alternative Society, as nearly everyone chose to see it. Thankfully the jury threw out the conspiracy charge, and understandably if regrettably found the three men guilty of the other obscenity charges. The savage penalties – gaol sentences of up to fifteen months and a deportation order for Australian Richard Neville[35] plus £2,200 in fines and costs – were seen by more than just the long-haired freaks as a vicious piece of authoritarian revenge: three former Cabinet ministers signed a Parliamentary protest. The Court of Appeal, meeting more swiftly than usual, soon quashed the more serious convictions because of defects in the summing-up by Mr Justice Argyle (who joined Melford Stevenson in the Left's demonology of injustice), though the Lord Chief Justice warned against any facile feeling that prison sentences were not appropriate for obscenity offences, and excluded magazines from the protection extended to books – that they should be considered as a whole.

Taken overall, the *Oz* affair was a setback for reaction and repression; but at lower levels, two moments in its story demonstrated the essentially political vindictiveness with which the authorities had approached the case. Even after *Oz* had been indicted, the Obscene Publications Squad continued to harass Neville; one raid led to his arrest and remand in custody for a cannabis offence, an outrage which was fortunately soon remedied by application for release to a judge in chambers. And when the three editors were remanded for medical reports between conviction and sentence, their hair was forcibly cut by Wandsworth warders; this piece of petty malice was, however, rapidly condemned by the Home Secretary, Maudling. Commenting bitterly on this summer of repression, Smythe of the N.C.C.L. wrote: 'Ultimately, all censorship is political. Censorship is for the powerful, and is a means of protecting their power'[36]. His reaction is an indication of how far the conception of freedom of expression had developed since Kidd and the others allowed the 1935 book prosecutions to pass unchallenged.

That Smythe was correct in making a political analysis of the issue was confirmed two years later when the Conservatives, in a characteristic aberration, decided to appease the Longford-Whitehouse lobby by introducing a Cinematograph and Indecent Displays Bill. Ostensibly this was aimed at preventing unsolicited mail of a sexual content and potentially offensive advertising outside sex cinemas. In fact, it went far beyond this. The advertising section would have given local authorities total powers over film societies and clubs then outside their control. The ill-drafted definitions of 'indecent' and 'display' threatened respectable institutions from libraries to galleries. Trial by jury was excluded, as was any defence based on 'public good'. The bill revealed an extraordinary reversion to pre-1950s attitudes. The N.C.C.L. was the first to notice the dangers, and organized such a fierce and widespread opposition that even Conservative M.P.s began to demand changes. Fortunately the bill was lost when the 1974 election overtook its passage through Parliament: the incoming Labour Home Secretary, Roy Jenkins, refused to revive it.

The N.C.C.L. was less swift in its response to the revival of the Incitement to Disaffection Act, however. Since the one case in 1937, it had become a commonplace to assert that the act was a dead letter. The danger in such complacency became devastatingly apparent when a 39-year-old Irish power station worker, Michael Tobin, was sentenced at Maidstone Crown Court to two years' imprisonment under this Act in April 1972 for possessing documents of a nature 'that the dissemination thereof' among the British Army would be an incitement to disaffection. Among these documents were copies (not written by Tobin) of letters which made extremely rhetorical attempts to persuade soldiers in Ulster to desert. Though it was quite clear that Tobin had signally failed to distribute any of these to any soldiers (and that the jargon in which they were written was more likely to offend than subvert a soldier), the prosecution insisted they were dangerous. It was another example of the poisonous atmosphere created in mainland Britain after four years of Ulster civil war that the judge, Mr Justice Thesiger,* could hand down the

---

*The same judge when, hearing an application for bail from the Angry Brigade defendants, asked, 'Is this an I.R.A. case?'[37]

maximum sentence, adding for good measure that it was extremely undesirable for the likes of Tobin to be employed in a public utility like a power station.[37] The N.C.C.L. let this pass without comment until nine months later, when with Amnesty they took up Tobin's case in a belated recognition of the important issues involved. His case was submitted to the European Commission on Human Rights. Encouraged by their success with Tobin, the authorities brought a similar successful prosecution against Pat Arrowsmith in 1974 for handing out leaflets to soldiers urging them not to fight in Ireland. This time, the N.C.C.L. response was swifter. After Arrowsmith had been gaoled for eighteen months, Martin Loney immediately announced a campaign to repeal the 1934 act, beginning with a private member's bill in Parliament. Writing to the Home Secretary, Jenkins, Loney said that the 1934 act was 'only of value to those who wished to restrict freedom of speech'. The reaction of the authorities was to bring similar prosecutions against fourteen other people.

Equally disturbing was the prosecution of black activist Tony Soares, who was tried in 1972 on four common-law incitement charges for publishing an article in the black power paper *Grass Roots*. (It was in fact a reprint of an American piece.) The article, on self-defence groups, did explain how to use firearms. But as with the trial of the *War Commentary* anarchists in 1945 (see above, p. 89.) the State chose to punish the mere expression of violent ideas rather than violent actions themselves. The conduct of the case against Soares had some alarming features: to discredit defence witnesses, the prosecution was allowed to smear them with their previous police records, even when these were non-criminal – that is, merely complaints about police behaviour. The jury was not happy about this, acquitting Soares on two counts and only convicting him on the other two by a majority.

Tobin, Arrowsmith and Soares had not actually inspired any revolutionary or subversive action; it is a grave flaw in our constitutional freedoms that the prosecution in these cases did not have to provide evidence that they had done so. Their cases show just how vulnerable the right to free speech is if you belong to unfashionable minorities with poor connections to the established media or liberal pressure groups.

Sometimes even these connections do not provide sufficient protection. The Left-wing paper *Socialist Worker* and its editor Paul Foot were heavily penalized in 1974 for publishing the names of two witnesses in a blackmail case after the judge had asked for them to be concealed. The Lord Chief Justice, Lord Widgery, sitting with two other judges in what was effectively a test case in a hitherto unexplored area of the law, ruled that such a request was legitimate, and flouting at a serious contempt. Although there is clearly a need to protect witnesses from publicity in certain kinds of court cases, there was considerable concern that the ruling could have far wider restrictive consequences for the press. And the *Socialist Worker* not unnaturally felt that the granting of heavy costs against it was a politically-influenced attempt to put the paper out of business.

Freedom of expression is perhaps the single most important civil liberty. The free play of ideas is the basis of all political, scientific and artistic activity. The British have not established this freedom as an inalienable right, as the Americans, in their constitution, have done. As a result some restrictions imposed in Britain would not be possible in America, though perhaps we should remember that the U.S. Constitution does not help the Americans to provide for themselves as free and independent a broadcasting service as Britain has. But clearly the abolition or reform of the official secrets laws, the obscenity laws and the incitement to disaffection law would increase the quality of free expression in Britain. Nonetheless, the experience of the early 1970s shows that threats to this freedom can be resisted. Since 1960, the expression of dissent in art, journalism and politics has been on a scale and of a quality unprecedented in twentieth-century Britain.

3. Freedom of Movement

Many of our civil liberties have an aristocratic origin. As they become increasingly popular, the earliest beneficiaries can adopt two attitudes to the change: to try and preserve the quality of the freedom as it becomes more widely available, or to fight against the advance, even to the point where the particular liberty is devalued for all. No civil liberty has suffered from this second negative tendency as much as freedom of movement. In this century Britain has moved at an ever increasing pace from an open society, welcoming anyone – political refugee or economic immigrant – and with no statutory barriers, to a frightened country clutching a protective shell of new laws and ridden with endemic xenophobia. It was, of course, easier to maintain a generous posture when it was Oxford graduates going out to rule the Raj rather than Pakistanis coming to run the Oxford buses. But still, the Conservative Governments of the last century felt far less anxiety about Marx and Lenin than their successors demonstrated sixty-odd years later about Cohn-Bendit and Dutschke. The relative revolutionary capacities of the two pairs says enough about the decline in British confidence.

The decline has, it is true, been more in attitudes towards foreigners entering the country than in the passage of natives to and fro, though even here there have been hiccups in the free tradition, as the Berlin Youth Festival trouble in 1951 and the Crawford affair in 1968 have shown. The historical irony is that the very asset which created confidence in the past, the empire at its height – with outgoing traffic – induced fear and tension as it shrank and disappeared, propelling black citizens (carrying their British passports or British subject status) embarrassingly in the reverse direction. In the eighty years between 1825 and 1905, Britain passed no legislation affecting the free movement of people in and out of the country, with the very special exception of the 1870 Extradition Treaty. Since then we have put nine acts restricting this liberty on the statute book, five of them between 1961 and 1972.*

There have been waves of immigration before the twentieth century – the Flemings, the Huguenots, the Irish – all of whom encountered varying degrees of social prejudice and hostility when they first arrived. But the authorities never felt any need to pass restrictive legislation as a result of these tensions.[1] This tradition went into reverse with the anti-Jewish propaganda at the time of the expulsions and pogroms in Eastern Europe at the turn of the century. In one sense, of course, it is no diminution of a Briton's liberty if foreigners are prevented from free access to this country. But it remains unanswerable that a freedom we once extended cheerfully to all has been churlishly withdrawn. Worse, people we were once happy to call British, with auto-matic rights of entry (when only a handful exercised it), have had their rights modified or taken away. Freedom may perhaps be divisible, but the cutback we have tolerated in this area is not only a black mark against our humanity but nourishment to the deeper repressiveness of racialism.

The first restrictions on free movement into Britain applied to aliens, those born outside the British Empire. They were the result of two periods of chauvinist hysteria, anti-Jewish in the early 1900s, anti-German around the First World War.[2] The three acts passed in 1905, 1914 and 1919 provided the executive with absolute – and arbitrary – control over entry into Britain. This was the statutory position in the early 1930s, when the next period of potential large-scale immigration loomed with Hitler's accession to power in Germany, and the subsequent flight of Jews from Nazi territory. The support these refugees could expect from some quarters in Britain could be gauged as early as March 1933 with this Parliamentary question from the Conservative M.P. for Tottenham: 'Will the Home Secretary

*Aliens Act 1905; Aliens Restriction Act 1914; Aliens Restriction Amendment Act 1919; British Nationality Act 1948; Commonwealth Immigration Act 1962; Commonwealth Immigration Act 1968; Immigration Appeals Act 1969; Immigration Act 1971.

take steps to prevent any alien Jews entering this country from Germany? Hundreds of thousands of Jews are now leaving Germany and scurrying from there to this country . . .'³. Between then and the end of 1938, 16,000 refugees were admitted into Britain, nearly a third of them only because they were *en route* elsewhere; this out of an estimated total of one million people trying in that period to escape persecution in Nazi Europe. (The French record in this was greatly superior to ours.) Even this paltry flow only came after intense pressure from the Left. As the N.C.C.L. pointed out, the regulations governing the arrival of refugees, particularly those requiring guaranteed maintenance, excluded most of the working-class refugees whose need to escape was perhaps greater than that of those better off. Inevitably this led to some illegal immigration, and the enthusiasm shown by some magistrates in hunting this down left a nasty taste. Similarly, the Home Office attitude towards those convicted of illegal entry (leaving them in gaol for weeks before deportation and after serving their sentence to discourage other potential illegal entrants) anticipated the comparable bureaucratic callousness that found it politic to shuttle East African Asians round the airports of the world in the late 1960s.

A League of Nations convention forbidding the return of refugees to Germany was eventually ratified by Britain, but a call from the N.C.C.L. and other groups helping the refugees for additional legal protection (particularly regarding deportation) went unheeded. As with the Uganda Asian crisis over thirty years later, re-settlement was a major problem, given the lacklustre economic conditions in Britain at the time; some relief was obtained by successful applications to the Dominions for help.* The Austrian and Czech crises of 1937 and 1938 increased the gravity of the problem, and a well-organized Parliamentary lobby was put together by the N.C.C.L. to attack it. This lobby

---

*H. G. Wells went with an N.C.C.L. delegation to both Halifax, the Foreign Secretary, and various Dominion high commissions to point out the special responsibilities for Czech refugees that fell on those who had signed the Munich agreement. Other efforts of the time seem less relevant – one Government inquiry went to investigate the chance of large-scale re-settlement in British Guiana.

broke through the red tape when the Government was persuaded to issue a special block of 350 visas to get a number of desperately threatened political refugees out of Czechoslovakia in 1938. But it is difficult not to agree with Paul Foot's harsh comment on the overall performance of the British Government in this period – that, as a result of its attitude, thousands of Jews perished unnecessarily in the concentration camps.[4]

When war broke out, it seemed at first that the widespread internment of enemy aliens that occurred in the First World War would be avoided. Liberals found little more to grumble about than minor inconsistencies between the various Home Office tribunals set up to decide the fate of those interned; and the only political debate fizzled around whether Anderson's assertion that the internment power derived from the Royal Prerogative was constitutionally more accurate than Hoare's belief that it was exercised under the obnoxious Regulation 18 (B). (Anderson turned out to be right.) However, the apprehensions of a few radicals like Frank Allaun (later a Labour M.P.) as early as February 1940, when he drew attention to the latent and dangerous hysteria even then evident in press scares about spies and sabotage[5], were unhappily realized in July that year. At the height of the invasion crisis, the Home Office felt obliged to introduce general internment of aliens. The absurd injustice of this was scathingly exposed by Frank Owen of the *Evening Standard* at an N.C.C.L. conference on the new emergency powers in August. He contrasted the fate of a Social Democrat mayor of a Vienna suburb, with a record of imprisonment at the hands of Dollfuss and Hitler, who was then locked up on the Isle of Man by the British, with that of a leading Austrian Fascist, Prince Stahrenberg, whose achievements in the cause of democracy included marching with Hitler in the abortive Munich putsch of 1923 and congratulating Mussolini on his Abyssinian victories – and who was now living in Claridges as an officer of the Free French Air Force. At least one Labour M.P., the veteran Josh Wedgwood, had the grace to attack Anderson, the Home Secretary, on this: 'Why will you not allow the other aliens from Austria who hate Nazism to fight? You keep them in prison and allow a scoundrel like Stahrenberg to fight for democracy.' Such was the anxiety created by the July measures that many of the Left feared that the Government would even send Dr Negrin, the former President of the Spanish Republic, back to a Franco prison.

Public resentment at this soon forced the Government to begin releasing internees in certain categories: those useful in key industries, the very old and the very young, the infirm, and those who could prove they had played 'a public and prominent part against the Nazi régime' – a fine-sounding but very limited definition which most ordinary anti-Nazis could hardly hope to qualify under. For most men between 18 and 50, the only way out was to enlist in the Pioneer Corps; yet alien volunteers had no international status – if captured by the Axis powers they were more likely to be shot than imprisoned as P.O.W.s.* Even friendly aliens – Poles, Czechs, Belgians – suffered the bureaucratic nonsense at this time. 400 of them were briefly imprisoned without any trial or explanation.

An additional source of grievance for the refugees developed as a result of the powers given (under the Allied Forces Act, 1940) to the six refugee governments in Britain, in particular the power to maintain their own armies on our soil. Several Labour backbenchers questioned the constitutional propriety of handing over considerable authority to what were in reality no more than 'societies of friendly foreigners temporarily domiciled here', especially as large numbers of the refugee populations denied that their so-called governments had any democratic base. (The Polish and Czech governments in exile, whose racial policies were unsavoury, to say the least, were particularly disliked by their British-based countrymen.) Strong objection was taken during a Parliamentary debate in August 1940 to the fact that the French and Polish codes provided death penalties for offences which were only punishable by imprisonment under English law.

The adverse publicity all this received soon induced the

*Only 2,000 of the total of 22,000 enemy aliens took this option. The reluctance of the others is understandable in the light of the Corps' record and early recruiting slogan – 'enlist or rot'. There was no guarantee that you wouldn't be used to undercut British labour, and some promises to release wives after enlistment were not kept.

Coalition Government to moderate its treatment of aliens: various committees were set up to supervise the release of the internees, which went on rapidly enough in late 1941 and 1942. In mid-1941 there had been 14,000 'enemy' aliens interned: a year later, this was down to 8,000; and by the end of the year, almost all the anti-Nazis had been released. In addition, the new Allied Powers (War Service) Act gave allied nationals the choice of joining the British forces if they preferred these to their own, and even those unfortunates who had already committed themselves to their own national armies under the mistaken impression that they had to were able to change their minds. It was, as the N.C.C.L. said, 'a much better bill than originally seemed probable.' The change in atmosphere between summer 1940 and autumn 1942 can be seen in the ease with which the N.C.C.L. persuaded the War Office in November 1942 to cancel orders forbidding the speaking of German by German and Austrian refugee recruits in off-duty time. In 1944 there was another successful campaign, this time to liberate the Polish Jews from the anti-Semitic Polish forces in Britain;* but the final fling of the Allied Forces Act came after the war had ended, in the summer of 1945. Dr Jagodzinski, a Polish lieutenant and journalist, who had been given leave the previous year to become a lecturer at London University, was arrested and charged with 'desertion'. It was widely realized that Jagodzinski's real offence in the eyes of the exiled Polish government was his public support for the new Warsaw régime. He was, however, released after public outcry at the continuing ability of foreign authorities of doubtful legitimacy to seize people on the streets of London.

The wartime powers then duly lapsed, but some of them had to be re-enacted seven years later thanks to the Cold War. The Visiting Forces Act was passed in 1952 to cope with the presence of large numbers of U.S. troops here. At the time the N.C.C.L. objected to the departure from previous international legal practice which regarded foreign soldiers as normally subject to domestic laws and domestic courts. The 1952 Act gave the U.S. forces sovereignty over their nationals; worse, it even restricted

*See below Chapter 6, p. 230.

a few British liberties. For instance, if a U.S. soldier caused the death of a British subject, the coroner's inquest could be dispensed with. In practice these early fears proved unfounded, though some fifteen years later the 1952 Act was to create a quite different civil liberty problem.*

The pre-war refugees suffered a threefold liability: they were part of a large scale movement; most, being Jewish, were ethnically identifiable; and many were Left-wing in politics. The post-war victims of British restrictionism did not usually incorporate all three disadvantages in one person, and it is necessary to distinguish the two separate prejudices that affected free movement in and out of Britain after 1945. The mass migrations of blacks from the West Indies and the Indian sub-continent produced such hysteria in some sections of the British population that a series of racially exclusive laws were passed to contain and finally throttle this movement. The second factor was the Cold War and succeeding anti-Left neuroses, which afflicted the Foreign and Home Offices with a despicable nervousness. The civil liberty response in both areas was inevitably defensive. Repressive legislation was opposed, usually unsuccessfully; individual cases were fought, sometimes rather more successfully. Only with the immigration appeals procedure was there a civil liberty initiative.

The anti-Communism of the Cold War years inspired an unprecedentedly and unashamedly political interpretation of the power to prevent the entry of aliens into Britain. A similar attitude lay behind the equally unprecedented warning to native Britons that their freedom to travel abroad depended on the arbitrary discretion of the Government, and not, as most had hitherto cheerfully assumed, on an elementary constitutional right. It was a devious but effective arrogation of abolute power; in theory, no Briton required a passport to leave or enter this country, merely a satisfactory form of identification. The theoretical right was practically useless since every other country required Britons to carry passports issued by the British Government. The Government could therefore prevent any citizen leaving the country without breaking any constitutional statute.

*See below, p. 154.

In 1948, the Labour Government began to point this out in the passports themselves, when newly issued passports carried the statement that they were the property of H.M. Government and could be withdrawn 'if the bearer ceased to be entitled to H.M.G.'s protection' – a nicely silky phrase. Their Tory successors became even blunter in 1953 – passports thereafter simply said the Government could withdraw them at any time. In July 1951, this arbitrary power was actually used against Dr Burhop, a scientist who wanted to travel to Moscow. The N.C.C.L. tartly pointed out that Magna Carta had expressly guaranteed the freedom of an Englishman to leave his country in time of peace, and considerable press protest ensued; a month later, the Foreign Office returned Dr Burhop his passport, but only after his written assurance that he would not travel behind the Iron Curtain without telling them first.

Not that the governments of the time really needed to go to such blatant lengths to restrict the free movement of British citizens. In August 1951, several hundred people left Britain to attend a World Youth Festival in East Berlin. Before they left, the Government had tried to discourage attendance, but had never indicated that it would actually prevent it. The French and Belgian authorities were given the names of about 100 young people, who were refused permission to cross these countries *en route* for Berlin and sent back to Britain. Consular assistance at the ports was refused. 300 others, who got as far as the American zone in Austria, met a similar refusal when they were imprisoned, and in a few cases beaten up, for not having the right papers enabling them to enter the Russian zone, even though the Russians indicated they were quite prepared for the party to proceed through their territory. Despite N.C.C.L. pressure, the Foreign Office refused to investigate the incidents, and the council set up an inquiry under Sydney Silverman and four others, including the Cambridge scientist Joseph Needham. Their report confirmed the deliberate and underhand obstructiveness of the Foreign Office.

The colonial governments were even worse for habitually impounding their citizens' passports. In 1953, this prompted the *Reynolds News* to make the noble if doomed comment that 'a colonial subject has exactly the same status as a subject born in the U.K. A threat to his freedom to travel is a threat to the freedom of all of us.' The only individuals to receive a generous benefit of the doubt at this time were a handful of South African refugees. The election of South Africa's first Nationalist government, under Malan, and the consequent hardening of that country's racialist policies, forced several prominent opposition leaders to flee to Britain: in particular the Indian political leaders Dadoo and Naidoo, and the champion of the people of S.W. Africa, the Rev. Michael Scott, came here without passports (withheld by the South African Government) between 1948 and 1950. Despite this, all three were welcomed in Britain. N.C.C.L. representatives at the docks satisfied the immigration officers of Dr Naidoo's *bona fides* when he arrived as a stowaway on a ship with an Indian crew in 1951. (Naidoo, married to a white woman, had been forced to leave illegally after the passing of the Mixed Marriage and Immorality Acts in South Africa.) His family, also travelling without passports, was later helped through in a similar manner.

One foreign Communist was also lucky. Gerhart Eisler was arrested in May 1949 on board a Polish boat at Southampton while *en route* for East Germany from the U.S.A. Eisler had jumped bail in America after receiving a three-year sentence for perjury.* The Americans applied to the Bow Street magistrates for his extradition; the N.C.C.L. and various Communist organizations got together a formidable defence group very quickly. (Pritt and Dudley Collard gave their legal services free, and three Labour M.P.s – Tom Braddock, Maurice Orbach and Sydney Silverman – stood bail for Eisler.) Eisler was released after the defence successfully argued that there had been no perjury as English law understood it, and therefore no grounds for extradition. Eisler was lucky this technical loophole existed; on the subsequent performance of the British immigration authorities,

---

*Eisler had escaped from the Nazis during the war, and made some inaccurate statements to the U.S. immigration authorities *en route* to Mexico where he had been offered asylum. When the Americans later tried to exploit this technical offence to harass Eisler, they provoked widespread protest even in the U.S.A.

if he had relied on the other N.C.C.L. plea on his behalf (that the U.S. prosecution was in essence a political one) he would not have got off. Indeed, the following year showed how far the Government was prepared to go to make life awkward for Communists and their fellow travellers. An international Peace Conference had been arranged at Sheffield for November 1950; the Labour ministers, including Attlee, had attacked it but had recognized they had no right to ban it. However, more subtle measures were found. As the date of the conference drew near, visas were refused wholesale, and large numbers of non-visa holders declared *persona non grata*.

The absurdity of some of these decisions, even on security grounds as understood by the Cold War philosophy then paramount, was glaring; a prominent Swedish Social Democrat was sent back to Stockholm, and a lawyer was given a visa to attend an international legal conference in Britain but not the Sheffield conference. Still, the Labour Government achieved its object. The conference had to be shifted to Warsaw.*

Encouraged by their Labour predecessor's success, the Conservative Government which came to power in the following year went even further. In 1952, no foreign delegates were allowed in to attend the council meeting of the World Federation of Scientific Workers; young dancers, singers and athletes were refused permission to be present at a Sheffield youth festival (composers like Malcolm Arnold and Michael Tippett, actors Miles Malleson and Alex McCrindle protested, but the Home Office refused to see or hear them); two Polish Supreme Court judges, invited by the Haldane Society, were denied entry; and Western lawyers coming to a meeting to discuss the arrest of the French Communist leader Duclos were all turned back at the ports.† As the N.C.C.L. commented, it had become painfully

---

*There was a further minor flurry over this. The Australian Government said it would withdraw the passports of any Australian delegates to Warsaw, and at one stage it looked as though the unfortunate Australians would have their papers seized as they passed through Britain; but after N.C.C.L. protests this extra tyranny was avoided, and even the Menzies Government later abandoned this policy.

†Pritt was convinced the lawyers' names were known to the immigration officers only because the Special Branch had tapped his phone.

clear that the authorities had a blacklist of groups who were not to be allowed foreign guests for their meetings.

In 1953 the Government undertook an extraordinary survey of aliens in the U.K., including some who had come in the 1900s and who had British-born children. Questions included 'What newspapers do you read?' and 'What do you think of Marshal Tito?' And in 1954 they strengthened their powers to deport aliens. The depressing quality of the petty anti-Communism afflicting the authorities in these years is perhaps best evident in the classic affair of Dr Joseph Cort. Cort was a young Yale scientist – and a former member of the American Communist Party – who came to work at Birmingham University in 1951. When the McCarthyite campaigns got under way in the United States, the American authorities began to harass Cort from afar. His passport was demanded, he was called up for the U.S. armed forces* despite having been disqualified from military service in 1946 on medical grounds (and subsequently being given permission to leave the United States by the National Service Board); and, finally, in 1953 he was threatened with loss of citizenship. Three months later the Home Office, which previously had regularly renewed Cort's work permit, suddenly refused to do so again, and turned down Cort's application for political asylum, despite the obvious possibility that he could face prosecution under the Smith Act for his Communist affiliations if he were deported back to America. This churlishness met with a lively protest, particularly in Parliament and the universities; E. M. Forster remembered his libertarian past and joined his name to a letter to *The Times*. But despite this support, Cort finally found it necessary to accept asylum in Czechoslovakia, much as Dutschke had to go to the more generous climate of Denmark sixteen years later. The N.C.C.L. declared defiantly but unfortunately over-optimistically: 'Let us see that this is the last time considerations of political expediency govern the granting of refuge to those in need.'

As the Cold War became less frosty in the later 1950s, this obstructionism faded, and the Home Office found alternative

---

*A favourite victimization of this period – the U.S. Army conscripting 'politically suspect' doctors as privates.

work coping with the rapid growth of black immigration and the clamour for restrictive policies that this aroused in part of the population. In 1955 one unfortunate group, the Left-wing Arab students studying here, seem to have combined politics and coloured skins at exactly the wrong moment, and found themselves bridging two repressive attitudes. Those from Iraq in particular were subjected to intimidating delays in getting their three month permits renewed. Undeterred by public protests at this petty tyranny, the Government went even further in 1956 and cheerfully accepted a request from the reactionary Baghdad régime for the deportation of three students. 'In the old days', said the N.C.C.L., 'aliens were asked to leave the country only if they became chargeable to public funds, if they made themselves undesirable on moral or criminal grounds, or if they were believed to be engaged in espionage. There has been no suggestion that these three have offended in any of these ways.'

There have been two kinds of large-scale immigration in modern British history; that provoked by political persecution, and that which is part of a wider economic process. The Jews in the 1930s and the Ugandan Asians in the 1970s belonged to the first category, the East Europeans of the late 1940s and the black Commonwealth immigrants of the 1950s and 1960s to the second. The latter was part of the larger European phenomenon of major population movements from the underdeveloped countries, movements which fuelled the various West European economic miracles. The history of Commonwealth immigration is its transformation over thirty years from a movement of free citizens into a contract labour system almost identical to the industrial helotry practised on the Continent.[6]

Between 1945 and 1950 some 200,000 Eastern Europeans were brought here to cope with the post-war labour shortage. They came under the auspices of either the Polish Re-settlement Act (designed to cope with Poles unwilling to return to Communist Poland) or the European Voluntary Worker scheme. The exploitative nature of the strictly controlled movement was sufficiently obvious to get Britain pilloried at the United Nations in November 1949, since other countries did not, at that time, restrict immigrants to particular jobs, and the restrictions were lifted two years later.[7] But in some other respects, particularly the care taken to teach them English, the Europeans were treated more favourably that their Asian successors. And although there were individual instances of resentment and, at least to begin with, sustained trade union suspicion, the Europeans settled and integrated fairly rapidly.[8]

The Europeans were aliens, and could be regulated without reference to the constitution; the blacks from the Commonwealth and the colonies enjoyed superior privileges. The 1948 British Nationality Act (welcomed by the N.C.C.L. for its improvement in the status of married women, and later seen by some Conservatives as the cause of the racial troubles) tidied up the complex citizenship provisions of the old Empire, and created a distinction between Commonwealth citizens and citizens of the United Kingdom and its colonies. Both remained, however, British subjects, entitled to automatic entry into Britain. Within four years of the passing of the act, and the coincidentally simultaneous start of the West Indian immigration, Tory M.P. Cyril Osborne began the campaign to stop up this entry channel.[9]

But through the fat years of the mid-1950s Osborne found little support, official or otherwise.* Occasionally government agents revealed that callousness that was to characterize the implementation of immigration control in the 1960s. In the autumn of 1952 the police attempted to deport two Malayan seamen, Eurasians with British nationality, because one failed to carry his passport. Lawyers briefed by the N.C.C.L. stalled this long enough for documentary evidence to come from Singapore,† and two policemen were subsequently disciplined for 'irregularities in connection with overseas seamen's documents.' And in September 1954 a Cypriot with 'valid only for travel to Greece' stamped on his British passport found his legitimate entry into Britain obstructed by a Newhaven immigration official until N.C.C.L.

*The inter-departmental dispute between the Home Office and the Commonwealth Office is discussed by E. J. B. Rose, in *Colour and Citizenship: Report of British Race Relationships*, Oxford University Press, 1969.

†When at one stage the N.C.C.L. threatened to apply for *habeas corpus* the Home Office wanted to settle the matter 'amicably' by landing the seaman as an alien, an idea based solely on the fact that the Malayan had once been to Houston.

telephone calls secured his release. But, basically, the free movement of British subjects of whatever colour went on unimpeded.

However, in 1958 after the Notting Hill disturbances, the Osborne position received a considerable boost: Lord Home, the Commonwealth Secretary, called for restrictions on West Indian immigration, and the Conservative conference passed a resolution making similar demands; even Butler, the Home Secretary, was prepared to talk of establishing deportation provisions for colonial passport holders.[10] During the next three years the Conservative Government retreated rapidly from the confidently liberal position it had adopted in the mid-1950s. Partly this was in response to pressure brought by some of the new M.P.s after the 1959 election – particularly from Birmingham – who were eager to see controls introduced, and partly to the emergence of pressure groups on the Right after 1960, urging controls in tones of varying degrees of racialism, which lent some force to the idea that public opinion was changing. In January 1961 the Home Office put forward proposals for introducing controls, but Butler was overruled in the Cabinet.* During the first nine months of 1961 the rate of immigration doubled, part of a circular reinforcement process whereby the Right clamoured for control, the immigrants rushed in to beat controls, the Right increased its campaigning frenzy as the immigrant flow increased, etc. Osborne and his Tory allies Norman Pannell and Harold Gurden stepped up the Parliamentary pressure; Tory by-election candidates made increasing, though not particularly successful, use of the immigration issue. At the Conservative conference in October a resolution demanding controls was passed overwhelmingly, and within a month Butler introduced the Commonwealth Immigration Bill in Parliament, less than eight months after his ministry had refused to countenance the restriction of the 'historic right' of free entry.[11]

The appalling implications of the proposals for civil liberty were immediately attacked by the N.C.C.L. Quite apart from an

---

*As a result Butler's junior, David Renton, had to announce in Parliament a few weeks later that 'the Government refused to contemplate legislation which might restrict the historic right of every British subject . . . freely to enter and stay in the U.K.'[12]

obvious hostility to the underlying distinction between two classes
of British subjects on a covert basis of colour and race, the
N.C.C.L. pointed to the alarming increase in official power.
These powers included absolute discretion given to immigration
officers, with no appeal against their decisions – particularly
odious considering that mental health and physical sickness
were grounds for refusing entry, and yet the immigration
officers would have no professional qualifications in these areas –
the blanket power to refuse entry to those with previous criminal
convictions, which, as the N.C.C.L. pointed out, 'pre-supposed a
continuance of guilt after sentence has been served'; the national
security clause, which since more than adequate security provisions existed already, could lead to the political screening of
immigrants; unlimited detention powers; the clause making it an
offence to harbour an illegal immigrant or to refuse to produce
documents, a proposal the N.C.C.L. regarded as an intrusion
into individual privacy which would increase the accommodation
problems for immigrants; the extension from one to five years
of the period within which an immigrant could not claim British
citizenship; and the deportation powers, which made all immigrants 'second-class citizens, here on sufferance', and which
might severely inhibit legitimate activities like strikes and
demonstrations. The intense opposition inside Parliament from
the Labour and Liberal Parties, and indeed from some Conservatives (largely because the Government totally fouled up the
application of the new law to the Irish), won some concessions,
notably the publication of the instructions to immigration officers.
The N.C.C.L. and others were later to gain another qualified
victory on the appeals procedure; but few could foresee in 1961
that the relatively mild measures of that act, opposed so bitterly
by a substantial section of the country, were to be succeeded by
many much tougher restrictions with much less opposition.
It is now clear that the 1961 Act irretrievably smashed a crucial
psychological barrier against illiberalism; within ten years,
black British subjects became as ill-protected at law as aliens,
and considerably worse treated in practice. What happened after
1961 in immigration law and practice has been the worst disaster
civil liberty has suffered in modern Britain, not just because it has

been a major factor in institutionalizing racialism, but because a powerful Government department has been given licence to dispense with normal judicial procedures and exercise a wide-scale discretionary power. And so far at least it has been used with a marked lack of compassion, humanity and justice.

Two aspects of the 1961 legislation were to prove persistently troublesome; the power to refuse entry and the deportation and removal powers. Indeed, within a month of the act becoming law in June 1962, the new Home Secretary, Brooke, was being savaged in Parliament for his handling of a deportation case. A 23-year-old Jamaican girl, Carmen Bryan, was recommended for deportation after being bound over after a (first offence) shop-lifting conviction. Brooke came under strong pressure to rescind this order, from a Parliamentary group led by Labour M.P. Eric Fletcher with the support of the liberal press. After forty-seven days in Holloway, Miss Bryan was released and the deportation threat lifted. The *Observer* pointed out that the act already breached one principle of British justice – that all are equal before the law – but that if it were to be enforced in this way it would soon break another, that no-one should be imprisoned without trial. The subsequent record of the Home Office in detaining immigrants without trial for months on end was to prove the *Observer* sadly accurate.

It was soon clear what an impossible task had been assigned to the immigration officers, and with what appalling callousness some of them tried to carry it out. Organizations like Amnesty International and the N.C.C.L. were often able to get arbitrary and unwarranted decisions reversed with a quick telephone call, but only when the immigrant under threat was well-informed or well-connected enough to get instant access to these bodies.* But for those who hadn't such resources, it was the next plane back. And worse was to come.

Throughout the early 1960s a peculiarly vicious and unpleasant anti-immigrant campaign had been mounted by Conservatives

---

*One South African, Youssef Omar, who fled from police persecution to Britain without a passport, had to sit out an eight-month campaign on his behalf by M.P.s and liberal groups before he was allowed to stay: a sad contrast to the treatment of Naidoo.

in a traditionally Labour West Midlands constituency – Smethwick. In the election of October 1964, quite against the national swing to Labour, Peter Griffiths earned the reward of an openly racialist approach by winning Smethwick for the Tories.* There was a lot of fine-sounding liberal indignation and concern at this result, but the crucial consequence was that the political opportunists on the Left decided to secure themselves against another Smethwick by borrowing some of Griffiths' clothes. The rest of his wardrobe was acquired by the opportunists on the Right who thought they could thus regain power. In February 1965 Douglas-Home upped the respectable racialist ante: he called for the deportation of illegal immigrants, voluntary Government-assisted repatriation, the inclusion of dependants in the overall entry quotas, and a reduction in these quotas. This lurch rightwards was matched by the Labour Government with its notorious Immigration White Paper in August 1965. Labour had early dropped its absolute opposition to controls; now after the failure of its attempt through Mountbatten to negotiate bilateral agreements with Commonwealth governments for controls at source, it actually strengthened the British controls. The White Paper reduced the voucher limit from 20,000 to 8,500 a year, abolished the right of entry for unskilled workers, and toughened the powers of immigration officers to refuse entry, particularly in regard to dependants. One of the worst features of the oppressive control system built up during the 1960s was the way immigrant families became a favourite target for those seeking to cut down yet further the inward movement, and it is to the lasting discredit of the Labour Government that it was the first to tread this path. Opposition to these policies was, while not inconsiderable, hamstrung by the narrowness of Wilson's Parliamentary majority; the decline in the quality and intensity of this liberal opposition since 1961 shows how rapidly a civil liberty can be eroded when few choose to assert it.

However, in 1966, with Wilson confirmed in power with a large

* Griffiths, a local councillor, prevented a Pakistani getting a council house mortgage because it would lead to a 'ghetto policy'. He also responded to the 1963 unemployment crisis by recommending the Home Office to deport all blacks who had been unemployed for more than six months.[13]

majority, the liberals began to fight back. The Prime Minister's promise to set up a committee to investigate the possibility of appeals machinery was eventually implemented under Sir Roy Wilson, and the N.C.C.L., amongst others, supplied him with ample evidence of the need for such machinery. They restated the basic civil liberty principle: 'Any administrative decision should be subject to scrutiny and appeal before execution.' This was endorsed by the committee's report when it appeared in July 1967. In practice, the main problems arose over the entry of dependants from India and Pakistan. Those under 16 or over 60 had a theoretical right to join next of kin in Britain. These age limits created constant borderline crises, leading to farcical situations where quite inadequate medical checks on age were attempted, and documents issued in India and Pakistan largely disbelieved by immigration officers.* The farce could become something grimmer when children were detained for days at a time in Heathrow in quite unsuitable conditions. On one occasion the N.C.C.L. tried to force this particular issue by sponsoring an application for *habeas corpus*, and although this was rejected, the Lord Chief Justice commented that the immigration officer has a duty to act 'not only impartially but also fairly', while Lord Justice Salmon added that his powers should be used in accordance with natural justice. A second tactic was to take cases to the European Commission on Human Rights, a court only recognized by Britain in 1966. One case, of a Pakistani boy sent back after only twenty-four hours at Heathrow, was found to be admissible by the Commission because Britain had not provided a proper hearing of his application to join his father. This was an important victory in the fight to reduce the arbitrary powers of the immigration officers.

In the long delay between the Wilson committee call for an appeals system (July 1967) and the appeals legislation in 1969 – at one point in 1968 it looked as though Callaghan, the Home Secretary, was prepared to abandon appeals legislation al-

*One letter from the Home Office to the N.C.C.L. commented rather acidly that 'not all official documents issued in some countries can be accepted as proof,' but, as the N.C.C.L. argued back, the fact that some papers were unquestionably forged should not put all papers out of court.

together – the implementation of controls deteriorated still further. The following examples come from N.C.C.L. files: the 68-year-old wife of the Deputy Premier of British Honduras was given a medical examination which included stripping to the waist; seven Chinese sailors with Indian-issued British passports were shuttled 12,000 miles back and forwards between Athens and London while four countries tried to work out whose was the responsibility (five eventually went to India, two to the U.K.); a Pakistani father resident in Britain returned from a trip abroad with his son, whose relationship and age were both disbelieved by welcoming immigration officers (the suspicions were only resolved by a check with the Inland Revenue); a Biafran forced to leave Lagos on the outbreak of the war was refused extensions for his work permit in Britain until N.C.C.L. pressure modified the Home Office attitude; two Indian girls were detained thirteen days at Heathrow while the Home Office disputed whether their mother was in fact intending to come to Britain; and a Pakistani student at Middlesbrough Technical College was given impromptu educational 'tests' by an immigration officer, and found wanting – until the N.C.C.L. intervened.

In 1967 various immigrant organizations and radical/liberal groups came together to found the Joint Council for the Welfare of Immigrants, with full-time officials at Heathrow and in London: this took over most of the individual casework from bodies like the N.C.C.L. and those M.P.s who had been prepared to pursue such unrewarding activity. Neither the J.C.W.I. nor the N.C.C.L. were happy with the form of the Appeals Bill when it eventually appeared in December 1968, though it did at last destroy the completely arbitrary power of the immigration officers by the creation of adjudicators and appeals tribunals. Detailed procedures were left to the Home Secretary; immigration officers were given new power to enter private homes; and the bill came nowhere near setting up the comprehensive welfare services urged by the Wilson committee and others. The draft instruction on aliens, published for the first time with this bill, showed how Commonwealth immigrants were in fact occasionally worse off than aliens, whose dependants under 18 or over 60 were automatically admitted – while for

Commonwealth immigrants the corresponding ages were 16 and 65. But the final nasty irony in the long campaign for appeals machinery came late in the bill's passage through Parliament. In May 1969, Callaghan suddenly added a clause making entry certificates compulsory for all dependants. This almost completely wiped out the advantage of appeals machinery for Commonwealth immigrants, who would now have to contest decisions from afar. The Wilson committee had rejected this idea three years earlier: 'It would be out of the question to impose on Commonwealth citizens a visa requirement under another name.' And Callaghan himself, six months earlier (November 1968) had argued against such certificates because they would discriminate against Commonwealth immigrants compared with aliens. The restrictive purpose of this manoeuvre, though denied at the time, was implicitly admitted in November 1969 by Callaghan when he boasted of the decline in immigrant entry figures.

The liberal lobby made a last effort to mitigate the consequences of Callaghan's opportunism by pressing for an expanded advisory service abroad. Merlyn Rees, one of the Home Office ministers, met the J.C.W.I. on 5 June 1969 and promised financial assistance for such services. In July, Sir Derek Hilton undertook an inquiry for the Government into this idea, but was criticized by the liberals for his inadequate research abroad. This proved a crucial point, for his report, published in October, argued that the existing High Commission staff could cope abroad so that extra Government finance need only be made available in Britain – a view vigorously rejected in a simultaneous report by Mary Dines of the J.C.W.I., whose recent lengthy visit to India and Pakistan had indicated the need for independent advisory services there as well as in Britain. Meanwhile, the appeals machinery was still being set up, and a large number of questionable decisions went untested. Christmas 1969 was a particularly bad period, when several *bona fide* visitors were refused entry.

Even when the tribunal began to work in 1970, it was not quite the independent judicial body hoped for by the liberals. The N.C.C.L. commented after its first year: 'Many see it as an extension of a government department . . . its proceedings are like those of a Star Chamber . . . on many occasions more reliance is placed on unsupported Home Office statements than on the first hand evidence of persons attending the tribunal.' The N.C.C.L. could, however, have claimed with accuracy that it had tried hard to obtain justice even in such an unpromising arena, and had not infrequently secured it. A Jamaican woman whose child had been left with relatives in the West Indies while she found a home in Britain was refused an entry certificate for him, but the N.C.C.L., by obtaining a report from the local Jamaican children's officer, had forced the Home Office to change its decision. A Mauritian woman who had settled here illegally in 1968 went to the police three years later when she learned that her husband had left Mauritius to come looking for her. The police passed the case to the Home Office, which referred it to an adjudicator. He argued that in view of the woman's despair at the idea of returning to Mauritius 'there were good compassionate grounds for allowing her to stay here' if the Home Office cared to exercise them, though no legal grounds for overturning their original refusal to let her stay on. After further N.C.C.L. representations, the Home Office agreed and the woman stayed.

One long-drawn-out case, of a Biafran called Udoh, showed the difficulty of fighting appeals from a distance. Udoh arrived in Britain in 1965 and, forced to remain here by the outbreak of the Nigerian civil war in 1967, did so in breach of his original conditions of entry. Despite pleas for leniency from the N.C.C.L. and others, he had to go to Eire (which was prepared to accept him). A deportation order was then made against Udoh. He appealed to the tribunal, but the Home Office refused him permission to return to appear in person, a peculiarly bad example of bureaucratic petty-mindedness. The N.C.C.L. defeated this, however, by sending their legal officer Larry Grant to Dublin to obtain a detailed affidavit, which persuaded the tribunal to reverse the deportation order and allowed Udoh to return to Britain in 1972. Smarting from this setback, the Home Office changed the appeal rules (appended to the 1971 Immigration Act) to discourage challenges to deportation orders which had been in force for under three years.

But even this early it was clear that the long campaign to get a satisfactory appeals procedure had only had a strictly limited success. The important principle that administrative officials should not have completely arbitrary powers had been regained, but the practical objective of securing a generous treatment of immigration applications was completely lost. Given the entrenchment of racialism in the country at large during those years, generosity was scarcely likely anyway.

This long tussle went relatively unpublicized. Save for the ammunition it provided for the Right to shout about 'evasion of controls', the technicality of admission procedure excited little interest – another warning of how easy it can be for authority quietly to choke off liberties in out-of-the-way areas. The two big racial crises in the years after the Labour White Paper in 1965 erupted, ironically enough, as a result of a last act of Tory imperial grandeur a few years earlier. In the negotiations over Kenyan independence in the summer of 1963 (in which Commonwealth Secretary Duncan Sandys played a leading part), the future of the Asian community was left fudged; but there is no doubt that the British Government promised to honour the obligations of British citizenship for those Asians who retained it.* About 112,000 took this option. Four years later, the consequences of that pledge provided Sandys, and more importantly Enoch Powell, with a racialist platform which not only shifted the public debate finally and decisively away from the genuine problem of racial discrimination inside Britain to the fantasy problem of immigration control, but also corrupted the style of political debate in this country in a manner from which we had not recovered several years later. The Rightward flow of the political argument between the two major parties, evident since 1961, reached its high-water mark in 1973 when a Conservative candidate† argued for compulsory repatriation of immigrants. At least, one must presume it was the high-water mark; the only

---

A trio of Conservative ex-Ministers, Macleod, Fraser and Lord Lansdowne, disputed Sandys' attempt to deny this in the angry debates surrounding the Commonwealth Immigration Act in February 1968.[14]

†George Young, Brent East, in his unsuccessful campaign for chairmanship of the Monday Club.

policy left unadvocated by respectable politicians was a Hitlerian final solution.

In 1967, Kenya announced that aliens would in future only be allowed to work there on a temporary basis. As a result, there was a rapid increase in the number of Asians coming to Britain. From early 1967, Powell, the Conservative M.P. for Wolverhampton S.W. and a member of the Shadow Cabinet, had begun to argue that regulating the flow of immigrants was no longer enough; repatriation and separate development were the answers.[15] Initially he met with little response: but from midsummer he and Sandys seized on the new Asian influx (which, following the 1961 pattern, accelerated in reaction to the Right's demand that the avenue of escape be closed*) to re-create the atmosphere of hysteria that Osborne and others had successfully worked up six years previously. For its part, the Labour Government followed its 1965 pattern: send an envoy to appeal to Commonwealth solidarity so that the blacks would keep their own people at home†, and when this fails, legislate repressively. In February 1968, they rushed the Commonwealth Immigration Act through Parliament, without any idea of the number of people involved or affected.

This completed the racialist logic of the 1962 act. That had restricted the right of entry of those holding either Commonwealth (e.g. Indian) or colonial (e.g. Fijian) passports, though both were British subjects. Now the one group of blacks retaining a right to free entry (because they held British passports) were shut out, too. Freedom to enter the United Kingdom automatically was denied to United Kingdom passport holders unless they had family connections with this country. £15,000 special vouchers were created to regulate the flow of those citizens who lacked this kith and kin connection.

The fury this aroused in the liberal community was greater even than that inspired by the 1961 legislation, partly because this was a Labour measure and the betrayal seemed the greater;

*In the two weeks before the Parliamentary debates, 10,000 Asians came to Britain.[16]

†This time Macdonald rather than Mountbatten: Wilson had a taste for despatching old colonial hands to scenes of former glory.

partly because the suffering it would cause was much more obvious; and partly because even to some Conservatives the devaluation of the British passport itself and the creation of two classes of citizens was in constitutional terms far more serious than anything done in 1961. The N.C.C.L. pointed out that the 'two classes' concept was very close to the Nazi Nuremberg Law of 1935 and the South African apartheid laws, while Labour lawyer Anthony Lester bitterly updated Junius: 'In questions merely political an honest man may stand neuter; but the laws and constitution are the general property of the subject. Not to defend is to relinquish.'[17]. The Government's lack of regard for the constitutional implications of the measure, and the indifference of the country at large to that lack of concern, is one of the most serious corruptions of British democracy this century. The International Commission of Jurists felt it necessary to note the collapse of Britain as 'a traditional bastion of civil liberty', and not surprisingly some liberals in Britain felt the time had come to get ourselves a written constitution and a supreme court to uphold it.

A brave rearguard action was mounted by the Liberal Party; a handful of Labour and Tory M.P.s (Dingle Foot, now Labour, spoke brilliantly, a reminder of his pre-war civil liberty role in Parliament); groups like the J.C.W.I., the U.K. Committee for Citizenship (led by East African Asian Prafu Pratel) and the N.C.C.L. (though Smythe felt later they should not have moved so far from their neutral role as actually to have organized a demonstration[18]); and even the Right-wing press. *The Times* stringently commented that the Labour Party no longer believed in the equality of man but 'in the equality of white British citizens'.[19] In the Lords, where the Bishops, led by the Archbishop of Canterbury, showed a commendable if unusual political indignation, the Government was nearly defeated.[20]

For the Asians in Kenya the effect of this was naturally severe. Thousands, forced to wait in queue for a voucher, consumed their savings in unwanted idleness, or if, as happened in many cases, they had insufficient resources to cope with the waiting period, they became destitute. The hardships prompted many to try and enter Britain illegally: 'queue-jumping', the Home Office called it with characteristic insensitivity. So began the infamous shuttlecock system, in which hapless airlines were forced to fly families and individuals round and round the world while Britain, the only country which ultimately could accept them, coldly calculated the deterrent effect of this on those thousands in East Africa who might otherwise have felt queue-jumping was worth it. The ingenuity of the Asians in finding a variety of routes was matched by the determined pressure of the British Government on any country willing to accept them even in transit. Oddly enough, it was the authoritarian régimes of France and Spain which proved most sympathetic to the Asians, perhaps because they cared less than the others for British diplomatic sensibilities. The Home Office's punitive attitude to successful 'queue-jumpers' – and all were eventually successful – persisted long after their arrival; they were not allowed to bring their dependants over, or if their families got in, anyway, their children were refused schooling. Such were the rights of British citizenship . . . second-class.

The N.C.C.L. and the J.C.W.I. tried hard to modify the consequences of this, and in the summer of 1970 the Government was strongly criticized in the press when several hundred Asians were stranded in Europe by the shuttlecock policy. The N.C.C.L. used the case of the Mohammed Khan family of Nairobi in its brief for the Parliamentary civil liberty group in November 1970. This once prosperous family were separated; the mother and two youngest children in Pakistan on dwindling savings (£15,000 to £3,000 in two years' enforced stay); one son in Britain on a three-month permit (having been shuttlecocked round the world for three weeks); the father and the other son both illegally in Britain, all as a result of the 1960 act. 'The Khans,' wrote the N.C.C.L., 'are decent respectable people who have been driven to the verge of destitution . . . by circumstances over which they have no control and by the manoeuvrings of governments . . . They are the victims of legislation which can appropriately be described as the British Citizens (Exile) Act 1968.'

The tactic of going to the European Commission of Human Rights was tried again, this time on a larger scale and with greater success. In 1970, twenty-three out of thirty-five complaints were treated as admissible by the Commission, on the grounds that the Asians had been subjected to degrading treatment; that they had been denied the right to security of person; and that they had suffered discrimination.[20a] By 1973, nearly 300 such cases had gone before the Commission.

In Britain itself, his success in stampeding the Labour Government on the Kenyan Asian issue encouraged Powell to play the black card on a wider scale. In April 1968, just as the Race Relations Bill was going through Parliament, he made his notorious 'Tiber flowing with blood' speech in Birmingham, and 'Powellism' was born. Repatriation became instantly and irreversibly respectable. Heath could and did sack Powell from the Shadow Cabinet, but within months he was himself advocating a policy not far removed from Powell's – Heath wanted to encourage voluntary repatriation and to impose harsher conditions on those wishing to come here. In a major speech at York in September 1968, Heath adumbrated on the future 1971 Immigration Act, proposing to wipe out the distinctions between Commonwealth and alien immigrants at the point of entry and drastically to reduce the security of immigrants already in Britain. At a humbler level, the London dockers marched for Powell, and thirty-nine Heathrow immigration officers publicly supported his views. Even this peculiarly sensitive rebuff to official policy went almost undisciplined by the nervy authorities; just one officer was transferred from the reception point handling Asian arrivals.

Once he had come to power in 1970, Heath was as good as his word. In the following year the Conservatives passed their Immigration Act, which replaced most previous legislation. This, and the rules appended to it in 1972, screwed the repression of black immigrants even tighter. As the N.C.C.L. commented once it came into force: 'In 1963 one could still argue that control of Commonwealth immigration was undesirable in principle and in practice: in 1973 it is an uphill task even to obtain support to unite families affected by immigration control.' The main intellectual justification advanced for the act – that it would bring some rationality into the immigration laws by removing false distinctions between aliens and Commonwealth immigrants –

was lost, partly because the United Kingdom's simultaneous entry into the E.E.C. created an extra category of people with rights of entry into Britain, and partly because a successful Tory backbench campaign preserved certain privileges for whites from the 'Old Commonwealth'. The act created as a result an even more complicated entry system, with eight different categories for people entering the country. Not surprisingly Labour critics like lawyer Anthony Lester and Shadow Home Secretary Shirley Williams were soon calling for a complete re-writing of citizenship law.

Perhaps the act's most serious fault was its persistence with the old international tradition of complete discrimination against women. Larry Grant of the N.C.C.L. wrote: 'The Act treats women so automatically as appendages of men as to deny them even the status of second-class citizens; they scarcely exist except as shadows.'[21] A British woman marrying a foreigner cannot automatically win him the right to live here; but a British man automatically does so for his foreign wife. For immigrant or alien couples, a similar distinction is preserved in the deportation rules. If a woman is deported, her husband can stay in Britain if he wishes; but if a man is deported, his wife has to go with him. Liberals and the women's movement finally caught up with this absurd situation in 1974. An energetic campaign to make women equal in immigration and citizenship law was pursued. Although Labour M.P. Lena Jeger was unsuccessful in her attempt to introduce a private member's bill on the issue, and although the Home Secretary, Jenkins, refused to bring in Government legislation (on the grounds that the Asian tradition of arranged marriages would lead to a new flood of black male immigration), the new Labour Government was far more sensitive than its Conservative predecessors, and Jenkins kept his promise to apply his discretion sympathetically. In the summer the Home Office altered the immigration rules to allow women to bring foreign husbands into Britain.

For black immigrants, the act created what radical critics understandably called a 'contract labour system'. Permits to work were for twelve-month periods only, and annually renewable. The immigrant had to stay in the same place and work for the same employer throughout, retaining his approval; and he could not bring his family with him. The opportunity this offered unscrupulous employers to depress the wages and conditions of such tied labour was strongly attacked by the N.C.C.L., the Institute of Race Relations and various radical groups.

Though the Government abandoned its original intention to make registration with the police compulsory for black immigrants (partly in the face of sensible police opposition to the idea), fears of a South African pass-law system were revived once the act came into force in 1973. Under the earlier immigration acts, Commonwealth citizens who entered Britain illegally were immune from prosecution and removal once they had escaped detection for six months (the time limit for a summary offence, which illegal entry was made under the 1968 act). The 1971 act removed this immunity, and removed it retrospectively – any illegal immigrant who entered after 1968 was vulnerable. Soon after it became law on 1 January 1973, the police began to enforce this provision in a style which created a nightmare for the black communities. Thirteen people were immediately picked up off the streets, at their homes or at work, and sent back to India or Pakistan without any judicial process, even though they had been here several years. In some cases their relatives were not told what had happened to them, and they were removed in their work clothes with only the money they had on them. *Habeas corpus* applications by the J.C.W.I. temporarily halted this devastating and totally unexpected development, which persuaded the hundreds of thousands of legal immigrants that they would have to carry their passports with them – 'the pass-law syndrome' – if they were to be sure they were not going to be suddenly put on planes back to India. Three test cases went up through the Appeal Court and Lords and although minority judicial voices were heard asserting the old common-law rights of Commonwealth citizens, the majority of the judges found inevitably from reading the act that Parliament must have intended this unprecedented backdating of penal sanctions. (This was strongly disputed by the opposition parties, who could point to highly misleading statements from Maudling and other

Home Office ministers in the debates on the bill which had given the clear impression that any immigrant already settled in Britain would not be affected. Maudling's successor, Carr, could subsequently only get round this by quibbling on the meaning of the word 'settled'.) Though the Home Office was clearly unhappy about the way the early cases had been handled, it refused under the Conservatives to accede to the widespread demand for an amnesty for those who had settled and worked here as normal citizens for periods sometimes as long as five years. After Labour's return to power in 1974, however, Jenkins rapidly announced the amnesty. Although this was welcome, the way the retrospective aspect had slipped through the legislative process was the most frightening example hitherto of the extent to which the British political system could tolerate the destruction of basic constitutional rights when they applied only to blacks.

The unwillingness of the Tories to make a liberal gesture on this issue was perhaps the result of their disastrous experience with a liberal gesture a year earlier. In the summer of 1972, Gen. Amin of Uganda suddenly expelled 30,000 Asians, who, like their fellow countrymen in Kenya, held British passports. This time the Government generously refused to prevaricate, and admitted the refugees within a few months – to the fury of its own Right wing, particularly the Monday Club. Powell's needling questioning of their strict constitutional need to admit the Ugandans – which the Government had used as its main argument – created problems for the Conservative hierarchy at their annual conference in 1972, where Powell achieved substantial support for his condemnation of official policy. The Conservative leaders subsequently determined there would be no more Ugandas; and the re-settlement policy was not an unqualified success. Bureaucratic harassment of the East African Asians, particularly in regard to welfare rights, was one unpleasant feature of this failure.[22]

In fifteen years, the inability of British politicians to break free of the numbers game on the racial issue had led to the most deep-seated damage to civil liberty in modern times: an acceptance by politicians and public of a new wide-ranging arbitrary power hardly checked by judicial or Parliamentary processes, and through this power the creation of an inferior class of citizens defined by race and colour. Unfortunately, this wasn't the only setback. In the aggressively radical 1960s, a political repression similar to that undertaken during the Cold War was attempted by the Home Office in dealing with aliens; and the old readiness to grant asylum and to tolerate foreign political activists declined even further.

One case early in the decade showed how easily the Home Office could negotiate legal stumbling blocks when it was determined to get rid of a politically awkward foreigner. In 1962 Dr Soblen, an American convicted in the U.S.A. on an espionage charge, had to be taken off an El Al plane at Heathrow because he had badly wounded himself trying to avoid his forcible transfer from Israel (whither he had illicitly fled) back to the U.S.A. Although he was in a London hospital, Soblen had not, technically, landed in Britain – the immigration authorities handed him the refusal to land two days after he went into hospital. (An *Alice in Wonderland* situation – you are here but you are not here, as it were – which was to become endemic in Britain's immigration practice in the next few years.) Soblen's lawyers therefore failed in their applications for *habeas corpus*. The Government refused to grant him political asylum, and issued a deportation order against him. Civil liberty lawyers argued that this was an attempt to extradite him even though proper extradition powers were not available in espionage cases. The Court of Appeal, hearing a second *habeas corpus* application from Soblen, agreed that extradition was not possible, but ruled that the Home Secretary was correctly using his discretionary power to deport an alien 'for the public good'. The discovery that the Home Office's discretion could be sustained so far by the courts prompted bodies ranging from *The Times* to the N.C.C.L. to call for the re-imposition of the judicial check on this power that had existed up until 1914. But the Government ignored them. However, the Enahoro case in the following year did lead to a useful change in the law as far as Commonwealth political refugees were concerned. The Fugitive Offenders Act of 1881 (which governed the extradition of Commonwealth subjects) did not exclude political offences; and in 1963, Chief Antony Enahoro was returned from Britain to Nigeria, amid widespread protests, to face a political trial. When Labour came to power in 1964, they set about persuading other Commonwealth governments that this was not a very good idea any more, and the 1967 Fugitive Offenders Act permits the Home Secretary to refuse to return anyone to a Commonwealth country if he feels the case is a political one.

The nuclear disarmament, Vietnam War and student agitations persistently tested successive Governments' tolerance of foreigners during the 1960s, and usually found it wanting. In June 1964, an American member of the Committee of 100, Bert Bensen, failed to get his permit renewed because he was a 'security risk'. He briefly disappeared, in the hope that an incoming Labour Government would view his case more sympathetically. (Labour M.P. Judith Hart had sponsored his attempts to stay.) But like other Leftists on other issues, Mr Bensen was soon disillusioned; the new Home Secretary, Sir Frank Soskice, persisted with the deportation order. This proved no isolated piece of reactionary obduracy on the part of Soskice; in 1965, he refused to allow four North Vietnamese women (including 2 M.P.s) into Britain at the invitation of the Medical Aid for Vietnam Committee because he regarded them as 'active exponents of North Vietnamese propaganda'. In the same year he turned away N.L.F. representatives from South Vietnam invited here by Bertrand Russell on similar grounds. The N.C.C.L. commented, tartly enough, that 'conducting propaganda is one of the advantages of democracy – it is what politicians are doing all the time. Propaganda is only dangerous when both sides cannot be heard.' The Labour Government's double standard on this was exposed when they granted the South Vietnamese Government facilities to send their propaganda experts on a tour of Britain in the same year. In 1968 the American Ralph Schoenman, a former leading member of the Committee of 100, played a joke game dodging the immigration officers in London for a few weeks, but the grim implications of the Home Office attitude – that Schoenman was dangerous and to be kept out of the country – survived the joke. In the same year, the German student Daniel Cohn-Bendit, who had become internationally notorious for his part in the May struggles in Paris, was briefly allowed into Britain for a

B.B.C. broadcast only after strenuous efforts on his behalf by M.P.s and the N.C.C.L.

Much more serious was the affair three years later involving Cohn-Bendit's revolutionary fellow-countryman, Rudi Dutschke. Dutschke had been prominent in the Berlin student struggle of 1967 and 1968; he came to Britain in 1969 to study and recuperate from a head wound. Callaghan granted him permission to stay, provided he did not take part in any political activity. Early in 1971 the Conservative Home Secretary, Maudling, revoked this, and Dutschke appealed to the newly created Immigration Appeals Tribunal. The proceedings were a disaster, and roundly condemned in the Press.[23] Because Maudling was justifying his decision on the grounds of national security, part of the case was heard in secret, with neither Dutschke nor his counsel present. The tribunal supported Maudling and justified their decision on the grounds that Dutschke might *become* a security risk. They could not produce any evidence that he had broken his promise about political activity, save that he naturally admitted that he had talked about politics. Maudling's response to the protests that followed this was to remove national security cases from the jurisdiction of the Appeals Tribunal. It is difficult to see how, after the Dutschke case, they could be considered likely to pronounce liberally in any such matter, but Maudling was not taking any risks. It was yet another extension of that arbitrary discretionary power that the Home Office seemed to have come to regard as its natural right. Speaking at a packed emergency meeting on the affair (attended by Labour M.P.s Michael Foot and Richard Crossman) Tony Smythe argued that 'civil liberty is not about the way you treat your friends but about the way you treat your enemies'. The N.C.C.L. concluded that few recent incidents had revealed to such an extent the 'ability of the powerful to bend the system to their own advantage'. Dutschke and his wife found asylum in Denmark.

One of Smythe's great strengths as general secretary of the N.C.C.L. was the consistency with which he put his precept about 'enemies' into practice himself. Three years before the Dutschke affair, he had been criticized by some of his supporters for his handling of the scientology issue, which again showed the extent to which immigration law could be used to restrict ordinary freedoms. The scientologists, an unpleasant, authoritarian pseudo-religious cult inspired and led by an American, L. Ron Hubbard, attracted considerable opposition in Britain when they began actively to proselytize here in 1967–8. In 1968 the Minister of Health, Kenneth Robinson, undertook an active campaign against the organization, and the Home Secretary, Callaghan, refused permission to hundreds of foreign scientologists to enter for a special congress. The N.C.C.L., despite its lack of sympathy for the cult, joined politicians like Iain Macleod in rejecting the Government's use of its unchallengeable administrative powers to attack a minority group in this way. Smythe wrote to Robinson: 'We have to accept that in a free society many organizations will exist and flourish which to the ordinary person are cranky, if not an outright menace ... the advantage of thinking in legislative terms is that in this way the case against scientology would have to be proved, a situation which clearly does not exist at present.' The scientologists failed to get a hearing at the European Commission of Human Rights and in 1970 the Court of Appeal approved a Government decision that scientology was not any form of 'religious worship'.[24]

The insecurity of the governments of the 1960s in handling immigration matters even extended to reviving the brief Cold War practice of restricting *white* British passport holders. In 1968, the Foreign Office refused to give the Australian journalist Wilfred Burchett, then exiled stateless in North Vietnam, a British passport, even though he had held one from 1946 to 1955. With even-handed injustice they also penalized a Right-wing figure, Sir Frederick Crawford, in the same year, withdrawing his passport because of his connections with the outlawed Rhodesian régime. The protests were that much stronger when it was a white Briton under restraint rather than foreigners, and a *Daily Telegraph* journalist, Ian Colvin, attempted to assert his Magna Carta right to leave the country freely without a passport, but was stopped at Heathrow by the immigration officers. Constitutionally this was wrong, but Colvin did not test it in the courts, and the Home Office evaded the issue in Parliament.[24a]

In the late 1960s and early 1970s, the most regular foreign

political victims of Home Office prejudice were American radicals, as the British authorities finally realized that these were actually more subversive than any old-style Communists. From 1967 onwards, young Americans who wished to avoid serving in Vietnam began to stay in Britain, either legally or illegally, as a way of resisting the military draft. The N.C.C.L. gave advice on how they could do this legally, and questioned Scotland Yard's enthusiasm in seeking out people wanted by the U.S. military authorities. The Home Office justified this as standard international practice, and that questioning was 'confined to asking them what their intentions were'. At one moment they refused entry to an American at Glasgow Airport because he was due to be inducted, until the N.C.C.L. protested. This victory had an important consequence: thereafter the Home Office announced that draft status would not be considered when entry or residence applications were being processed. As for actual deserters (rather than draft resisters) the Visiting Forces Act of 1952 enabled the U.S. military police to arrest these and return them to the United States without seeking extradition; and the British Government refused to accept that conscientious objection to the Vietnam War provided grounds for granting political asylum. Many U.S. deserters in Britain consequently lived a semi-underground existence (unlike in Sweden, where they were granted right of refuge). In 1970, Lord Gifford attempted to promote a bill which would amend the 1952 Act to provide a right of appeal, but this failed to pass even the Lords.* With the winding down of the war in the succeeding years the problem disappeared; but the act, and the way it was enforced in a few cases in the late 1960s, was a peculiar anomaly that should have received more critical attention than it did. Once again, the civil liberties of unpopular foreigners were allowed to wither away unlamented in modern Britain.

Occasionally, official sensitivity to the new radicalism could become farcical. In 1969, Robert Williams, an American black leader who had fled from North Carolina eight years earlier when facing a trumped-up charge and then lived in exile in Africa, decided to return to the United States to clear his name. In September he stopped over in London to transfer to a T.W.A.

*It did inspire the first ever lobby of the Upper Chamber.

flight, and was promptly detained and searched for arms. He was at first served with a removal notice which would have sent him, as he wished, by the next available flight to America; he was then taken to Pentonville*, and kept incommunicado through the week-end. West Indian groups, the American Civil Liberties Union and the N.C.C.L. took up the case, and persuaded Home Office ministers to go and see Williams at Heathrow on the following Monday – just as he was about to be shipped to Cairo. Williams was detained a full week before being allowed to proceed, as he had always intended, to the United States. It never became clear what was behind this absurd situation, though it looked as though the airline had been unduly nervous and as though the State Department knew more about Williams' intentions in coming back than the C.I.A. did. But, as far as Britain was concerned, the bizarre business underlined the ease with which bureaucratic injustice could be meted out unchallenged and without redress in immigration matters.

In the following year the jokey agitator Jerry Rubin came to Britain for a David Frost TV show, created a stir by taking it over and behaving in a manner correctly calculated to offend most of the viewing audience, and then disappeared to Belfast for a few days while the immigration authorities were trying to get him out of the country, after fifty Tory M.P.s had called for his immediate deportation. It was scarcely an important case – Rubin had no wish to stay here – but the heavy-handed reaction of the authorities almost justified Rubin's irreverence. Rubin was one of the Chicago Eight, the radicals tried for conspiring to disrupt the Democratic Convention of 1968, and eventually cleared of all charges; in 1971, another of the Chicago defendants, Dave Dellinger, a lifelong pacifist, was refused entry altogether; and at Christmas 1972, Jane Fonda, the radical actress, and yet another Chicago defendant, Tom Hayden, came to talk to peace groups and found themselves being grilled at Heathrow for several hours. It took interventions by Lord Brockway and Tony Smythe to secure Hayden a seven-day entry permit. No reason was given for this treatment, which contrasted badly with the ease with which the couple completed the rest of their European tour.

*The unfortunate Williams at first took this to be a hotel.

Soon afterwards the radical priest Daniel Berrigan was admitted without problems, after the N.C.C.L. had obtained prior assurances from the Home Office that he would not be harassed. The N.C.C.L. commented sarcastically on the contrast between Hayden's treatment and the much facilitated entry of millionaire American Howard Hughes a few weeks later without a passport. 'We are not complaining', said the N.C.C.L. in its bulletin, 'we simply wish that other visitors were treated with the same courtesy and friendly assistance.'

More seriously, a US/Taiwanese refugee, Tzu-Sai Cheng, failed to win asylum here in 1973 despite a lengthy legal battle. In 1970, he had been convicted in New York of conspiring to assassinate the son of Chiang Kai-shek when he visited America. Cheng fled to Sweden, but in 1972 the Swedish Government accepted that it was bound to return him to the U.S. under their extradition treaty. On the flight from Stockholm, Cheng was taken ill and had to be landed in London and rushed to hospital. He then appealed for asylum; Home Secretary Robert Carr chose to let the courts decide whether his case could be considered a political one, and therefore outside the 1870 extradition treaty. Despite the support of groups like Amnesty, Cheng failed narrowly to convince the British courts that he was a political refugee; the Lords decided in April 1973 by a 3–2 majority that because he was being returned to the U.S. rather than Taiwan, the political nature of the case did not apply. (Cheng had always maintained, however, that there was a danger he would thereafter be sent from America to Taiwan.) Lord Simon, dissenting, argued powerfully against the 'marginal and anomalous judicial erosion of traditional immunities' that this judgment implied. There was a final unsuccessful effort by M.P.s Neil Kinnoch and Robert Hughes to persuade Carr to override the courts as Callaghan had done with the Greek student after the Cambridge Garden House Hotel trial. Cheng went back to America under armed escort.

Carr's decision to allow the courts to determine Cheng's fate was at least defensible: later that year he, or his Home Office advisers, reverted to straightforward arbitrary exercise of administrative power when seven Chilean students sought asylum here. The students had fled from Chile after the military coup in the autumn. Many other European countries had welcomed Chilean refugees without qualms; even France had admitted a thousand of them. These seven came to Britain because they wished to study here, though they had been to other countries on their way. The Home Office refused their request, on the extraordinary grounds that they should have sought asylum in the other countries first. It was an argument which the N.C.C.L. justifiably scorned as revealing an 'intellectual shoddiness fully commensurate with the moral shoddiness' of the operation. The council condemned Carr's decision as one of the blackest spots on the Conservatives' civil liberties record.

The anger aroused on the Left over the Chilean episode eventually secured a more honourable outcome, however. Two months after Labour returned to power in 1974, Jenkins reversed Carr's decision and allowed the refugees to remain in Britain.

Freedom of movement has shrunk drastically in Britain since the war; and just as alarming as the actual decline in quality of this freedom has been the indifference demonstrated by the mass of the British to the loss of this traditional liberty. It has been of course largely foreigners and blacks that have been affected; but the toleration of the vast increase in the arbitrary powers of Government departments and agencies, particularly since 1960, just because the powers were being applied to foreigners and blacks, poisons British liberties in a subtle way that may only be recognized by the natives when it is too late and they find the arbitrary powers being used against themselves.

Part Two

Civil Liberty and Justice

The English legal system is traditionally supposed to have placed greater emphasis on the liberty of the individual than those in most other countries. Freedom from arbitrary police power, the protection of those arrested and brought before the courts, *habeas corpus*, the presumption of innocence, trial by jury; all are features in which pride has been understandably taken. Since the late 1950s, this reputation has increasingly been called in question, as the police and the courts grappled with that phenomenon already noticed in the area of political freedom – a greater use by ordinary people of rights and liberties until then largely the preserve of educated and powerful minorities. As a result, the law has suffered the worst of two worlds. Traditional rights have continued to work generously for professional criminals, who have the money and expertise to secure them, but these same rights have often been denied to those who really need them – the poor, the weak and the inadequate. According to the perspective adopted, the answer is either to call for a reduction in the absurdly generous rights given defendants so that criminals can be dealt with properly – as the police, most of the judiciary and the political Right have done; or it is to seek to make those rights a reality for the under-privileged, as social workers, radical lawyers and the political Left have tried. Those concerned with civil liberty fell naturally into this second group. By the early 1970s, the consequent polarization produced the worst crisis in English justice this century.

Another contributory factor in this crisis was the infection of the legal system with the great social disease of the 1960s, the productivity ethic. For the policeman financial reward, promotion and improved status are usually achieved by results –

turning over a large number of arrests and convictions.* If his job is a job like any other, it will be measured by output like any other. This is a disastrous pressure on a law enforcement officer. For the courts, unhappily aware of the growing public dislike of the cost of the legal process, it became increasingly important to churn out cases as fast and as cheaply as possible. Both the courts and the police have succumbed to a concept which, even if it is justified when applied to the production of motor cars, is downright dangerous when applied to the production of prisoners. Crime has increased, too; the police and the courts have found it easier to deal with the minor criminal, or with those who are not really criminal at all, than the big villains. The productivity has sometimes been at the expense of the innocent.

The way the police and the courts work has always concerned the N.C.C.L. and the few active civil liberty lawyers, but until the late 1950s the concern was almost exclusively political; the anxieties were over the way the law dealt with Left-wing protest rather than over the quality of justice itself. Only occasionally did the problematic nature of the legal machinery become an issue for the radical watchdogs. The next two chapters will look at the way a profounder, less partisanly political, understanding of the civil liberty problem presented by the police, the magistrates and the judiciary has developed since the late 1950s.

---

*In 1971, there was a successful campaign to prevent a Kentish bobby being transferred from the village he had happily policed for twenty years because 'my superiors say I don't summons enough people, outside those I have to summons.' With that attitude the constable wouldn't have lasted twenty months in the Metropolitan Police, let alone twenty years.[1]

4. The Police

For many years, the N.C.C.L. implicitly subscribed to the Left-wing view of the police as the repressive agents of ruling-class power. After all, the police themselves occasionally hint at such an analysis; in 1971, the Police Federation chairman Reg Gale talked of the way the law worked 'in favour of the rich and against the poor'.[2] However, similar obvious generalities had never seemed to lead anywhere, and in the late 1950s a new attitude developed amongst those concerned with civil liberty. Banalities about class were discreetly shelved and replaced by specific, attainable reform proposals: the existing protections for those in police custody, codified in the Judges' Rules, should be enforced strictly, and an independent system of dealing with police mal-practice should be set up – someone other than the police should police the police. These two demands subsequently dominated civil liberty discussions of the police.

The larger idea of the democratic control of the police has rarely excited interest in Britain. Traditionally, the existence of autonomous local constabularies has been seen as a safeguard against a national, Government-controlled force; and in theory these local forces are under the supervision of their local authority paymasters. In practice the police have regulated themselves. Most Chief Constables know how to handle the local politicians, and the relationship with the Home Office is a subtly indirect one of circulars and memoranda, with no constitutional strength whatsoever. Even the one force for which there is direct Parliamentary responsibility, London's Metropolitan Police, is in no sense run by the Home Office, whose officials are not very happy dealing with Scotland Yard. The general acceptance of this professional élitism has limited public discussion of police accountability to procedural devices, like complaints tribunals, rather than a frontal attack using the wider concept of popular control.[3]

While the constitutional argument has therefore been very restricted, the more mundane details of police behaviour have aroused considerable criticism in three main areas: stop, search and seizure powers; the quality of police evidence; and corruption. Particular public *frissons* develop, as in the early 1960s and again ten years later, when bent coppers spectacularly hit the headlines; but these intermittent anxieties miss the point that even good policemen regularly break the rules the public have managed to impose on them. There is a subtle spectrum of policing, from those who ignore the rule book in the interests of catching criminals through the man who bends the evidence to nick someone who, if not guilty of what he is accused is probably guilty of something similar anyway, to the totally corrupt policeman who fixes evidence on a large scale either to extort money from those he is victimizing or to do favours to those from whom he is receiving bribes. Whatever their individual honesty, however, all policemen are under the same pressure; bend the rules to deliver the goods in the form of convictions, and since we make it so easy for the police to secure phoney convictions we should not be surprised if many of them do so. How many is unknown – and immeasurable. The mythologies of Right and Left – that there are a few rotten apples in an otherwise impeccable barrel, or that the entire force is bent and only a few occasionally get caught – are equally sustainable.

The quality of police evidence, and its honesty, is crucial because most people who are convicted are convicted by it. Much of this evidence relates to how an accused was detained, what was found on or near him, and what he said under interrogation. It is the abuse of police power in these circumstances – arrest, search and questioning – that has created the most intractable police-civil liberty problem in recent years. Whether the following cases, which make up the civil liberty history of the police since the 1930s, are the tip of the iceberg or the isolated exceptions is impossible to say.

Stop, Search and Seizure Powers

One clear erosion of civil liberty has occurred with the extension of the police right of arbitrary search since 1967. The police can normally only search people or premises with a warrant issued by a magistrate, but they have exceptional powers for searching without warrant on 'reasonable' grounds when they are looking for drugs, firearms and stolen goods. 'Reasonable' is of course capable of wide interpretation, a fact the police know how to exploit. Irregular use of stop and search powers was generally tolerated until the 1960s, when the harassment of particularly sensitive groups – the radical young and the blacks – provoked a counter-attack. However, even before the 1960s, the judiciary and public opinion would occasionally wake up to reality, and temporarily disapprove of it. In the 1930s, the N.C.C.L. campaigned against the widespread use of 'loitering with intent' and similarly vague charges, which justified almost random street searches. Between 1930 and 1938, more than a fifth of the 38,000 people arrested on these charges were not proceeded against. In 1932 there was a particularly widely-publicized case. Flying Officer Fitzpatrick was walking in the West End after midnight carrying a suitcase. This was enough to get him stopped by plain-clothes detectives, who assaulted him when he refused to answer questions (since he did not believe they were police officers); he was taken to the police station, but released after some hours. This treatment of a respectable pilot was not appreciated by Parliament, and the Home Secretary, though defending the action on the right of the police to question people suspected of committing a felony, apologized to Mr Fitzpatrick in a personal interview. In 1936, the N.C.C.L. again stirred up a press and Parliamentary campaign on the issues, but the real check to police power came in 1938 with another individual case. A young actor called Ludlow won £300 costs and damages from the police for assault and false imprisonment. He had been waiting at a Chelsea bus stop with an overcoat he was taking to the cleaners when he was arrested on suspicion for failing to give a satisfactory explanation for the coat. Though he was not subsequently charged, Ludlow brought a successful action against the police. Lord Chief Justice Hewart found the police did not have reasonable grounds for suspecting Ludlow had stolen goods and hence for using their 'stop, search and detention' powers under the 1839 Metropolitan Police Act. Summing up, Lord Hewart – not always known for his concern for civil liberty* – said:

Is it easy to imagine a more gross indignity offered to a perfectly innocent and respectable professional gentleman? It is a perilous thing when great powers, with the knowledge, maybe, of great force behind, are recklessly, foolishly or over-zealously employed ... one of our most priceless possessions is liberty of the subject. If once we show any signs of giving way to the abominable doctrine that because things are done by officials some immunity must be extended to them, what is to become of our country?

Subsequent Parliamentary questions on the matter elicited the Home Office assurance that an 'elaborate code' of instructions on these powers had been issued to the police. Though gratified by Lord Hewart's stand for freedom, Kidd of the N.C.C.L. did make the tart comment that had the victim been unemployed instead of a respectable professional gentleman the incident would have attracted little or no attention.[4]

In theory, the police have no right to seize anything not relevant to the offence they are investigating. In practice, this protection is frequently ignored. There are valid common-sense arguments for tolerating this abuse; if the police accidentally find genuine evidence of a criminal offence, it is pedantic to say they cannot use it because they were not acting in connection with that particular offence. But there are greater reasons for trying to preserve this inhibition and keeping the police in line. They can, after all, go back and get another search warrant; even the eighteenth-century courts were opposed to the idea of general search powers. And toleration of the abuse provides much easier opportunities for planting evidence and 'fitting up' in general.

Two important cases in modern times have confused the legal situation on search and seizure powers. In 1934, the police

*See above, pages 25 and 26.

arrested Wal Hannington of the National Unemployed Workers' Movement on a sedition charge, taking away various documents from the Movement's office when they did so. They were subsequently sued by another N.U.W.M. official, Elias, for taking these papers. Though the judge ruled that the police should release these after Hannington's trial, he held that they were entitled to seize anything which was evidence of any crime by anybody. (In this case, a possible prosecution of Elias.) In academic legal circles, this judgment has been criticized for years, but since the case did not go to appeal its validity was never tested. However, in 1969, the Court of Appeal considered the extent of police search powers and re-defined them more strictly in their decision in *Ghani v. Jones*. Investigating the murder of a woman, the police entered her father-in-law's home with a warrant and seized the passports of three of her relatives. They refused to return them when these wanted to go to Pakistan; however, the Court of Appeal ordered them to do so because they were not evidence relating to a murder charge.[5]

The limited value of this protection, and the extent to which the police could cheerfully ignore individual rights, was seen a couple of years later during the intensive search for the Angry Brigade. For the police it was vital to get information about friendship patterns among the libertarian groups on the far Left. On several raids, undertaken with warrants to search for explosives, the police took away material, which helped them build up a profile of the personalities and politics of a network that had previously escaped the notice of the Special Branch. In March 1971, the N.C.C.L. protested to the Home Secretary about these indiscriminate seizures – explosives were never found at any of the places raided on these warrants, and the N.C.C.L. argued that the police knew they would not be, but wanted to exploit the warrants to get access to information about political groups. An attempt was made by members of the Prescott/Purdie defence committee to sue the police for taking documents relating to the defence case after one such raid – even leaflets and posters were taken. The police argued that they were evidence of a possible crime (conspiring to pervert the course of justice) and the judge accepted the argument, on the grounds that the police would not hold the material longer than necessary. No-one was ever charged with this offence, but the transparency of the police manoeuvre appeared to worry few people outside the libertarian Left and the N.C.C.L.

Matters worsened during the police investigations into the I.R.A. bombing campaigns in London and Birmingham in 1973. There were so many information-gathering raids that even the Irish political organizations in these two cities were unable to catalogue them all. The victims were often Republican sympathizers (though this should scarcely have been grounds for depriving them of their civil rights) but sometimes bizarre searches were carried out. In September that year, the Irish Centre in London was raided. It is a welfare organization run by the clergy: as the N.C.C.L. pointed out, it was rather as if the police looking for the Angry Brigade had raided the Salvation Army. Although the terrorist bomb attacks were extremely serious crimes meriting intense police activity, the wholesale jettisoning of normal civil liberty protections should not have been part of the police response. Indeed, the constitutional defences against arbitary police power are needed even more at such critical moments than in ordinary times.

Obviously, in a serious matter like terrorist bombings, the police have no difficulty obtaining search warrants from magistrates, but the liberality with which warrants have been dispensed in recent years on more trivial occasions, particularly in relation to drug searches, attracted considerable criticism. The failure of magistrates to probe the grounds for police requests – often simply anonymous tip-offs – led to serious abuses. One magistrate became disgusted at her own laxness when she discovered the police repeatedly – and unsuccessfully – raided the new council house home of a black family on her warrants purely on the 'tip-offs' of racist neighbours who resented their presence on the estate.[6] In 1968, the raid on the home of Lady Diana Cooper after similar anonymous information created such an outcry that the Home Office had to issue a directive about such information. The N.C.C.L. pointed out that they had several cases of less famous figures similarly harassed at the same time, and with similar lack of justification, who failed to received the apologies that Lady Diana obtained from the police and from Home Secretary Callaghan. Often the police would search anyone whose name was found in the address book of someone arrested on a drugs charge.[7]

The most damaging result of the public hysteria about drugs in the middle 1960s, however, came from the creation of a statutory power for the police to stop and search people in the street, granted in the Dangerous Drugs Act of 1967. This was a wider power than even the 1839 Metropolitan Police Act gave for suspicion of theft, as in the Ludlow case, since then the victim usually had to be carrying something. It led to such widespread evidence of random police harassment of young people and blacks that the Home Office set up a committee to study police powers under the chairmanship of Conservative M.P. William Deedes in 1969. Even the extremely moderate recommendations of this committee did point out that the police would have to accept that dress and hair style were insufficient grounds for searching young people for drugs. A minority of the committee argued that the stop-and-search powers should be repealed altogether.[8] As early as November 1967, the N.C.C.L. had collected evidence of the abuse of the new powers, and urged their withdrawal, in a report *Drugs And Civil Liberties* which appears to have influenced the Home Office decision to review the situation. Police behaviour in this regard improved in 1971 after two disastrous trials involving the Drugs Squad had revealed appalling irregularities, but the Government still refused to take the opportunity provided by the Misuse of Drugs Act that year to abolish the offensive power totally. However, the Home Office did initiate a detailed study of the effectiveness of street searches which was published in 1973. The official figures showed that nearly 30,000 people had been stopped under the drug laws, of whom less than 8,000 had been arrested. The N.C.C.L. questioned whether such a low success rate justified the sweeping powers, and argued that there should be a return to the old law requiring 'reasonable suspicion' before the police could conduct a search. The N.C.C.L. tried its own survey a year earlier by asking for all Chief Constables' reports; it only received eighteen from the forty-six different forces, and only five of these contained statistics on street drug searches. The success rate ranged from a third (Essex, Mid-Anglia) to less than five per cent (Leicester and Rutland).

One *cause célèbre* arising from the drugs legislation of the middle 1960s deserves mention, though it is not strictly an example of police misuse of search powers, but simply of a bad law working badly. In 1967, the Oxford police found cannabis at a house occupied by various people but tenanted officially by Miss Stephanie Sweet, a schoolteacher, who in fact lived elsewhere, rarely visited the house and knew nothing of what was going on. Nonetheless, she was convicted and fined for having premises where cannabis was smoked. There was considerable public criticism of the injustice of this, and the Divisional Court felt obliged to take the unprecedented step of reversing its own refusal of leave to appeal to the House of Lords. In January 1969, the Lords ruled that *mens rea* – evil intent or knowledge – must be proved even in statutory offences of this nature and that the courts should not cause hardship to the innocent if it served no purpose in enforcing public welfare legislation.[9]

In 1971, Parliament passed another statutory measure – the Criminal Damage Act – which contained a clause extending police powers of search and seizure yet again. The police could obtain a warrant to look for anything they believed was intended for use in committing criminal damage. The N.C.C.L. lobbied against this and in Parliament the former Labour Attorney-General Sir Elwyn Jones warned: 'It is dangerous for the law to be couched in such terms as to encourage fishing expeditions by the police into houses . . . for a general look and search in the hope of finding something.' The new power was soon abused. In March 1972, after the I.R.A. bomb attack on the Aldershot barracks in which seven people were killed, the police in London raided the homes of sixty people using warrants executed under the Criminal Damage Act. Many of those raided were members of the Left-wing International Socialist group. The police could have had no evidence of any criminal associations against these, only their political background and connections: and even these had little to do with the Provisional I.R.A.[9a] It was symptomatic of the generally low level of concern for civil liberty in Parliament that such a measure should have been enacted. Overall, the police rights to stop and search were greater than they needed to be, and certainly too great for a country that was supposed to be concerned about the liberty of the individual.

Police Evidence

The quality of police evidence became increasingly suspect in the 1960s. It may not actually have become worse than it was before, but certainly public concern about police methods of obtaining evidence increased sharply. Two particular injustices were apparent; people were being pressured into admitting to crimes they had not committed, and evidence was being fabricated by the police. Pressure to make false or damaging statements came in various ways – illegal detention ('arrest for questioning'), ignoring Judges' Rules, particularly in regard to the caution and to permitting solicitors to be contacted, plea-bargaining ('if you plead guilty to the lesser offence we'll drop the bigger one') and straightforward physical brutality. 'Fitting up' was just as varied: planting, verballing (the fictitious police version of an interrogation), doctoring notebooks. A further injustice, though not one that was always the fault of the police themselves, was created by totally inadequate identification procedures. A glimpse into police attitudes to evidence was graphically provided during the trial of a Thames Valley detective for corruption (he was acquitted) in the summer of 1971. The detective cheerfully admitted that he 'did away with the rule book', that he had no scruples in dealing with criminals ('Perhaps I have been indoctrinated') and pointed out that he was in no way special or different from other detectives. 'This is part of the practice of other police officers in the country to get information.' The judge was naïve enough to be shocked: 'The evidence in this case has exposed an alarming state of affairs that is extremely damaging to the public.'

Illegal detention is a long-standing police malpractice against which there are few remedies except a vigorous solicitor prepared to seek *habeas corpus*, or sufficient funds and nerve to undertake a private prosecution for false arrest. Strictly, no-one need go to a police station unless arrested; if arrested, you have to be told the reason. Detention for questioning is therefore in theory impossible; in practice, 'helping the police with their inquiries' is a daily event. Civil liberty protests are usually easily dismissed: in 1956, the N.C.C.L. complained to the Home Office about the frequency with which people were being held for two days just for questioning; seventeen years later, they were quoting the example of an inspector who said in court that he had once held a man for seven days before charging him. The practice continued nevertheless.

Periodically, the courts have re-asserted the citizen's right not to be detained without reasonable stated cause, and for brief periods police behaviour in this respect would subsequently improve. Part of the problem has been the wide availability of very loosely worded or wide-ranging offences from which a policeman could usually expect to pick something which would justify his action if he had to. In 1936, two Liverpool men, Ledwith and Crothers, were detained for several hours (but not charged) after the police had 'observed' them for twenty-five minutes and then decided they were about to commit a felony. Ledwith subsequently sued two constables for false imprisonment, and the Liverpool judge ruled that the police argument did not provide a legal defence for their action. The Court of Appeal upheld this, and Lord Justice Scott took the opportunity to attack meaningless old legal descriptions – 'rogue and vagabond', 'loitering with intent' – that had come down with a succession of vagrancy laws from as long ago as 1349. 'It seems to me wrong that these old phrases should still be made the occasion of arrest and prosecution, when in their historical meaning they are out of keeping with modern life in Britain.' And the court concluded that it was not enough that a policeman honestly believed that his captive was a 'loose, idle or disorderly person', for instance, but that he should actually be classifiable as such. It was a rare, and important, restriction on the usual police defence that they had reasonable grounds for what they did, and it led to a dramatic decline in the number of such arrests. Welcoming this decision, the N.C.C.L. drew the conclusion that thousands of people, mostly from the less privileged sections of the community, must have been wrongfully convicted in the previous 100 years.[10]

The 'loitering with intent' charge was too useful for the police for it to rust away, however; one West End Central policeman has described how in the early 1960s it was 'quite common for a person to be arrested (on this charge) just because a police officer did not like the look of him or needed to keep his arrest record in good shape'.[11]

Early in 1973, the Court of Appeal re-affirmed another vital protection against illegal detention: the citizen's right to leave the police station at any time he wishes unless he has formally been arrested. In the case of *R. v. Inwood*, the court held that people could leave even if they had been cautioned. The N.C.C.L. commented, however, that the court had left the police a vital loophole in that they had said there was no 'magic formula' for indicating to a suspect that he was no longer a free man. 'By detaining him without making an arrest,' said the N.C.C.L., 'the police are able to use his subsequent detention as a mere fishing expedition.' The extent to which this was happening had become clear during the bombing campaigns in London in 1970–73. Partly because the police were confident that when dealing with bombers the public would tolerate more rule-bending than normal, and partly because the bomb-suspects were often politically sophisticated and prepared to argue for their rights, the police became remarkably frank in admitting to illegal detention. On 11 February 1971, the police investigating the Angry Brigade attacks detained six people; one, Prescott, was kept forty-eight hours incommunicado (and was later convicted for his part in the conspiracy), and the others were released after spending periods of up to two days at Barnet police station. They were not voluntarily helping the police, nor were they free to go; yet they were never formally arrested or charged. Among them were women who had been picked up, with some public fuss from barristers and lawyers, at the Bow Street magistrates' court, where they were either witnesses or friends of women's movement defendants on trial for a demonstration at the Miss World competition in 1970. With N.C.C.L. help, they subsequently brought a civil action against the Bomb Squad for false imprisonment and assault.

Two years later, after the big London explosions by I.R.A.

units from Belfast, ten people were held for four days before being charged. The N.C.C.L. was preparing a *habeas corpus* application when they were at last brought to court. The N.C.C.L. was critical, not of the police action in arresting the ten without a warrant, but of the unlimited time available to the police to hold them without bringing a charge against them. 'No wonder the police . . . feel able to declare that "detaining people for interview is normal practice" even when there was no suggestion that anyone would be charged in the near future.' The police are often able to get away with this attitude because of the cost and difficulty of bringing actions against them: but they cannot always get away with it. In 1966, two London policemen were ordered to pay £8,000 damages to two West Indians for false imprisonment; indeed, one of the policemen had paid out damages on similar charges two years earlier.[12]

The police understandably value a fudged division between detention for questioning and arrest because they can interrogate freely only until they have cautioned the suspect. This is clearly a real help to them in nailing criminals, but also helps them to pressurize the weak and fix evidence against guilty and innocent alike. The nature of police questioning was at the heart of the fierce debate in the early 1970s about the Judges' Rules. These were first introduced in 1912, at the request of the police who had found problems with the conflicting views of judges as to what kind of interrogation would produce admissible evidence. They are a code of practice which has no legal force whatsoever; any judge can at his discretion accept evidence obtained in breach of the Rules. They were extended in 1918; subjected to an unsuccessful attempt at clarification in 1930; revised in 1964; and the object of controversy after the proposals of the Criminal Law Revision Committee – that they should be greatly modified in the interests of the police – had been published in 1972. The main C.L.R.C. recommendations were the abolition of the caution; the replacement of the Rules by administrative directions; the abolition of the right to silence in court; and a relaxation of the restrictions on 'inducing' confessions. From a civil liberty perspective the position, even before the C.L.R.C. report, was extremely unsatisfactory; the existing rules were inadequate as a protection for those in custody since the police could often break them successfully. In the same year as the C.L.R.C. report, Lord Chief Justice Widgery, in the Prager case, allowed damaging evidence – statements made by the accused before he had been cautioned – even though he assumed they had been obtained in defiance of the Rules; and the Court of Appeal agreed with his decision because they similarly felt that the statements had been made voluntarily. It is this question of the willingness of the accused to answer questions that most courts are concerned with, rather than technical breaches of the Rules. (The *New Law Journal*, commenting on the decision, unfavourably contrasted the English situation with that in the United States, where since the Supreme Court's *Miranda* decision in 1966 it has been impossible for the police to use statements obtained in breach of a strictly defined rule as evidence in a trial – with no discernible setback to legitimate police activity.)

Though the English attitude is pragmatic enough, decisions such as those in the Prager case ignore the common-sense point that without any institutional safeguards for those arrested the police are always likely to want to chance their arm with improper pressure during interrogation. Impropriety was defined in 1972 by the N.C.C.L. (out of its own long experience of allegations against the police) as 'No information about rights and facilities; uncertainty about rights and obligations, if any; no communication with solicitors or friends; no refreshment; disregarding of procedure in interrogation and taking of statements; questioning of young people.'

The lack of supervision of police questioning makes it impossible to tell whether the frequent conflict of evidence between what the police officers say took place during interrogation is more accurate than the accused's version. The police have traditionally relied on their superior credibility as honest men and women; but by 1970 this was sufficiently in doubt for a prominent judge – Mr Justice McKenna – to warn of the dangers publicly:

If (the police) agree to tell an untrue story, they know each will be available to confirm the other's evidence in the trial, and that the only written record will be their notebooks, each book telling the same story in identical words. They know that they will go into the witness box as men of good characters, likely to be believed.[13]

A frequent abuse is the 'verbal', the police version of their questioning recorded some time afterwards by two or more officers in identical form and differing, sometimes widely, from what the accused said happened. Among criminal lawyers, 'verbals' have long been notorious; in 1960, a committee of the Surrey and Southwark Sessions Bar asked for the entire Flying Squad to be transferred to other jobs because of the extent of their 'verballing'[14], and even two Royal Commissions (1929, 1962) have commented uneasily on the strength of the allegations about 'verballing' made to them. The West End Central detective already quoted, describing the extent of police irregularities for *Release* years later, finally decided to resign from the force in 1963 because he did not wish to 'verbal' and consequently none of his colleagues would go out on jobs with him.[15] Another more famous West End Central detective, Det. Sgt Challenor, met his comeuppance in 1963 as well. The Challenor case was a low point for the police image;* and the detective was, needless to say, a dab hand with a 'verbal', though they now have an odd ring to them; one of his victims was supposed to have said in the police station, 'Can I speak to you, Guv? . . . I'm knackered, anyway. But don't get the wrong idea. This is all a take-on. Joe Oliva, myself and a few of the boys are only taking the mickey out of him. We wouldn't have had his money. It was just frighteners.'[16] The judge in the subsequent trial clearly doubted Challenor's veracity, and when the extent of the detective's dishonest and perjured career was later exposed, the man thus 'verballed' was pardoned – after several months of a prison sentence. In the end, when Challenor had been the subject of two inquiries and a prosecution, the pattern of his 'verbals'

became some of the most telling evidence against him . . . looking at his cases altogether lawyers found recurrent phrases which were suspicious . . . it was not likely that a number of people in separate cases on different occasions would make similar statements using the same colloquialisms.[17]

Discussed more fully on pps. 182 and 185 below.

In their criticism in 1972 of the C.L.R.C. report, Release lawyers pointed out that the most damning evidence of the extent of 'verbals' was the disparity between the police and defendant versions even when the defendant was pleading guilty.[18] One of the most sensational individual examples of the injustice that could arise from this abuse came in 1967 with the Colenso diamond affair. A young man, David Knight, was convicted of stealing the diamond from the Natural History Museum solely on the conversation he was alleged to have had with two detectives, Smith and Harris. The diamond was never found. Knight denied the 'confession' he was supposed to have made when the detectives interviewed him in his home, but he was convicted and spent three years in prison. The N.C.C.L. campaigned strongly on his behalf; and in 1972, after Smith and Harris had separately been convicted on perjury offences in other cases, the Home Office agreed to set up an inquiry. The N.C.C.L. argued that Knight's case fully confirmed the need to make any confession of guilt inadmissible as evidence unless it was made before an independent authority, such as a magistrate or a solicitor – an idea they had been advocating since 1959.

An even more astonishing, though happily less serious case, involved Satnam Kane of Southall. In 1973, Kane 'confessed' to stealing some money from his employer. It then turned out that the money had never been stolen at all. Kane claimed he had been forced to make the confession: the police said he had done it willingly. A subsequent investigation failed to find grounds for prosecution of the police involved; not surprisingly, for, as the N.C.C.L. said, when the matter in dispute occurs during police interrogation there are only two witnesses, the interrogator and the interrogated, and it is impossible after the event to establish who is lying. This provides those policemen who wish to fabricate evidence with almost certain immunity against punishment, and, as the N.C.C.L. said, 'very seriously increased the temptation to behave improperly.'

Defence lawyers frequently question the accuracy of identical police notebook records of alleged conversations; but twice in the early 1970s came alarming evidence that the doctoring of police records went far beyond the mere re-editing of conversations. In

November 1971, a Leeds detective-sergeant, Kenneth Kitching and a former detective-inspector, Geoffrey Ellerker, were convicted of assaulting an unemployed Nigerian who dossed around in Leeds – David Oluwale. Oluwale had been found floating in the river a few hours after Ellerker and Kitching had made one of their regular harassments of him (harassments which regularly included pissing on him, kicking him, beating him up and dropping him miles out in the Yorkshire countryside). They were acquitted on a manslaughter charge. The only way these two had been able to sustain this brutal campaign against Oluwale over a period of years was by the wholesale fixing of notebooks and station records, which involved the complicity of other policemen. This collusion was one of the most sinister features of the affair, though it should be remembered that it was ultimately one of the Leeds police who eventually forced the business into the open.[19]

In the same month, November 1971 – such a bad moment for the police that Home Secretary Maudling was compelled to announce a tightening up of disciplinary procedures – the conviction of members of the Salah family for drug offences on a large scale was quashed by the Court of Appeal, and six former members of the London Drug Squad were subsequently tried for perjury because of the way they had fixed the evidence against the Salahs. Chief Inspector Kelaher admitted ordering his subordinates to change their notebooks 'in the interests of security' and his number two, Det. Sgt Pilcher, was found to have inserted whole new pages into his book.* The extent of this practice is, again, not measurable, but that two detective-inspectors in two different forces could have simultaneously been using it for so long does not encourage the idea that it was not widespread in the C.I.D. throughout the country.

Not surprisingly, civil liberty groups began to agitate for improved methods of monitoring police interrogations. The only existing sanction was police apprehension that the courts might refuse to admit evidence improperly obtained, but the courts of the 1960s and early 1970s showed great reluctance to do this. Those in custody would have been better protected if the loosely

---

*Pilcher and two other detectives were gaoled for perjury.

worded right to contact a solicitor as soon as 'convenient' after arrest was respected by the police, but for many years this has been a discretion the police have constantly abused. (On understandable grounds, since the normal advice of a solicitor to a suspect is to say nothing.)

In 1940, the Liverpool Recorder, Mr E. G. Hemmerde, who had been thirty years on the bench, attacked what he regarded as the extraordinary increase in 'confessions' tendered by the police in the previous few years. The occasion for his criticism was a written statement which a defendant agreed he had made – in the absence of a solicitor – but which in court he said was untrue, and made only because the police promised to get him released. Hemmerde refused to accept it as evidence, and protested at what he saw as strong signs of police collaboration in its preparation.*

Thirty years later, Chief Inspector Roy Habershon, in charge of the Bomb Squad looking for the Angry Brigade, was to describe the right to a solicitor as a 'legal nicety' for which he had little concern, after he had refused several people taken in for questioning permission to contact solicitors; indeed, he told one solicitor's clerk who arrived at Barnet to be present during the questioning of one of his clients that he would only be allowed to see him after the police had finished with him. Similar problems arose in 1973 when the Belfast Ten bombers were likewise denied legal help for four days. The Release lawyers reported persistent difficulty in tracing clients held by the police on drug offences; and in the same year (1972) an academic study by Michael Zander found that most suspects were prevented from telephoning their solicitors.[20]

The only other protection is the caution, particularly the early or 'short' caution, which is supposed to indicate to the suspect that he is no longer simply helping the police with their inquiries but that they now have the beginnings of a case against him. In fact there is little doubt that the police usually delay this caution until their case is well advanced. Even so, the N.C.C.L. and Release both felt that, formality though it was, it was still worth preserving when the C.L.R.C. proposed to abolish it. More

*The only cases the defendant could recollect were the fourteen already known to the police.[21]

important than the caution, perhaps, were the radical ideas for checking on what happened during police interrogations: tape recordings, examination in front of a magistrate (as in France), or duty solicitors.[22]

One police objection to tape recordings was the possibility that the suspect would suddenly shout in mid-interview 'Stop hurting me', and thus convince a jury he was being beaten up. Perhaps there would have been more sympathy for this point had there not been enough instances to indicate that the least subtle pressure used by the police to acquire evidence was straightforward physical assault. A succession of highly publicized cases after 1957 where police violence was evident, or at least strongly suspected, was an important factor in the pressure leading to the Police Act in 1964. Ten years later, violence was one of the abuses that led the police authorities and the Home Office to consider independent reviews of police disciplinary inquiries.

In 1957, a quite mild (by subsequent standards) slap on the face of a 15-year-old boy, Walters, by two Thurso policemen led to a Parliamentary enquiry and a report criticizing this kind of behaviour.[23] In 1960 Gunther Podola (later convicted of murdering a policeman) had to be put in hospital for several weeks after the treatment he received from the police, which prompted the suggestion that people suspected of committing serious crimes against the police should be kept in prison rather than police cells.[24] In 1962–3 the Woolf, Sheffield, Glasgow and Challenor affairs contributed strongly to what must have been a nadir in police-public relations. In November 1962, Herman Woolf, an artist, was knocked down by a car. In hospital he was found to have some cannabis on him, and the police arrested him on a drugs charge. After a day in the police detention room at West End Central he was found in a coma. He was returned to hospital without any diagnosis of a fractured skull – yet when he died thirteen days later that was found to be the cause of death. None of Woolf's friends or relatives had been told what had happened to him, even though he had been registered as a missing person and even though his diary – in police possession – gave his ex-wife's name and address. The story did not surface until a year later,* and ultimately an inquiry by the Portsmouth Recorder, Norman Skelhorn (now the D.P.P.), acquitted the police of direct responsibility for Woolf's death. The report did however criticize the surgeon who made an incorrect diagnosis, a constable who failed to notice that Woolf's condition was deteriorating badly, a detective who illegally searched Woolf's home and also failed to notify the Criminal Records Office (which would have activated the missing persons machinery); it also deplored the practice of charging 'insensible or semi-sensible people' – a brief glimpse of police behaviour that is almost comic in its grimness.[25]

Four months after the questionable circumstances of Woolf's death came the unquestionable brutality of the Sheffield 'Rhino Whip' affair. On 14 March 1963, two detective-constables beat up four men with a truncheon, a gut-like rhino whip† and their fists. One of the men received seventy-five different blows; the whole business was watched by an inspector who 'displayed callous amusement' and who subsequently said in public, 'These things go on fairly frequently, don't they?' The object had been, the police said, to induce confessions of crime. They had not expected the victims to complain in court, but they did; and thanks to a brave campaign by the *Sheffield Telegraph* – and despite the efforts of senior Sheffield policemen to cover up the business – a public inquiry eventually led to the dismissal and prosecution of the two policemen. (One of them explained, in the classic but still sinister excuse, that he had merely been carrying out instructions.) The inquiry's report blamed the Sheffield police for putting too great a pressure on their detectives to obtain results (the productivity ethic again), pressure which went as far as to encourage violence as part of the drive against the 'crime wave', and for concocting a false story in court. When they were forced to investigate what happened, some senior officers commiserated with the men they were investigating, and even the Chief Constable shook them by the hand. It was

*The N.C.C.L. had been unable to use the information they had: eventually their founder-member Claud Cockburn ran the story in *Private Eye*.

† Carried, according to the detective who wielded it, 'in case of conflict between coloured informants.'

inconceivable, as Ben Whitaker subsequently wrote, that after this the Home Secretary would introduce a Police Bill 'proposing to leave similar inquiries in the hands of the police.'[26] Inconceivable; but, nevertheless, exactly what happened.

Throughout this period, at West End Central, Det. Sgt Challenor was including physical violence as part of his wide range of techniques for securing convictions. And, in November 1963, a man died after receiving injuries in a Glasgow police cell. P.C. Nimmo, who admitted to 'punching the man in a momentary loss of temper', was afterwards found not guilty of culpable homicide.[27]

Though all this had a discernible effect on public attitudes to the police – juries became far less willing to accept police evidence after the perjury demonstrated in the Sheffield case – any change in police behaviour could have been only temporary, since the disciplinary procedures were totally inadequate. Within a few years, the N.C.C.L. became very worried by the fast deterioration of relations between the police and the black communities, in which police violence played a large part.[28] Two cases, in which the N.C.C.L. took an active role, achieved particular notoriety. In 1969, a senior Nigerian diplomat, Gomwalk, took his family shopping in Brixton on a Saturday morning in a new Mercedes he had bought at a cut-price diplomatic rate in West Germany; it still bore the West German number plate. He parked it on a double yellow line, a sad mistake on his part; he ended up being accused of having stolen it. Gomwalk alleged that he was taken to the police station with considerable violence and racist abuse; eventually, he managed to convince the duty inspector of his identity and was released. Meanwhile, the police had had to break up a large crowd of angry Brixton blacks who had not liked what they had seen happen to Gomwalk; and they broke it up violently. It did police/black relations in London no good at all, and the large battles between the police and hundreds of young blacks at Peckham and Herne Hill on two occasions in the next few years have to be understood in this context. Callaghan, the Home Secretary, was rather quick to defend the police in the Gomwalk affair; the well-documented account produced later by the N.C.C.L. was brushed aside with the usual dismissive 'conflict of evidence' excuse much loved by the Home Office in police matters.

The following year, and only five miles away across South London, came the episode involving the Quaye family. In April 1970, Susan Quaye, the daughter of a Ghanaian railway worker and his white wife, was arrested after an incident in Greenwich Park in which a white girl lost a purse containing 75p. Two policewomen then went to search the Quayes' home in Blackheath, but were refused entry because they did not have a warrant. The Quayes themselves walked down to Greenwich police station, but were not allowed to see their daughter. The police alleged that the Quayes accused them of planting evidence; the Quayes that the police threatened them. On their return they found the police waiting outside their home in force (the police denied the number of twenty-two described by several defence witnesses, but there was no doubt that there were a lot of policemen to execute a search warrant for a 75p purse) and Mr Quaye was arrested and handled with what he alleged was considerable violence. His wife and other daughter were also arrested. At their trial, Susan Quaye was acquitted on the theft charge; and although the Lambeth magistrate, Beaumont, felt it necessary to impose light sentences on the others for assaulting the police,* these were afterwards quashed by the Appeal Court because of the conflict of evidence. The Quayes were lucky in their connections: they were members of the Communist Party and they knew their local clergyman, Paul Oestreicher, well. He was an executive committee member of the N.C.C.L., who supported their case strongly, and arranged for the appeal to be handled by the radical solicitor Benedict Birnberg; they also impressed the Court as witnesses. Most blacks with complaints against the police are not so fortunate.[29]

Not that, in the late 60s and early 70s, police violence was directed only at blacks; the defence in the Angry Brigade trial alleged, with convincing photographic evidence, that Greenfield had been beaten up when first arrested, and there were three quite

*The magistrate added the revealing comment that 'it would not have happened if Mr Quaye had not stood on his legal rights and allowed the policewoman to search the house.'

mundane cases handled by the N.C.C.L. in 1969 in which police violence had been arbitrary and unprovoked; but the blacks were the most vulnerable community in their relations with the police, and as a group were most likely to fight back, physically and politically. Nor was it just the police. In 1972, at the height of the 'mugging' scare, there was the case of the Oval Four, which involved the London Transport railway police in a nasty way. Four blacks from South London were arrested at the Oval station by plain clothes policemen as they were returning from a political meeting, and accused of attempted theft and assault. They claimed to have been beaten up and a white woman who came to their defence was also charged with assault. They received prison sentences, but these were quashed on appeal. The persistence of treatment like this (and its judicial equivalent, the twenty-year sentence given to Paul Storey of Birmingham for mugging) convinced the black communities they were being victimized, and partly explains the appalling state of race relations in certain parts of Britain in the first years of the 70s.

The lack of concern shown by the police after the publication of a well-documented analysis of a dozen cases involving Ealing police and immigrants by the Runnymede Trust late in 1973 was characteristic of this deterioration. Scotland Yard tried to rebut the charges of police misbehaviour by referring to the failure of the D.P.P. to bring prosecutions in any of the cases quoted. But, as the N.C.C.L. frequently pointed out, many of the complaints against the police did not require criminal prosecutions as remedies, merely adequate disciplinary action.

In at least two parts of London, however, the Metropolitan Police had worked hard to restore reasonable relations between themselves and the local black communities. The situation in Notting Hill, which had been very bad in the late 1960s, had been transformed by 1973 after new senior officers had been sent to the area with a new, conciliatory policy. A similar improvement occurred in Lewisham, where the hostility between the blacks and some local police had been spotlighted in a report by the S.E. London group of the N.C.C.L. The N.C.C.L.'s demand for reform had been supported by Lewisham Council in 1972. Again, the Metropolitan Police command took prompt action by introducing new officers to the area, and allegations against the police dropped noticeably.

The difficulty in assessing the honesty of police evidence has always been its intangibility; what was said is often incapable of definitive proof, and physical attacks do not always leave tangible marks. But even tangible evidence can be bent – usually by planting it. There was an epidemic of complaints alleging this in drug cases from the young and the blacks in the late 1960s. In the summer of 1971, a very serious situation developed in Liverpool, largely exposed by the local B.B.C. radio station, Radio Merseyside, and the 'free' local press, in which there was large scale harassment of the blacks by the police. One Liverpool policewoman described on the radio how she saw the situation: 'In certain stations, particularly in the city centre, brutality and drug planting . . . takes place regularly . . . after hearing the word "agriculture" used on a number of occasions I asked what it meant. The reply was "planting", but you can leave that to us.'[30] In two instances that year, respectable Liverpool blacks were acquitted on drug charges after they had claimed they had been planted by the police.

Planting is such an obvious excuse for a guilty man caught with the goods that it is rightly heard with scepticism in many courts. Unfortunately, the career of Det. Sgt Challenor showed just how prevalent it may become in particular stations, when insufficient senior control is exercised. The downfall of this extremely successful 'Soho gang-buster', as the press described him, came when he was one of 1,355 officers policing the demonstrations during the week of Queen Frederika's visit in 1963. Outside Claridges on the evening of 11 July, Challenor, working with a team of twenty-eight aides, made eight arrests.[31] Three of them were people booing royal cars; one, Donald Roum, was arrested outside Claridges carrying a banner; and four were boys completely unconnected with the demonstration who just happened to be walking in the West End that evening. Three of them, including Roum, were knocked about by Challenor. He also presented all of them with half-bricks to sign for – 'a present from Uncle Harry' – giving Roum 'his' out of his own pocket, wrapped in newspaper. By mistake – for Challenor, a disastrous one – Roum was not given bail overnight. His wife contacted Martin Ennals of the N.C.C.L. (Roum was a council member) and he arranged for N.C.C.L. solicitor Stanley Clinton Davis (later a Labour M.P.) to meet Roum straight from police custody and get his coat forensically examined for brick dust. There wasn't any, naturally. From that moment a long chain of events led the courts, the police and the Home Office to recognize reluctantly that something had gone wrong in twenty-four cases involving Det. Sgt Challenor in the period August 1962 – July 1963. Five free pardons were granted, ten appeals upheld, six people found not guilty, and three had no evidence offered against them. Seven of these were paid compensation. Challenor and three other officers went for trial in June 1964 on charges of perverting the course of justice; Challenor was found unfit to plead through 'insanity' and the other three were convicted and given sentences of up to four years.

To remedy these injustices had taken a tenacious campaign by the N.C.C.L., who were the only people who could make the connections between what happened to Roum and other non-political cases fabricated by Challenor, with eventual and slow-moving support from the press and some M.P.s; on the official side there was a Scotland Yard inquiry by the Chief Constable of Wolverhampton, and finally an independent inquiry by Mr James, Q.C. The Home Office, which had at first been extremely churlish to the N.C.C.L., eventually sought their help in sorting out the mess. There were three particularly alarming features in the Challenor story: firstly, that what turned out to be perfectly justified allegations of planting of offensive weapons (knives, bricks, hatchets – Challenor must have kept a private armoury somewhere) were rejected so readily by the courts until Roum provided unchallengeable evidence, because the odds in favour of even bent policemen being believed were so overwhelming; secondly, the disgusting prevarication of Home Secretary Brooke during several months of press and Parliamentary agitation, which unduly lengthened the time spent in prison by several of Challenor's victims; and finally, the toleration, to put it at its mildest, extended to Challenor and his methods by his colleagues and superiors at West End Central. It is sobering to consider how long Challenor could have gone unchecked had he not picked an N.C.C.L. activist for an easy victim.

1963 was a bad year for police fabrications; several officers at Hornsey were found to have planted weapons on suspects by another inquiry, conducted by William Mars-Jones, Q.C. And in another N.C.C.L. case, a schoolteacher, Leslie Stratta, was acquitted on a charge of assault (by spitting at a policeman) when scientific analysis proved that the spit stain could not have been caused by Stratta, though it could have been by another policeman. Stratta received £750 compensation, but to the irritation of the N.C.C.L., the Home Office tribunal reinstated the two officers because the allegations of false statements were 'not proved' – not surprisingly, perhaps, since the tribunal did not feel it necessary to hear evidence from Stratta himself.

All these examples of the abuse of police power demonstrate just how much the ordinary citizen is at the mercy of the police once alone inside the station with them. The urgent need to create an independent monitoring service has been regularly proposed by the N.C.C.L. since 1959, with increasing support from other legal and civil liberty groups. However, far from convincing the Government and judicial authorities that this reform was needed, in 1972 the N.C.C.L. had to initiate a campaign against the C.L.R.C.'s proposals to weaken the few existing protections provided by the Judges' Rules. The groundwork for the proposed changes had already been done by other legal notables. In 1965 Robert Mark (later Metropolitan Police Commissioner) argued that the caution was a useless protection for the innocent, and that if it were abolished and the accused forced to testify in court, it would shift to the criminal lawyer 'that part of the task of the police officer that seems to arouse most distrust and criticism of the police . . . namely, the interrogation of the accused.' Mark had a good case, except that he did not suggest how his 'absolute prohibition of duress' could be enforced any more successfully than the existing prohibitions; and it was the lack of this success that justified the right to silence. In 1971, Lord Chief Justice Parker forecast the abolition of the caution and the removal of other '"anomalies" which unduly helped the prisoner.' A few months later his successor, Lord Widgery, told a London legal conference that we could no longer afford to invite a suspect to keep quiet during interrogation, and that it was equally unacceptable – since it led to the same result – to have the suspect's solicitor present during interrogation. Lord Widgery did, however, agree that it was a good idea to have an independent third party involved in the process. Since we do expect the police to catch and convict criminals, there is a great deal of reason to the Mark/Widgery arguments; but a vital objection had been made by Mr Justice McKenna a few months before Widgery's speech, when he pointed out that it was 'cruel to compel a man to choose between confessing his guilt, committing perjury, or standing mute and suffering whatever penalties you care to attach to his silence.' The existing right to silence, both in police custody and in court, should therefore be preserved. The N.C.C.L., in its riposte to the C.L.R.C., went further than McKenna, and argued that an immediate improvement in the situation could be achieved simply by giving the Judges' Rules the force of law, which would make much of the police evidence then improperly obtained inadmissible. 'The Judges' Rules', wrote the N.C.C.L. 'would not be as discredited as their authors – the judges – now say they are if the judges had been more insistent that they should be complied with by the police.'

Release felt however that mere enforcement of the Rules would not be enough. They wanted tape-recorded interrogations, and either duty solicitors at police stations, or, better still, an examining magistrate as in France. The examining magistrate had already been suggested as a reform by the N.C.C.L. in 1959, by Justice in 1967, and rejected by the C.L.R.C. in 1972, on the grounds that the formality of the procedure could lead a suspect to refuse to answer a question ('an amazing suggestion, implying that the brutal informality of the police station could discover the truth,' commented Release.) Release understandably felt that until an effective monitoring system was in force, the right to silence had to be preserved.[32] Another idea, originally submitted by the N.C.C.L. along with the suggestion of the examining magistrate to the Royal Commission on the Police in 1960, was to take the role of prosecutor away from the police, which 'would reduce the temptation to embroider the evidence'. The Scots had always done this, with no obviously disastrous results for either justice or the police. The N.C.C.L. revived the idea again during the debate on the C.L.R.C. report.

On one kind of evidence, the C.L.R.C. did agree with its radical critics: identification procedures. The C.L.R.C. proposed that where the prosecution case depended wholly or substantially on disputed identification evidence, the judge should warn the jury against convicting solely on such evidence. The N.C.C.L. felt that although this would have been an improvement on current practice, such evidence should be made altogether inadmissible, unless corroborated by superior evidence such as fingerprints. The N.C.C.L. had good ground for their argument. For over twenty years they had campaigned against the injustices caused by unsatisfactory identification procedures.

In 1949, the council had taken up the case of John McGrath. In September of the previous year, the police stopped a lorry containing stolen butter in Southwark. One man, Bromfield, was arrested, but the driver escaped. Six days later, McGrath was arrested and picked out as the refugee driver by two policemen at an identity parade. At his trial, McGrath provided an alibi supported by five witnesses, but he was convicted and sentenced to three years in gaol. A campaign by the N.C.C.L., by McGrath's union, and the Labour M.P. for Bermondsey, Bob Mellish, acquired fresh evidence supporting the alibi and discrediting the identification; the Court of Appeal quashed the conviction.

Five years later, the N.C.C.L. was involved in another *cause célèbre*. In January 1954 three men, Emery, Powers and Thompson, were convicted for brutally attacking a policeman in Marlowe one night the previous October. They were found guilty on the evidence of the policeman, who identified them from photographs. Thompson sought the help of the N.C.C.L. in getting legal aid for his appeal; and the N.C.C.L., looking into the case, found further evidence supporting the alibis of the three – that they had been in Ashford at the time. The N.C.C.L. and the men's M.P., Sir Hugh Linstead, were preparing an application to the Home Secretary based on this when another man in prison confessed to the crime. Early in 1956, the Home Secretary granted pardons to the three men, with several hundred pounds compensation each. As a result of this miscarriage of justice, the N.C.C.L. made its first call for an overhaul of identification procedures.

However, they then let the problem rest for a few years – no mention of it was made in the N.C.C.L. evidence to the Royal Commission on the Police in 1959 – but in 1964 there were a couple of cases of mistaken identity which sufficiently alarmed the council for them to raise the matter with the Home Office. More and more such cases came to the N.C.C.L.'s legal panel in the next few years. In 1965, the Donovan Committee on Criminal Appeals drew attention to the danger in relying on identification evidence alone, and a Justice report repeated the warning and demanded the publication of the 'somewhat informal' rules governing police procedures. In 1967, the N.C.C.L. began to campaign for reform in earnest after several bad cases had come to its notice. Ray Barnett was convicted of a wounding offence solely on identification evidence and despite his alibi witnesses, and a young Bradford man spent four weeks in prison after six women had identified him as the man who stole their money until another man confessed to the thefts. But the biggest case of all, and one which became a long-running national scandal, involved a policeman as victim. P.C. Frederick Luckhurst had a spotless record, yet was convicted of the theft of £139, substantially on the identification evidence of just one person. The parade took place eleven weeks after the alleged theft, and the other witness did not pick out Luckhurst, while a police colleague of Luckhurst's who had been on duty with him at the time of the theft provided him with an alibi. At the appeal, the Lord Chief Justice, though disturbed by the improbabilities in the prosecution case, refused to overturn the jury's verdict. After considerable public protest, the Home Office set up an inquiry – conducted by a police officer, which annoyed the N.C.C.L. – but its report (unpublished) failed to clear Luckhurst. A full-scale Parliamentary debate in 1969 was the last, and unavailing, attempt to remedy the injustice.

In April the previous year, the N.C.C.L. had included Luckhurst, Barnett and the Bradford man among fifteen recent examples in a memorandum to the Home Office asking for a change in the rules. This was followed a month later by a Justice report with further instances. In one murder case, sixteen innocent people were picked out in five parades. The situation became absolutely farcical later in 1968 when a Scotland Yard inspector was identified by a City of London constable as the suspect in a parade. The case – against the inspector's neighbours, which is why he was in the parade in the first place – was dropped. After an internal inquiry, the Home Office finally published the rules for a revised identification procedure. This was given a qualified welcome by the N.C.C.L., but they were more impressed by what appeared to be a simultaneous change of practice by the Court of Appeal, which began consistently to quash convictions based largely on identification evidence: 'When the only evidence,' the court said, 'in one case consists of identification, however positive, it is right to look at the matter with very great care.' ('The understatement of the year' was the N.C.C.L.'s comment.) The council however continued to press for the complete inadmissibility of such evidence when it was the only evidence, and for the judges to warn juries of the dangers inherent in identification evidence at any time. This last point was taken up by the C.L.R.C. in their 1972 report.

Despite this, the injustices continued. Only after the almost simultaneous publication of two more examples – the Virag and Docherty cases – was positive action taken. Luke Docherty was convicted in 1972 for stealing curtains in Sunderland at a time when he had in fact been on a coach with forty other people. Because of a mistake on his lawyer's part, only two of the coach party testified in support of Docherty's alibi: and they were not enough to outweigh the jury inclination to believe other witnesses who 'identified' Docherty as the man in the Sunderland shop. The Appeal Court at first refused to hear evidence on appeal from the other coach trippers on narrow technical grounds: only after Justice had taken up his case was his conviction quashed by the Appeal Court, following a directive from the Home Office to re-hear the case. Docherty received compensation for his nine months in prison. In Virag's case, the correct procedures had been carried out, yet Virag was still mistakenly identified by eight witnesses, five of them policemen: it took two-and-a-half years for the Home Office's own internal inquiries to reveal the discrepancies in his case. The glaring failures of identification evidence in these two cases forced the Home Office to set up a committee under Lord Devlin, which included several lay members, to reconsider the law and the procedures in their entirety.

Corruption

The corruption that exists in the police can be put down to three factors: the freedom given the C.I.D. to mix socially with criminals, the opportunity made available by the English judicial system for the police to bend or invent evidence, and the monotonous regularity with which Parliament passes morality laws that half the country have little intention of observing. In the 1930s it was the licensing laws, particularly as applied to night-clubs; in the 1940s and 1950s, the gambling and prostitution laws; and in the 1960s, the gambling, drugs and pornography legislation.* Periodically there are public scandals, and attempts to clean up particular police departments, but there is little reason to believe that corruption will disappear as long as these three factors continue. The first is perhaps a necessary evil, though one that could be better supervised than it has been in the past.† The second two are capable of some reform, by creating a strict monitoring process for police interrogations, and by Parliament restraining itself from proscribing relatively harmless pleasures. Both would probably have a more enduring effect than occasionally putting in new top brass to mount a purge.

In the 1930s Lord Byng, the Metropolitan Commissioner, suspended nineteen Soho policemen on corruption charges, and

*There are obvious parallels with the more extreme circumstances in the U.S.A. – the prohibition era in Chicago, and the endemic New York corruption revealed in 1971 by Knapp.

†Williamson, when head of the Manchester C.I.D., would never allow the name of an informer to be kept a secret by a subordinate, as the London detectives prided themselves on doing. The secrecy clearly increases the possibility of corruption.

many were subsequently dismissed from the force. Corrupt relationships, of a minor nature, were 'quite widespread'[34] among the police and bookmakers, prostitutes and night-club owners in central London at the time; one Soho detective sergeant, Goddard, became as notorious as Challenor was to become in the same area thirty years later. Challenor took bribes or extorted money to drop or ameliorate charges. He secured bail for one of his victims on the payment of £50 from the boy's father, and unsuccessfully tried for another £50 from the same source later on. Another man had paid £100 to Challenor not to bring evidence against him.[35] A few years earlier, three chief constables had been forced to resign for various irregularities. In the late 1960s, the rumours that the Kray and Richardson gangs only survived at liberty because they bribed key policemen gained some credibility when three south London detectives were exposed by *The Times* in 1969 for attempting to secure money to drop charges. A peculiarly sinister remark came from one of them, Simmonds: 'I am a member of a firm within a firm.' Two were subsequently convicted at the Old Bailey. A provincial policeman, Frank Williamson, was appointed the Home Office Inspector of Constabulary with a special brief to investigate corruption in the London force, and a couple of years later another provincial officer, Robert Mark, took over as Metropolitan Commissioner; a large part of his brief was to clean up the C.I.D. Mark certainly attempted to reorganize it thoroughly, and created a new department (A.10) to deal with allegations of irregularity immediately. Early in 1973, the head of the Flying Squad, Commander Drury, was forced to resign after the *People* had questioned the wisdom of his going on holiday with a notorious Soho figure, Humphreys, the owner of pornographic bookshops and night-clubs. Drury described the relationship with Humphreys as exactly the kind of thing efficient policemen had with good informers; Humphreys, put out by this account of him as an informer, retaliated by alleging that his friendship with Drury had cost him several thousand pounds. A Scotland Yard inquiry found no evidence of serious irregularity by Drury. However, a major investigation into allegations of corruption against several other Metropolitan policemen made by Humphreys was undertaken after his conviction in 1974 for assault. In a drugs trial the previous year there were allegations that detectives had tried to extort money from drug dealers; and suggestions of a whole complex of corrupt relationships between the police and the drug world were made in other cases. There were grounds for believing that the extent of the corruption in various élite squads had been covered up by Scotland Yard to avoid adverse public reaction. The N.C.C.L. had commented with concern in 1972 on Williamson's premature and unexplained resignation from his job of looking into corruption. But the possibility of provincial officers like Williamson and Mark eliminating dishonesty through successful internal inquiries and reforms was irrelevant to the more fundamental need to remove the opportunities for corruption provided by the lax control of police methods and the absurd attempt to enforce laws defied and derided by substantial sections of the population.

Police accountability

Police policy has been lost in Britain as a subject for democratic debate – it has indeed rarely been an issue. The police have a straightforward policy, in theory – to uphold the law. Their enormous discretion in doing so means that some laws are upheld more rigorously in some places than in others. Occasionally an individual citizen can force a particular issue by going to the courts for an order requiring the police to enforce a law they have allowed to fall into abeyance. Raymond Blackburn, the former Labour M.P., twice did this successfully – in 1966 and 1973 – over the gambling and pornography laws respectively. But largely Chief Constables lay down policy, and have to justify it to nobody.

The more negative concept, of correcting abuses, has of course been debated much more thoroughly. There are three forms of redress available. Private prosecution for false arrest, assault, etc., where this is relevant and where the victim has sufficient funds and confidence to embark on it; the custodianship of the courts, which in theory will refuse to allow the police to offer evidence improperly obtained*; and the investigation of formal complaints, which may eventually lead to criminal prosecutions. It is in this third area that there has been the one great civil liberty initiative – securing a form of investigation into police abuses that is ultimately independent of the police themselves.

A series of incidents in the late 1950s – the prosecution of the Chief Constable of Brighton and some of his senior officers in 1958, the dispute between the Chief Constable of Nottingham and his Watch Committee in the same year, and other irregularities in Cardigan, Worcestershire and London led the Home Secretary, Butler, to yield to Parliamentary pressure for a Royal Commission on the Police in 1959. Several bodies, including the N.C.C.L. which suggested the idea when the Commission was set up, argued for some kind of independent investigation in their evidence to the Commission. At that time complaints were handled by the Chief Constable of the force concerned, making him investigator, judge and ultimate defendant as well, since any adverse findings reflected on him as the man responsible for the condition of his constabulary. (Rarely, in extremely serious cases like the Sheffield affair, the Home Secretary could set up a cumbrous independent investigation.) The chief constables themselves did not much like this conflict of rôles, and suggested to the Commission a combination of county court judges and outside chief constables as the right kind of inquiry teams. Like the N.C.C.L., the Law Society and the Magistrates' Association called for genuinely independent investigators. The N.C.C.L. wanted such a tribunal to be able to authorize compensation, and the hearings to be in public. Eventually the Royal Commission recommended – and the Government accepted in the Police Act of 1964 – a revised complaints machinery, without however making this independent of the police in the manner asked for by radical critics. The Home Secretary was given more flexible power to appoint independent inquiries able to call witnesses; but this would be an abnormal procedure. Chief Constables had to record all complaints, for inspection by Home Office officials every year,

*There is a fundamental contradiction between the lawyers' simultaneous belief that the courts provide adequate control *and* that trials and police discipline are separate matters.[35]

and they could, if they wished or if the Home Office advised them to, ask another force to provide an officer to conduct the investigation into serious complaints.

Though this was an improvement, it soon turned out to be insufficient. In December 1965, Lord Devlin, the new chairman of the Press Council, was suggesting a Police Council on similar lines. On the police side there was resentment at the Home Office pamphlet telling the public how to set about making complaints. One man who made a complaint, Peter Forbes (he alleged that a detective inspector had stolen £10) was prosecuted for criminal libel and gaoled for three years.* The N.C.C.L. not surprisingly pointed out that it was scarcely going to encourage people to make legitimate complaints if they could expect a prison sentence when they couldn't prove them, and the Chief Constable of West Sussex announced he would take civil action against anyone making an unjustified complaint against officers in his force. In 1966 the demand for genuinely independent complaints tribunals grew stronger: the Archbishop of Canterbury, inspired by his experience with the National Committee for Commonwealth Immigrants, was an important new voice on this side, but Jenkins, the Home Secretary, felt unable to take any initiative. Gradually, however, the police themselves began to ask for independent machinery of some kind, since the system had become increasingly discredited. (There was one brief setback in 1967 when it seemed the police might abandon their numbers – which were a necessity for any real complaints system. Jenkins' successor, Callaghan, scotched that fairly quickly.)

In 1968, there was an extraordinary example of the complacency with which the Home Office tolerated police officers being the judges in their own cases. A man sentenced to four years' imprisonment had alleged during his trial that his confession had been obtained under duress after he had been beaten up. The inquiry into this was undertaken by a senior officer who had previously – and unsuccessfully – brought charges against this man. The Home Office conceded in a letter in January 1969 to the

---

*The judge quite inaccurately accused the N.C.C.L. of fostering the idea of the complaint in Forbes' mind.

N.C.C.L. (after the D.P.P. had, as usual, found insufficient evidence to bring a case against the police) that it would have been 'more appropriate' for someone with no record of involvement with the complainant to have undertaken the inquiry, but they refused to reopen the matter. However, Labour M.P.s began to press hard for a study of various proposals for independent inquiries, and in August 1969, after the all-party Civil Liberties group of M.P.s had tabled a motion in the Commons, Callaghan at last set up a Home Office group to look into the idea again.

This worked against a backdrop of increasing public police scandals, and little public evidence of police attempts to keep their house in order. Out of 10,300 complaints in 1969, 235 led to criminal prosecutions, but most people just got a note saying there was no case to answer. Since they were not asked to offer evidence themselves, or hear how their case was investigated, this left many of them somewhat dissatisfied. The Leeds cover-up case in 1970 – two detectives were gaoled for nine months each after their handling of a road accident in which a senior Leeds officer had knocked down and killed an elderly teetotaller whom the detectives alleged smelled of drink – dented the police image badly. The N.C.C.L. pointed out that the case only emerged in public because two police constables had resisted pressure from above and taken the matter to the coroner, which did not justify optimism about the impartiality with which internal police inquiries were conducted.* In December 1971, Maudling finally reported to Parliament on the study group's recommendations, and proposed only minor improvements. Crucially, he rejected the notion of independent tribunals, on the grounds that the D.P.P., to whom papers had to be sent if there were possibilities of criminal proceedings, was a sufficiently independent element. But as the N.C.C.L. argued, there were very different tests to be applied to a prosecutable offence and a merely disciplinary one – the latter being the bulk of the complaints received. Another suggestion, put forward by Justice as well as the N.C.C.L., that there should

---

*The state of the Leeds force at the time was so bad that five local M.P.s forced the Home Office to set up an inquiry despite the Chief Constable's petulant opposition to a 'gaggle of politicians'.

be an independent review of minor complaints after the police inquiry if the complainant was not satisfied, was also flatly rejected. However, in 1972 the Parliamentary Select Committee on Race Relations urged an independent element in the handling of complaints against the police, and the following year Maudling's successor, Carr, finally promised to introduce a new system with a genuine independent factor.[35]

Even while Carr's experts were considering what form this should take, a serious situation in Bristol demonstrated just how mistrusted the existing system had been. Following police raids in the city first on Left-wing activists, then on squatters, in 1973 (raids which once again featured the use of search warrants for explosives to obtain information), a number of complaints against the police had been made through the Bristol N.C.C.L. An external investigation was ordered: but the police handling it came from Liverpool, a city where the Bristol Chief Constable had served for thirty-five years, part of that time as a close colleague of one of the two officers sent to investigate the Bristol force. To point up its concern at this, the Bristol N.C.C.L. held its own public inquiry into the complaints about the searches and the way they had been carried out.

Nationally, the N.C.C.L.'s main concern was that the *ex post facto* independent review body proposed by Sir Robert Mark and apparently supported by Carr would do little to solve the problems, since such a review body could only comment on the procedures adopted by the police investigators. If it criticized these, there would be the unsatisfactory result of a dissatisfied complainant, a policeman with no chance to clear his name, and a demoralized force. The Police Federation also criticized this idea, since it would place a policeman in double jeopardy. The N.C.C.L. argued for a system which would allow a complainant to be legally represented and which would include an adjudicatory tribunal which could enforce remedial action in cases which did not require criminal prosecutions.

However, this latest study still failed to provide an answer. The experts could not agree on a positive solution: all their report suggested in 1974 were five principles for the Home Secretary to consider in formulating policy. The five did not include the crucial one – a genuinely independent element. The report was inevitably attacked by the N.C.C.L. and other radical groups. The new Labour Home Secretary, Jenkins, was however more determined than Carr to create a genuinely independent vetting system. In the summer of 1974 he indicated he was proposing to set up a statutory commission to supervise the investigation of complaints.

To judge from the relative public profiles of the police in 1930 and 1970, it would seem as if the quality of Britain's police had deteriorated drastically. But although the crisis in relations between the police and some communities was real enough, the real change was in the healthy public recognition of the actual problems of police work* and of the contradictory pressures – to be efficient and productive at the same time as being blameless guardians of individual liberty – imposed on them by society. In the 1970s, the danger was that having at last perceived the problem, the answer provided by the authorities and accepted by the public would be to regard police malpractices as inevitable and tilt the balance even further towards efficiency and productivity and away from liberty and justice.

*Reflected in TV series like the B.B.C.'s *Softly Softly* and its imitators in police realism – which might indeed have increased public toleration of rule-breaking and bending by the police.

5. The Courts

In their daily working, the courts have not been as damaging to civil liberty as the police; indeed, on many occasions lawyers and juries and less frequently judges have been liberty's best and last defenders. The English have always believed their legal system can satisfy the right to a fair trial; unfortunately the conditions necessary to secure that right have not always been observed. No-one should suffer injustice because thay cannot afford the cost of legal action; the innocent should not spend time in gaol; the operation of the courts should guarantee equal treatment for both parties; and those meting out punishment should not try to get round the limits of the law to increase or impose penalties which they happen personally to find appropriate. In modern Britain these four conditions have not always obtained in English courts – particularly the first two. Most recently the courts have suffered the same pressures as the police – to be efficient and productive. Except, that is, where the structure of the legal profession itself is concerned; archaic procedures and lunatic expense continue there almost unchallenged.

This pressure has particularly affected legal aid. As it became increasingly available, there were corresponding adverse threats to its availability. The courts disliked the heavier work-load, dubious activities like plea-bargaining increased as they tried to reduce it, and trial by jury became increasingly seen as an expensive and time-consuming luxury. But other attempts to make justice more widely accessible succeeded without this counter-effect: juries were democratized, barbaric punishments eliminated and court procedures liberated. The most serious flaw has been the slowness with which the legal profession has begun to turn itself from a rich man's consultancy service into a freely available (indeed, a free) social service.

The Cost of Justice

In criminal cases in the United States and Scotland, a defendant has an automatic right to be legally represented: in England he does not. In civil actions, the poor and the under-privileged often lose out to wealthier opponents because they cannot afford representation. In both criminal and civil law the situation began to improve in the late 1960s, but even so England was far from securing what the N.C.C.L. described as a 'basic bastion of civil liberty' – a comprehensive system of freely available legal advice and representation.

A large measure of the blame for this must lie with the legal profession itself – in particular, the barristers. They have resisted the structural changes in twentieth-century society more successfully than any other profession: even medicine was forced to become a social service.* In the 1970s Britain still retained a legal system based on private practice, a system in many ways completely unsuited to the demands made on it. Only the new experiments with publicly-financed law centres offered a sense of change in the right direction.

Civil law retained the stamp of an institution concerned essentially with property matters to long after the social revolution of the nineteenth century had brought entire new areas of concern – and entire new classes of the population – into the courts. The provision of aid for the unrich has suffered from the class basis of civil law since such schemes were started in the thirteenth century. Indeed the medieval *in forma pauperis* procedures survived until 1914, when a limited Poor Persons legal aid scheme was set up.† The scheme was taken over by local committees of the Law Society in 1927, but the exclusion of county court work – the vast bulk of civil cases – remained. As the 1930s advanced, it became increasingly difficult to get solicitors to take on civil

---

*Perhaps because lawyers are regularly one of the largest occupation groups in Parliament and can always lobby effectively in their own interests.

†A progressive suggestion in the Lawrence Report – that the poor should be represented by state-salaried officials – was defeated by the private practice enthusiasts of the legal profession.

legal aid work at all. Ironically enough, what transformed this scandalous situation was the huge increase in divorce requirements brought about by the liberated habits of the population during the Second World War. Financial limits were dropped for all ranks in the armed forces from sergeant downwards, and legal advice was given free by the Services Divorce department. A similar scheme was necessarily extended to civilians (the other half of the divorce, usually) by the Law Society. Both were extremely successful.

At the end of the war, the lawyers – reluctantly recognizing that civil legal aid on a substantial basis had come to stay – took steps to make sure it remained under their control, and in no way threatened the private enterprise nature of their profession. In 1945 the Rushcliffe Committee recommended a legal aid and advice scheme in which applications would be vetted by Law Society committees (as to their 'merit') and the National Assistance Board (for the financial criterion). Those who survived these hurdles would be given certificates and could then pick a solicitor from a voluntary panel. These recommendations were enacted by the Labour Government in the 1949 Legal Aid and Advice Act. Rushcliffe's one radical suggestion – that the supervisory committees should contain some laymen – was strongly supported by the N.C.C.L. and some Left-wing lawyers, but defeated by the mainstream legal lobby. The N.C.C.L. also reacted bitterly to the postponement, for economic reasons, of the full implementation of the scheme and its restriction to High Court actions only. In 1953, the Council joined with several social service organizations in a campaign, organized by the National Council for Social Service, to get the Act brought into force properly. Within a year, this pressure was successful in getting legal aid extended to county court cases. In 1960, civil legal aid was made available for appeals to the House of Lords, and for some magistrates' proceedings (like maintenance applications) in the following year.

Rushcliffe's most revolutionary proposals were in the area of legal advice, before court proceedings had started. The 1945 committee had come close to 'socialized law' with their proposals of a blanket 2s. 6d. fee, no means test, evening office hours ('often the only possible time for working people') and branch offices in large towns: the cost to be met by the Government. These ideas were defeated, not by the lawyers, but by the Treasury, and have never been implemented, even though they went on to the statute book in 1949. Legal advice has been available in various piecemeal forms, from charitable organizations like London's Toynbee Hall, from the Citizens' Advice Bureaux, and from trade unions and political parties. The Law Society introduced a voluntary scheme for cheap advice in 1959. But none of these was nearly adequate for the needs of the country.

The legal aid scheme did however work reasonably well, at least until inflation made the income qualifications absurdly unrealistic. In 1957, there had been a seventy per cent increase in prices above the 1945 level on which the income figures determined legal aid were based. This inevitably put millions of people who were originally intended to benefit from the new law beyond its reach. There were minor improvements in the financial restrictions in 1959, but the pace of inflation meant the pattern of injustice was soon repeated. In the mid-1960s there was criticism of the fact that eighty per cent of civil legal aid went on divorce cases, but those who attacked this forgot that in divorce matters incomes were treated separately, which brought many more people within the pecuniary limits of the scheme. Examples of the petty injustices created by these limits were produced by the Cobden Trust report prepared for the N.C.C.L. in 1969. A middle-aged widow, wrongfully evicted by her landlord, was unable to take county court action as advised because a contribution of £54 towards the cost, as required by the Law Society legal aid committee, was more than she could afford. An office cleaner, permanently injured after falling on badly-lit stairs, could only obtain legal aid for an action for damages if she paid out £107 of her own money. She couldn't find this, not surprisingly since her husband earned only £13 a week and she only £4. In 1969 there was the widely publicized case of Donald Macdonald of Dounreay, who contracted leukaemia, probably while working at the atomic reactor there. Despite receiving only £6 a week Social Security benefits, Macdonald was refused legal aid to bring an action against the Atomic Energy Authority because his car was valued at £700 and, as 'disposable capital', put him outside the legal aid limits. Even though Macdonald naturally argued that the car was vital to someone in his condition, the law still required that he should sell it if he wanted to undertake a civil action.[1]

In the 1960s, the N.C.C.L. and other radical groups concerned with the machinery of the law began to debate various reforms: the idea of a National Legal Service was one which had a brief fashion. But the one that took root was the concept of the local law centre, following the success of these in the U.S.A. The neighbourhood law centres in America are staffed by qualified lawyers paid for either by state governments or charitable foundations, are located in the working-class areas and are open at hours that ordinary people can get to them. In 1970, the first English centre was opened in North Kensington and soon demonstrated that it was fulfilling a real need. Money for more was made available to local authorities through the urban aid programme, and within the next four years another dozen were started, mostly in London.

The Law Society was one institution at least that was positively influenced by all this. In 1968, it produced its own surprisingly radical reform proposals. Legal advice would be available for only a few pounds, the actual fees calculated on a means-test basis; and the income limits were set sufficiently high to include a large section of the population. In addition, they wanted liaison officers to be appointed to bridge the gap between social service agencies and solicitors. The Society rejected, however, the idea of state-financed law centres as 'socially divisive', and consequently its own liaison officers were seen by some social workers and radical groups as a compromise attempt to head off these centres. The advice scheme was on the other hand widely welcomed: the most substantial criticism was the doubt as to the number of solicitors who would be prepared to operate it. The Government accepted the scheme in 1971, and it went into operation in 1973.

Another improvement introduced by the Law Society scheme was that for the first time ordinary people coming before one of the many tribunals (rent, industrial injury, etc.) created since the war would get legal advice beforehand (though given the often complex nature of the law, the advice alone could be meaningless).

In 1967, the N.C.C.L. had begun to campaign for legal aid to be extended to tribunals, which had increasingly taken over from the courts in areas like redundancy, supplementary benefits and so on. Nine years earlier, in 1958, the Franks Committee had recommended that legal representation should be allowed for parties appearing before these tribunals, and that legal aid should be be made available for such representations. Characteristically, the Conservative Government adopted the first recommendation but not the second. The inequitable result was predictable. In 1967, a survey found that in one week of hearings at a rent tribunal seventy-four per cent of the landlords were legally represented while only eight per cent of the tenants enjoyed this advantage. Similar discrepancies were found at Social Security Tribunals, where ministries and employers had lawyers to speak for them and the claimants didn't. In the following year, Professor Harry Street – himself an experienced tribunal chairman – pointed out that in rent actions a wealthy property company would appear buttressed by solicitors and valuation experts, but for a tenant 'to have comparable help would cost 50 guineas a day.' A Child Poverty Action Group report in 1969 highlighted the importance of the Social Security Tribunals for the poor, and the serious deprivation that arose from the lack of legal aid on such occasions. In 1968 less than twenty per cent of appeals before supplementary benefit tribunals succeeded; yet when in the following year the C.P.A.G. began to represent appellants (in a random manner) nearly all their cases were won. The non-availability of legal aid and advice, concluded the C.P.A.G., meant that 'the rights of the poor are grossly restricted'. Despite this pressure from the radical lobbies, legal aid was not made available for tribunals when the Law Society reforms were implemented by the Government, though advice became much more widely available for preparation of cases to go to the tribunals. However, in 1974, the Lord Chancellor's advisory committee took up the point, and much of the evidence it heard argued strongly for extending legal aid to tribunal work.

In criminal courts, legal aid in some form or another has been provided on a more regular basis than in civil actions throughout this century. From 1903, it has been possible for judges to grant legal aid under the Poor Persons' Defence Act.* Magistrates' courts, however, were not included in this dispensation, and to get legal aid defendants had to disclose their defence in advance – which could be highly damaging to their chances of acquittal. This reactionary condition was abolished in 1930, but the judges – and the committing magistrates – still retained enormous discretion in granting legal aid, and this inevitably led to abuse. In addition, it remained difficult to get aid for appeals, and almost impossible for appeals from magistrates' verdicts – and magistrates have always handled the vast majority of criminal cases. The N.C.C.L. began to agitate for improvements in this area after its experience in the John McGrath affair in 1949,† at the time that the Rushcliffe Committee's proposals were being enacted. But the discretionary power available to magistrates (a power perpetuated by the 1949 act) continued to be the main target of the N.C.C.L. and other civil liberty groups, particularly since many magistrates demonstrated a deep-rooted hostility to what they regarded as a foolish waste of public money.‡ In 1956, during the identification campaign in the Powers case, the N.C.C.L. again found the injustices that arose from this weakness in the 1949 act: Thompson, one of the three men eventually pardoned in this business (see above, p. 189), had had great difficulty in getting legal aid to prepare his defence at the trial. And then the inflationary progress of the 1950s affected criminal as well as civil legal aid, making the income qualifications unrealistic and consequently ensuring that legal aid was too sparingly granted. The judiciary itself became alarmed at what was happening. The first improvement was to increase

*This was passed to thwart a private member's bill proposing something much more radical – free counsel at quarter sessions and assizes.

†McGrath was refused leave to appeal because he had incorrectly drawn up the documents on his own, as he had had to do since he couldn't afford a solicitor.

‡In 1968, one magistrate wrote, 'To me, it always seemed a farce that society, having been outraged by a crime, should have to pay money to try and get the criminal found not guilty.' Such naivety about the nature of crime, the police and justice goes a long way to explaining the ninety per cent conviction rate in magistrates' courts.

the fees lawyers received from criminal legal aid in 1960, which prevented a return to the 1930s situation, when lawyers were reluctant to take on such work. In 1961, aid on appeals became generally available, though still not sufficiently so in the vital preparation stage. The Lord Chief Justice, Lord Parker, began a formidable campaign to pressurize the magistrates into giving aid more frequently. In 1963, he told them, 'In almost every case the interests of the prisoner can only be safeguarded by legal representation, and as you know, subject to a means qualification, he is entitled to it.' In the same year, they were finally empowered to grant aid in all criminal proceedings heard by them. The N.C.C.L., however, knew that the discretionary nature of this power meant that the right to legal aid would scarcely be automatic, and called for firm and clear instructions to be issued to magistrates to override their traditional prejudice against legal aid. For their part the magistrates, in the form of the Magistrates' Association, replied by calling for contributions from defendants towards the cost of their defence. These contradictory pressures, over the inadequacy of aid and over the cost of it, led to the setting up of a study committee under Lord Justice Widgery in 1964. Its report rejected the idea that a body independent of the courts should decide who got legal aid (which would have effectively killed the magistrates' discretionary powers) on the grounds that it was too cumbersome a procedure: worse, they accepted the proposal that defendants should pay something towards their own defence. This Establishment response was characteristic of the attitude to civil liberty in the 1960s: when a 'right' becomes too widely available and too frequently asserted, find some way to cut it back.

In 1967, the Labour Government enacted the Widgery proposals in the Criminal Justice Act that year. There were some benefits: legally-aided defendants could now choose their own solicitors, and aid could be granted for the preparation of appeals at the discretion of the Court of Appeal. But the new contribution scheme was described by the N.C.C.L. as 'one of the most serious attacks on civil liberty in recent years . . . this retrograde step is likely to cause innocent men with family responsibilities to fight criminal charges without legal representation.' The argument in favour of contributions – that some pause had to be given to the ever-increasing cost of legal aid – was of doubtful force, since it was estimated that contributions would recoup only one per cent of legal aid costs. After the first year of the new scheme, the N.C.C.L. complained that it had resulted in several instances of injustice. 'It is not applied uniformly, and works unfairly in that it is the innocent who suffer.' The most serious injustice was that it placed yet another discretionary weapon in the hands of the courts, and yet another method of imposing a form of punishment when defendants had been acquitted of formal charges.

Although legal aid was granted more generously after 1967, the N.C.C.L. and other radical groups stepped up the campaign to get legal representation for all as a right. Analysis of the Home Office figures in 1970 showed that the magistrates' discretion was used as arbitrarily as ever. Manchester magistrates refused legal aid in only six per cent of the cases they heard, but in Liverpool there was a fifty-eight per cent refusal, and in Bootle it ran at an astounding ninety-four per cent. In London there was a glaring contrast between Bow Street, where seventeen per cent of the cases were denied aid, and Marlborough Street, where sixty-eight per cent were. (However, the persistent criticism of Marlborough Street magistrates for this seemed to have a small effect: two years later the court's refusal rate was down to forty-seven per cent.) The N.C.C.L. protested vigorously to the Home Office about these discrepancies, along with Release, which was very concerned at the customary refusal of aid in drug cases: and there was an adjournment debate on the issue in the Commons. Among the cases quoted by the N.C.C.L. was that of a man on a drugs charge who, because he had been unemployed for three months and therefore had no money, had had to change his plea from 'not guilty' to 'guilty' when he was refused legal aid: and the amazing Derby instance when a man on a murder charge had initially been refused counsel at the committal proceedings.

One proposal that began to attract support at this time was the idea of a duty solicitor at all magistrates' courts, as in the sheriff's courts in Scotland. A pilot scheme in Bristol run by the local Law Society in 1972 was a success, even with the police and the courts.

Another unsatisfactory result of the 1967 act was the failure to make legally-aided advice readily available for the preparation of appeals. The act had intended to make this easier, but the N.C.C.L. found from its correspondence with prisoners that in 1970 over two-thirds of them had had no help from their lawyers in preparing their appeals, and that the situation worsened in the following year.

The automatic right to legal representation had not been won in England even after more than twenty years of agitation. As the Cobden Trust report argued in 1970:

The 1949 Act, with its relatively generous scales, its apparent inclusion of tribunals and its promise of legal advice for all, represented a high point from which there was a retreat ... not enough money has been made available to enable legal aid to keep pace with inflation, still less to progress.

The innocent in prison

A major civil liberty campaign developed in the late 1960s over the extremely unsatisfactory way magistrates were using another of their discretionary powers – the granting of bail. In theory the English bail system, which does not demand actual payments before release, is more generous than the American system, which does: and those arrested by the police and brought before a magistrate should – again in theory – normally be released on bail pending trial. In practice, magistrates have proved far too ready to accept unquestioningly police objections to bail, and it became clear in the late 1960s that many thousands of people who were ultimately acquitted or given non-custodial sentences were spending months in prison awaiting trial because bail was being persistently, and for no discernible reason, refused.

Here again, the productivity ethic was frustrating justice. The Release lawyers commented bitterly on the cursory way its defence cases had been treated in magistrates' courts, under the pressure of the vast lists to be heard[2], and the Cobden

Trust survey on bail in 1971 found that the average time taken to hear bail applications was three minutes: many unrepresented defendants were sent to prison or remand centres unheard. For many years previously, the N.C.C.L. had from time to time expressed concern over what it understandably saw as the misuse of the bail procedure, particularly when it was used as a way of imposing brief prison experience on people who would otherwise have received at most a fine; in 1956, for instance, it protested at the week's remand given a 17-year-old girl who subsequently received only a probation order, and indeed had her conviction quashed on appeal. Throughout the 1960s, the N.C.C.L. drew attention to particular abuses in political cases, where police and magistrates seemed on occasion to combine to teach demonstrators a lesson. (See above, p. 67.) This political orientation eventually brought home to the N.C.C.L. the wider implications of the bail situation in the late 1960s, and influenced them to undertake some of the first serious research on the subject.

Ironically enough, the 1967 Criminal Justice Act had by then already tried to remedy the bail injustices by making it axiomatic that the accused should be released except in precise and defined circumstances. However, the magistrates continued to show their subservience to the police, whose motives for opposing bail were not always proper, to say the least – in 1964, the N.C.C.L. had attacked the police habit of threatening to oppose bail unless a confession was made. In 1969, 44,267 people were detained in custody awaiting trial, of whom 2,079 were subsequently found not guilty and another 22,233 were not sent to prison. Not surprisingly, there was an intimate relationship between getting legal aid and getting bail: those who were legally represented at magistrates' hearings stood a far greater chance of obtaining bail. In that year, the N.C.C.L. suggested various reforms, including a standardized procedure for magistrates hearing bail applications, and automatically informing the accused of their right to appeal to a judge in chambers if bail was refused.*
In the following year, one N.C.C.L. case illustrated the extreme

*A further problem was that legal aid was not available for this kind of application.

consequences that could follow when bail was refused. A man was charged with conspiring to rob, and possession of a firearm. He had no previous convictions, yet the police sucessfully opposed bail four times before they withdrew their objections – after the defendant had spent a month in prison. At his trial, the judge stopped the hearing and directed the jury to acquit him. But by then he had lost his job and council house, his wife had had a mental breakdown, and his son was having to have psychiatric treatment.

In 1972, the N.C.C.L., shuddering at the prospect of an increase in the magistrates' powers to remand from eight days to twenty as proposed in the Criminal Justice Bill, successfully lobbied to get this clause defeated in Parliament. They also gave evidence to a Home Office working party on bail, which reported in 1974. Though this repeated the theoretical objectives of remand policy – that there should be a basic presumption in favour of granting bail – and also recommended a standard procedure for the courts, it was criticized by the N.C.C.L. for rejecting the fundamental changes needed to prevent thousands of innocent people spending unnecessary time in gaol.

A variation of the abuse was the development of the practice of remanding for social or medical reports. The number of prisoners so remanded increased substantially after 1967: people who needed only a few minutes of conversation with a psychiatrist or doctor were kept three weeks in prison at a cost of £25 a week to the State. In 1973, the Magistrates' Association became anxious at the extent of the habit. A Holloway survey found that out of fifty-one first offenders remanded for reports, none had subsequently been given prison sentences. In the same year the Lord Chancellor, Lord Hailsham, attacked the practice of remanding a convicted person: 'To give them what is called a taste of prison ought never to be done.' The concern shown by those in authority was timely: the year before, a Billericay magistrate had remanded a woman for two weeks' medical reports, simply because her husband had said she hadn't 'seemed well'. After N.C.C.L. protests she was released, but she should never have gone to prison in the first place.

The remand situation was further aggravated in the late 1960s by the long delays between committal and trial. The prosecution of Egbuna and two other Black Panthers in 1968 was another political case which alerted the civil liberty activists to a wider problem: Egbuna spent five months in Brixton awaiting trial. Just as bad was the delay in hearing appeals. One prisoner who had his sentence reduced found that he had already served three months *more* than his reduced term because it had taken so long – twenty-one months – for the appeal to be heard. The Beeching Commission proposed the replacement of the old assizes and quarter sessions with new Crown Courts, in the hope of speeding up justice, at least between committal and trial: after the establishment of the new courts in 1972, the waiting time was reduced to an average of two months outside London, though it was still an unsuitably long five months in the capital. Right-wing critics found that the iminent breakdown of the legal machinery was due to over-generous legal aid, which led to an increase in the number of defendants choosing trial by jury, and to an increase in appeals: the N.C.C.L. responded to this obscurantism by comparing it to 'introducing a Health Service to meet the needs of those who would otherwise be denied the medical aid they need, and then complaining that because of the use that is made of it the service can't cope any more.' It was the classic English civil liberty situation of the mid-twentieth century – progress, in that civil rights were increasingly available for and increasingly used by the mass of the people; setback, because the increased activity produced a threat to the civil rights themselves.

Justice inside the courts

For similar reasons, the move to improve the 'productivity' of the courts had by the early 1970s threatened three vital areas of procedure in the trial process itself: the attempt, formalized by the C.L.R.C., to abolish the 'right to silence' (the long English tradition that it is wrong for the accused to convict himself out of his own mouth); an increase in plea-bargaining, where judge and counsel 'arranged' deals resulting in a lower sentence in return for a guilty plea; and the erosion of the right to trial by jury.

Because the law had always been stacked against defendants, they had not, until 1898, been allowed to give evidence at all, as a form of protection for their limited rights. The English developed a tradition, as part of the 'innocent-until-proven-guilty' concept, that the prosecution had to prove their case without any co-operation from the defence at all. (For this reason, the police were forbidden to interrogate prisoners after they had been charged which led inevitably to the perennial problem of police-induced 'confessions'.) After 1898, a defendant could give evidence, either unsworn from the dock, in which case he could not be cross-examined, or on oath in the witness box: but judges continued to instruct juries that if a defendant did not choose to give evidence this did not in any way incriminate him. In 1971, for instance, Ian Purdie, accused of taking part in the Angry Brigade conspiracy, chose not to go into the witness box, and was acquitted. However, in the 1960s, a formidable section of judicial opinion began to feel that this was all out of date and irrelevant: what had an innocent man to lose by giving evidence? In 1971 Lord Widgery, who with the D.P.P., Sir Norman Skelhorn, and the incoming Metropolitan Police Commissioner Robert Mark, had long been one of the leading exponents of this school, told the American Bar Association Conference in London that a jury should not be deprived of the right to draw inferences from a man's decision to keep silent. It was not, he said, 'respectable' to keep silent; rather, it was something that required explanation. In the following year, the C.L.R.C. recommended that defendants should no longer be able to make unsworn statements, and that refusing to give evidence on oath could count as a corroborating factor against him. This ruthless attitude was logical enough since they also proposed that keeping silent during police interrogation should be seen as an implication of guilt. But as with the other pro-prosecution proposals (see above, Chapter Four, pp. 187–9) these ideas came under such heavy attack, not only from the N.C.C.L. and Release, but also from the legal profession itself, that the Home Office had to defer action indefinitely. Lord Devlin compared the C.L.R.C. proposal to changing the process of civil actions so that defendants would be required to go to the plaintiff's solicitor, submit a defence to an undisclosed statement of claims, and then be prepared to answer questions about it.* The N.C.C.L. and Release both raised the problem of the unscrupulous policeman in such a situation, able to ask a damaging question and also able to ignore the answer, thus achieving a fabricated silence which would heavily suggest guilt. Release further warned that if the Criminal Bar Association felt that abolishing the 'silence' rule could lead to injustice in jury trials, then the situation was bound to be even worse in magistrates' courts where police evidence was already receiving far too uncritical acceptance.[3]

Even more than police interrogations, plea-bargains are amongst those murky areas of the law that are impervious to analysis because they happen in secrecy. There are two forms of bargaining: a defendant will change a 'not guilty' plea in the expectation of a lesser sentence; or the prosecution will abandon a major charge (carrying a heavier penalty) in return for a 'guilty' plea on a lesser one. The 1967 Criminal Justice Act made the second of these rather easier than it used to be.[4] Because such agreements are made privately between counsel and judge in the judge's room, it is never publicly known what exactly happens. The N.C.C.L. rightly attacked the activity as undermining open trial by jury, and the courts themselves have always been embarrassed by any hint of 'secret' trials. In 1970, the Appeal Court laid down stringent conditions for negotiations between judge and counsel, making it clear that judges should never offer a lower sentence in return for a plea of 'guilty.' Publicly, the judiciary have always said that abuses of these procedures are rare, but outsiders may be forgiven if they feel that the discussion of the subject since the late 1960s by the lawyers and judges themselves suggests that impropriety has been rather more frequent than their public disclaimers would suggest.

That the N.C.C.L. connected the abuse of plea-bargaining with undermining jury trial indicated the increasingly valuable civil liberty role of juries in England. Two contradictory developments affected jury trials at this time: there was a campaign from the

*Release commented sardonically that at least in this situation the solicitor would faithfully and accurately record the answers, which could not automatically be said of the police.[5]

Left to extend the jury service to all adults, and pressure from the Right to restrict the number of offences which could be brought before a jury.

During the war, juries were abolished for civil cases and their numbers reduced from twelve to seven in criminal prosecutions because of the scarcity of manpower. (Women, of course, could not make up the deficiences because so few of them qualified for service.) However, peacetime provisions were restored in 1947, and the following year the Juries Act abolished Special Juries, made up of those entitled to call themselves 'esquire', whose services you could obtain to hear a civil case for the payment of 12 guineas. The N.C.C.L. had always attacked these as an upper-class anachronism; and during the Parliamentary debates on the 1948 act, they also called for the payment of jurors in compensation for loss of earnings, and the abolition of the property qualification.

As part of this campaign the N.C.C.L. did a survey of one Paddington ward which showed that there were only forty-one jurors out of an electorate of 7,784. The Labour Government accepted the idea of payment for jurors, but the property qualification was preserved. Shawcross, the Attorney-General, admitted that he could not oppose the principle that jury and electoral qualifications should be identical, but said that there had been insufficient time to investigate the proposal. The rating reviews of 1956 and 1963 increased the proportion of working-class householders on the jury rolls, but still exempted large sections of the population – most blatantly, women. In 1963, a Home Office study group on the issue was set up: in its evidence to this, the N.C.C.L. repeated its argument that trial before one's equals was a nonsense while half of the adult population was excluded from service. The Council also wanted the selection of juries to be modernized, using genuinely random electronic selection rather than the human discretion of the sheriffs, who were known to pick entire panels from just one neighbourhood. In 1965, the Home Office committee recommended the extension of jury service to all those on the electoral rolls, and also the exclusion of ex-prisoners. The 1967 Criminal Justice Act implemented the second idea, but the truly democratic jury only became a reality seven years later with the implementation of the Criminal Justice Act of 1972 in April 1974.

But while this advance was being won, pressures from above were simultaneously threatening its value. In 1967, the Criminal Justice Act created the possibility of majority (10-2) verdicts, which the N.C.C.L. criticized bitterly as a retrograde step, disputing the Government's assertion that important criminals were escaping punishment because individual jurors were being subverted and calling on the Home Office to provide the facts that would substantiate this. However, there seems no reason why a majority verdict from a democratic jury should lead to injustice, and since 1967 there has been no evidence that it has: the N.C.C.L. fear was unfounded. However, the N.C.C.L.'s other suspicion, that the step was just the start of an attempt to erode the basis of jury trials, was a more important anxiety and better grounded. (It did not help their case in this respect that some of their own members – notably the publisher, John Calder – were simultaneously calling for the abolition of juries in obscenity cases.) Juries were certainly reluctant to convict in the wave of politically-based conspiracy trials after 1968, which could not have endeared them to those in authority.

However, the most persistent critic of the jury system was Sir Robert Mark, whose hostility was based, not on political prejudice – indeed, he went out of his way to point to the need to preserve juries in trials of a political nature – but on his concept of rationality and efficiency. In his controversial B.B.C. lecture in 1973 he doubted the value of juries in fraud cases, a point already made in the previous year by Mr Justice King-Hamilton after a six-month fraud case at the Guildhall. But Mark's claim that there had been no serious study of the 'sacred cow' of juries was inaccurate: an Oxford study in 1972 found that oft-repeated assertion that juries were too easily outwitted by clever criminals and their lawyers was true in only a tiny number of cases; that in fact judges were responsible for a third of the acquittals, and much of the blame for the high acquittal rate was due to prosecution inadequacies.[6] Another academic study published after Mark's speech by Michael Zander of the L.S.E. concluded, on the basis of a number of cases at the Old Bailey and the Inner London Crown Court, that juries acquitted the genuinely guilty far less frequently than Mark suggested. The Lord Chancellor, Lord Hailsham, arbitrarily abolished the right of defendants to know the occupations of jurors in 1973, which came on top of the restriction of the right to challenge potential jurors on the grounds of political prejudice after Mr Justice James' liberality towards the defence in this respect had been criticized in the main Angry Brigade trial in 1972. Hailsham also called for the revision of the right to jury trial in motoring offences – a point considered by a special committee on juries set up in 1973 – as part of the way to ease the 'log jam' in the courts. The N.C.C.L. retorted that the log jam could be better dealt with if trivial prosecutions were discontinued, and that the maximum sentences for motoring offences would have to be drastically reduced if magistrates only were to hear them. 'Fundamental liberties,' said the Council, 'are not to be eroded for the sake of administrative convenience.' And, in 1974, Justice added its voice to those warning against any attempt to curtail trial by jury in order to ease the congestion in the courts.

There has, however, been one unalloyed success in liberalizing court procedure – the creation of the 'McKenzie' principle in 1970. In a divorce case that year, a young Jamaican (McKenzie) wanted to continue the action without his solicitors but with a young friend who happened to be a barrister. The judge hearing the case told the lawyer he could no longer assist, and he left the court. The Appeal Court subsequently ruled that everyone has the right to have a friend present in court prompting, taking notes and generally advising, and that the Jamaican had been deprived of that right by the judge. This development was imaginatively seized on by various radical groups in the next few years, particularly those with a libertarian outlook, like the Claimants' Unions. It was sometimes used as an alternative to legal aid, with the occasional bizarre consequence, such as when one magistrate who insisted on granting legal aid had to give way to one who would accept 'Mackenzie' advisors instead. The defendants in the Angry Brigade trial in 1972 made a sustained use of 'Mackenzie' men and women as part of the aggressively political style in which they fought the case. The flexibility of the new procedure marked a real advance in the demystification of the law, though it was only really of use when the defendant was articulate.

Punishment

Punishment has not in this period been a civil liberty issue in itself: that some kind of penalty will be exacted has generally been accepted by groups like the N.C.C.L., and only with the formation of specialist radical groups like R.A.P. and P.R.O.P. in the early 1970s has this orthodoxy been seriously challenged. However, two subsidiary aspects of punishment have created serious civil liberty problems: degrading treatment, particularly physical punishment; and, more serious because more persistent, the way in which certain discretionary powers have been abused by judges and magistrates to inflict punishment with non-penal procedures like costs, remand and binding over.

Physical punishment – birching – was accepted in Britain until 1948; its use was largely confined to juvenile offenders, though it was in theory permitted for adult offenders in crimes like robbery with violence. The abolition of corporal punishment had been voted by the Commons in 1933, but defeated by the Lords. In 1938, a Home Office departmental committee again recommended abolition, and the Criminal Justice Bill published that year would have effected this had not the war intervened. In 1938, forty-eight boys were dealt with in this way: the trend towards reform was then violently interrupted by what the N.C.C.L. called 'the brutalizing effects of the war'. In 1942, over 300 boys were judicially punished by birching. However, this illiberal development was checked the following year when the N.C.C.L. turned the case of a Herefordshire boy, Dean Craddock, birched for a trivial offence, into a *cause célèbre*. A special conference was organized, and was well attended by child and penal specialists: even in wartime, it attracted considerable publicity. Four years later, a similar case in Birmingham prompted a similar response, and this time the pressure was sufficient to win the inclusion of a clause abolishing the practice in the Criminal Justice Act of

1948. Thereafter only the Isle of Man and the Channel Islands retained laws permitting flogging; and in the 1960s its intermittent use in the Isle of Man (less frequently in the Channel Islands, where the practice was tacitly abandoned until its sudden revival in 1974) regularly attracted mainland press outrage. In 1972, two 15-year-old boys were each given three strokes after an assault conviction: this time the N.C.C.L. tried to put an end to this last vestige of public brutality by taking the cases to the European Commission for Human Rights as a breach of Article 3 – 'no-one shall be subjected to torture or to inhuman or degrading treatment or punishment.'

A more subtle injustice has persisted for years in the way magistrates and judges have availed themselves of opportunities presented by the lesser mechanisms of the judicial process to impose penalties on those who would otherwise escape punishment and to increase them in cases where the statutory maximum appeared – to the arbiter – inadequate. This tradition has already been noted in the punishment of political protest (see above, Chapter One); as with bail, the wider civil liberty implications of such abuses tended to cause concern in the N.C.C.L. only after the political aspects had been a source of agitation for years.

The cost of innocence, however, was sufficiently scandalous to have worried the N.C.C.L. in its own right. The 1948 Criminal Justice Act had given the courts the discretion to award costs to those acquitted on indictable offences. The reluctance of the judges to make use of this opportunity was immediately obvious, and the subject of angry comment: but what was not known for some years was that, in November 1949, the Home Office had circularized the judiciary secretly instructing them to award costs only in exceptional circumstances. When this became known in 1952, the N.C.C.L. criticized the constitutional implications of this relationship between the Government and the judges, as well as the injustice of the action itself. In the same year, the Costs in Criminal Cases Act was passed, which again failed to make costs mandatory for those acquitted. In 1959, after some demonstrators had been penalized by the refusal of costs, the N.C.C.L. unsuccessfully sought the amendment of this Act, and ten years later again they were still fruitlessly urging the automatic provision of costs for the acquitted: 'If the principle that it is for the prosecution to prove its case is upheld then no person should be made to suffer financially if the prosecution fails.'

At least the legally-aided defendant could not be victimized in this way: not, that is, until the 1967 Criminal Justice Act introduced the idea of legal aid contributions. (In civil cases there was, in fact, a strange injustice caused by legal aid: a successful unassisted plaintiff was unable to recover all his costs from a legally-aided defendant because of restrictions on payments from the legal fund imposed by the 1949 Legal Aid Act. In 1964, these restrictions were to some extent eased, but the situation was not finally remedied until an Appeal Court decision in 1969. Given the narrow limits of legal aid for so many years, this was an injustice which affected more than just the wealthy.) The power to impose contributions after 1967 gave the judges and magistrates a useful new weapon against those they felt had been wrongly acquitted or unsatisfactorily punished. The Cobden Trust survey made for the N.C.C.L. showed, after two years of making the acquitted contribute to their own costs, the effects of penalizing the innocent in this way. In one example, an unemployed man who had spent three months in gaol awaiting trial on a receiving charge was eventually acquitted, but he was ordered to pay £140 towards the cost of his defence. When he refused, the court took out a summons against him. In 1969, four demonstrators facing riotous assembly and other charges were acquitted on all save one minor count, for which they received a suspended sentence – yet all were forced to pay £40 towards their costs. In another case, a young man was acquitted of indecent assault and had a £55 contribution order imposed on him, which led the *Law Guardian* to comment that 'the scales of justice are still weighted against the poor'; even more scandalous, a 14-year-old boy, convicted for his part in a £2 10s. robbery, received a probation order *and* a £315 contribution order for his defence costs. However, such unpleasant anomalies forced the Government to issue a practice directive to the courts in 1972 restricting their power to make such orders.

Another much abused discretionary power was the binding-over facility granted J.P.s since 1361. Again the N.C.C.L. had regularly objected to the way this was deployed against political protesters. After the notorious Portsmouth case of the sixpenny protesters in 1969, the Home Office undertook to review these powers. But the abuses continued, and the N.C.C.L. now discovered they were not only confined to political cases. The Council was particularly concerned at the frequent use of binding over procedures (then running at the rate of some 9,000 a year) and also that these could be used not just when a defendant had been acquitted but when people were not accused of anything at all. In 1970, a man who admitted offering lifts to two 14-year-old schoolgirls (which they refused) was bound over for three years, even though there was no suggestion that he had committed an offence or had even attempted to commit one. Two years later, the Council helped finance unsuccessful appeals against two particularly glaring abuses of the binding-over powers. Six young people were bound over against their wishes, and after the assault charges against them had been withdrawn, simply because the South London magistrate handling the case seemed to want to get it over in a hurry. In the other case, a man acquitted on an insulting words and behaviour charge at Woking was told at the very last moment that he would be bound over for two years, without being given any warning of the last-minute penalty or any opportunity to argue against it. At his appeal before the Divisional Court, he argued that binding over was a stigma – in effect a suspended sentence – and that had he been convicted he would have had a chance to address the court. Lord Widgery disagreed, since the magistrates were not obliged to announce their intention of imposing the penalty, even though he thought it might have been wiser of them to have done so. The survival of this medieval punishment, which did not even require the commission of an offence, and which could be imposed entirely at the discretion of the authorities, was an extraordinary feature of English justice in the 1970s.

One other discretionary injustice survived a rather shorter time, however: perhaps because it occurred at a more sophisticated level of the legal hierarchy. It had been the practice, widely resented by prisoners, to add up to sixty-three days to an unsuccessful appellant's sentence to cover the time he had received favourable treatment in prison while awaiting appeal. When, in 1961, the Appeal Court issued a practice note reminding appellants that the court had the power to increase as well as decrease sentences, and indicating its intention of doing so where appropriate (part of the productivity drive to reduce the number of appeals) the N.C.C.L. urged that the 'sixty-three day' practice should in turn be abandoned. In 1965, the Donovan Committee recommended that the power to increase sentences should be abolished, and that time served pending an appeal should normally count as part of the sentence. These reforms were enacted a year later.

All these discretionary powers have proved the biggest threat to liberty in the courts – English flexibility become a vice. What should be the automatic rights of every citizen have been privileges accorded at the whim of the judiciary. Their independence from the executive, which is usually a virtue, has meant that they have been able to defy those attempts by Government to limit their discretion, as in the 1967 Criminal Justice Act. Were the courts to accept that legal aid and costs for the acquitted were essential components of justice, that innocent-until-proved-guilty meant that those accused of offences should be granted bail in all but the most serious circumstances, and that the archaic power to bind over should be far more stringently restricted, they would be acting in their own supposed tradition as the ultimate guardians of English liberty.

Part Three

Civil Liberty and Oppressed Groups

Minorities can suffer various fates. They can be actively persecuted; publicly discriminated against; unofficially discriminated against; ignored; and supported by positive action to enable them to surmount the built-in disadvantages they endure simply by virtue of being a minority. Minorities in twentieth-century Britain have never faced active persecution, but they have all experienced most of the other conditions. Needless to say, the last – positive support action – is realized rather less than the others.

Minorities in Britain are of three kinds. There are the minorities that are really majorities but have suffered historical repression of such magnitude that they have only recently begun to act like majorities – women, and the Catholics of Northern Ireland. There are the ethnic minorities – the various black immigrant groups, and the gipsies. And there are the institutional minorities: the mentally deficient, young servicemen and prisoners, whose rights are inevitably seriously restricted.

A significant characteristic of mid-century Britain has been the rapid growth of minority politics, which has naturally had a profound effect on civil liberty. The next two chapters describe the impact on our civil rights of the various campaigns and movements to eradicate minority injustices. The most important of these in this period was the movement against racialism (Chapter Six). Although both women and the Northern Irish Catholics are numerically larger groups than the blacks, the impact of their rebellions has either been more muted or has become significant only recently. They are described, along with the civil rights issues raised by the gipsies and two institutional minorities, in Chapter Seven.

6. Race Discrimination and Incitement to Racial Hatred

The cancer of racialism has proved, not just incurable, but capable of unfortunate side-effects amongst those who have attempted surgery. Two important measures, the Public Order Act of 1936 and the racial incitement provisions of the 1965 Race Relations Act – both owing something to successful liberal pressure – have done more to restrict liberty than to combat racialism. The cynic and the anarchist may regard this as the inevitable consequence of government. It is also the result of a confusion between the genuine need to counteract discrimination and a more spurious desire to stifle unpleasant opinions.

Incitement to race hatred preceded racial discrimination as a recognized political issue; and this historical priority determined the approach to both problems until the middle 1960s. Traditionally the authorities regarded racial issues as a public order problem,[1] and with some justification, since prejudice generally manifested itself in outbreaks of rioting or physical assault, from the anti-Irish terror in nineteenth-century Glasgow to the 1958 disturbances in Notting Hill. The Jew-baiting of the 1930s may not have been the most violent moment in this history of spasmodic hatred, but it was the first to arouse a sustained political opposition.

Reacting to the virulent tactics of the Blackshirts, a number of Labour and Liberal M.P.s, with the support of a variety of political organizations, urged the Baldwin Government to take action.* The crucial occasion was Mosley's attempt to march

*A good example of Blackshirt activity, quoted by Herbert Morrison in a Parliamentary debate in May 1936, was the beating up of two men in Hackney late at night and their hospitalization for two weeks. Morrison also named a professional boxer who seemed to get much of his sparring practice knocking down Jews in Hoxton.

in London's East End on 4 October 1936. The contention of the Home Secretary, Sir John Simon, that the police had no power to prevent the march beforehand convinced some of Mosley's opponents that such powers would have to be provided by Parliament. Partly in response to their prompting, the Government introduced the Public Order Act. Though this outlawed political uniforms, as the critics had demanded, and extended police powers over demonstrations, as they had *not* demanded, the Government refused to included a clause which would have made it a criminal offence to incite racial or religious hatred.

Not all of the anti-Fascists thought it wise to ask for new legislation of any kind. Ronald Kidd pointed out that had the authorities used their existing powers under statute and common Law against Mosley with the same eagerness they used them against Left-wing activists, the problem would not have arisen; and he gave a warning that legislation would in fact further weaken civil liberty.[2]

He was right, of course, but the idea that racial violence might be curbed by Parliamentary action had taken root. It is of fundamental importance in the history of the campaigns to secure anti-racialist legislation that many of those who pioneered these campaigns after the war conceived their ideas in the period of the Blackshirt street battles.

Some of these pioneers were also involved in the groups formed to support colonial independence; and the concept of racial discrimination was imported into Britain as part of their political equipment. The two concepts, incitement and discrimination, began to run in harness during the war. The preparation for a 1941 N.C.C.L. conference on civil liberty in the colonies included a questionnaire on racial and religious discrimination. One of those who attended the conference was the Labour M.P. R. W. Sorensen, who ten years later was the first man to introduce a bill on race in Britain.

One consequence of the exigencies of war was that black people suddenly appeared in Britain in large, or at least noticeable, numbers; the American blacks in the U.S. forces, and the West Indians who came to join the R.A.F. or to work for the Forestry Commission or in the factories.[3] The scale was small, but the friction caused anticipated in remarkable detail the larger troubles of the next thirty years.

The 'colour bar', as it was more graphically known in those days, showed itself in hotels, pubs, dance halls – and the workplace. In October 1939, the press and several M.P.s took up the case of three black Paddington civil defence workers, including a clergyman, who had been forced out of their stretcher party jobs because some of their white colleagues objected to serving with them. In 1941, a Trinidad chemist and a Ceylonese clerk both found themselves in the papers because prospective employers (London Transport in the latter case) had refused them work on the grounds of their colour.* In July 1943, Learie Constantine met with a snub from the Imperial Hotel when he tried to stay there with his wife and child, and won a famous moral victory in court a year later. (Mr Justice Birkett felt he lacked the authority to grant substantial material damages – Constantine was granted five guineas and limited costs.[4]) But Constantine won only because it is an ancient common-law offence for an 'inn' to withhold available accommodation; it mattered not at all that Miss O'Sullivan, the manageress, had told him they 'would not have niggers in the hotel because of the Americans staying there'.

The Americans often seemed to provide an occasion for British prejudice. In September 1942, black soldiers were unable to get into an army dance in Eye, Suffolk – and they were also banned from the town's reading room. In February 1944, the magistrates of Ledbury in the same county deferred the renewal of all pub licences because some of the licensees had refused to serve black soldiers. Occasionally, however, the Americans' own prejudice met with a more commendable local response. A black sailor was attacked by compatriots at a Southend dance in May 1944 for presuming to dance with a white girl, and was subsequently ordered out by officers present; whereupon the local Southend people there got so upset that the white Americans, some hundred of them, were themselves forced to leave.

---

*The managers of 1941 at least had the honesty – or effrontery – to put in writing, 'not fitted because of complexion'. They have since grown more subtle.

A major political and diplomatic issue developed around the prejudice shown in another of the Allied armies camped in Britain – the Poles. The treatment suffered by Jewish soldiers in the Polish army had drawn persistent criticism from British liberals: in May 1944, the exiled Polish government felt obliged to set up a formal enquiry into anti-semitism in its forces which would for the first time include Jewish members in the investigating team. Their report was never published, but over 200 Jews were transferred to the British army. A third group, which had actually deserted the Polish force in protest at the way they were being persecuted, was amnestied but denied the chance to transfer to a British unit. They volunteered for any 'dangerous work' which would further the aims of the Allies but also get them out of the clutches of the Poles; and Tom Driberg M.P. led negotiations with various ministries to get them jobs in the pits. Additional pressure was applied to the Polish authorities in Edinburgh by the local branch of the N.C.C.L., and in the autumn of 1944 the recalcitrant Jews won the right to be British miners rather than Polish soldiers.

While these particular fights were being fought on behalf of Jew and black, the first attempts had been made to devise legislation which would cover all such cases. Worried by a spate of anti-semitic wall slogans in the winter of 1942–3, the N.C.C.L. annual conference in March called for legislation 'whereby individuals and organizations disseminating anti-semitic and fascist propaganda, or racial antagonism in any form, shall be guilty of a criminal offence'.

During the debate, Pritt immediately located the central problem for any libertarian: 'the universal and absolute right for everyone to express their opinion'. He had a confidently authoritative answer – that 'if the whole business and purpose of Fascism was to destroy civil liberty, one could not concede fascists the civil liberty to advocate the destruction of civil liberty.' Pritt also emphasized that all kinds of racial hatred, and not just anti-semitism, should be the object of the new law. This was to counter any suggestion of 'favouring the Jews', and this led him to enunciate what was to become the classic doctrine of positive discrimination: 'In order to treat a person fairly, you sometimes have to give the appearance of doing him a favour.' His precedent was Article 123 of the Soviet Constitution.

Three years later, Pritt repeated his proposals but in a far harder form. He wanted specific acts of Fascist propaganda, particularly anti-semitism, made punishable; power given the Home Secretary to declare an organization 'fascist' and there-after have it suppressed by a Court order; and to deprive, tem-porarily at least, members of proscribed organizations of their right to organize, stand for election or write for publication. He brushed aside the rather natural objection that it is not the busi-ness of libertarian organizations to recommend the restriction of anyone's liberties, and certainly not in their interest to increase the arbitrary power of the Home Secretary. Yet Pritt managed to persuade the N.C.C.L., the Haldane Society and a sub-committee of the Parliamentary Labour Party to support his case. The proponents of anti-racialist laws have never again argued them-selves into such a repressive position, but too many have followed the logic, if not the detail, of Pritt's extremism.[5]

When, in the following year, 1947, the International Conference on Human Rights urged legislation on incitement and discrimin-ation in housing and employment, the Labour Government was sufficiently impressed by the accumulating demands to attempt a test incitement case under the existing laws on sedition. These made it illegal to intend 'to promote feelings of ill-will and hostility between different classes of His Majesty's subjects'.[6] In August, at a time when British troops were under frequent attacks from Palestinian Jews, the editor of the *Morecambe and Heysham Visitor* wrote in an editorial:

There is very little with which to rejoice greatly except the pleasant fact that only a handful of Jews bespoil the population of our borough ... there is a growing feeling that Britain is in the grip of the Jews ... violence may be the only way to bring them to a sense of their responsi-bility to the country in which they live.

The author, Caunt, was tried before Mr Justice Birkett (of the Constantine case) at Liverpool Assizes. The judge emphasized that the jury had to be convinced of Caunt's intent to provoke violence, and reminded them of their responsibility for protecting the freedom of the Press. Caunt was acquitted, and went away to write a rather gloating anti-semitic editorial to celebrate his triumph. The defeat destroyed all enthusiasm at the Home Office for anti-incitement legislation.*

Though anti-semitism attracted the greater part of radical interest in the immediate post-war years, the 'Colour Bar question' was revived by two separate but converging developments – the beginning of West Indian migration to Britain in 1948, and the increase in the agitation for colonial freedom which followed the independence of India and Pakistan in the same year. Naturally, the colonial problem preceded the domestic one: politicians concerned with the former found themselves extending the colour bar concept to this country almost accidentally. Sorensen introduced his 1950 bill on discrimination because of the experiences suffered by Commonwealth students.[7] Brockway formulated a Human Rights bill in the same year as a result of his work for the Movement for Colonial Freedom. And in 1952 'Racial Unity', the first multi-racial group specifically concerned with fighting racialism at home and abroad was founded (largely by the white radical allies of the black colonial politicians). Harold Wilson, Hastings Banda, Fenner Brockway and the Aga Khan were prominent early members. The style of 'Racial Unity' may have been somewhat genteel – 'splendid garden parties' tended to be favoured as fund-raising events – but it did take up individual cases of discrimination in Britain. Success led to a touching optimism: 'We find that very often (discrimination) is largely through ignorance rather than any deep prejudice.'

Just as in 1947 Labour responded to the anti-Fascist pressure to try an incitement case, so now, though in opposition, they heard the increasing fuss about discrimination and deliberated what they should do. A sub-committee of the National Executive invited Dr Kenneth Little, an Edinburgh University anthropologist, to advise them on the need for a bill. He duly recommended it, and with considerable insight, also recommended conciliation machinery similar to that of the American Fair Employment Practices Commission. At the same time (1952) the M.P. (later

*Pritt saw some sinister pro-Fascist civil servant behind all this, proposing a test case which he knew would fail.

judge) Sir Lynn Ungoed-Thomas warned against drafting a bill simply for propaganda purposes, but felt that action against specific abuses, such as leases, dance halls, pubs, and employment would be worthwhile.[8] However, Labour refused to come to any official decision on a race policy for another six years. The party committed itself to legislation only in the wake of the 1958 disturbances.

Partly this delay may have been because the pressure for legislation slackened off in the mid-1950s. The incitement faction continued to make occasional noises, but with the decline in anti-semitic activity after 1949 they seem to have lost most of their inspiration. Examples of discrimination naturally increased with the build-up of immigration, but for the most part these were countered, where they were countered at all, at an individual level. Such an approach worked within the existing legislative framework, the one exception being Brockway and the M.C.F. The Labour M.P. introduced the first of his series of private members' bills on discrimination in 1956.

The two responses – individual casework and legislation – were complementary, however, and the evidence provided by particular cases increasingly furnished the arguments for changing the law. It seems likely that the nature of the casework activity begun in the 1950s considerably shaped the provisions of the 1965 Act. Predominantly, this was concerned with discrimination in public places – pubs, hotels, dance halls – rather than housing and employment. The most successful legal tactic used against discrimination before 1965 was devised to cope with the black man's frequent inability to get a drink in the saloon bar. This was the resort to brewsters sessions.

The idea was first mooted in 1951, when a Paddington pub was found to be regularly refusing to serve 'colonial citizens'. The brewery at first indicated its disapproval of this, but subsequently declared 'there is so much to be said for the tenant's point of view that we do not feel inclined to take any further steps on the matter'. The N.C.C.L. took the case to the Colonial Office* and their welfare officer eventually persuaded both pub

*This, and its sister ministry, the Commonwealth Relations Office, were generally more sympathetic to immigrant problems than the Home Office,

and brewers to change their attitudes. But, during the negotiations, the N.C.C.L. made it clear they would challenge the licence at the local brewsters sessions if the ministry were unsuccessful. Three such challenges were in fact made two years later. Two, in Manchester, were only partially successful. Although the licensing justices publicly deprecated discrimination, they renewed the licences of two pubs where African students had been refused drinks even though the licensees' lawyer had defended the discrimination and had refused to give any assurances that it would not be repeated. (A publican is entitled by law to refuse to serve anyone without giving a reason.) In the third case, however, the Desborough Arms in Paddington publicly renounced its colour bar after a protest at the local brewster sessions.

This precedent was sporadically followed for the next twelve years. The high point in this strategy was reached in 1958, in the Milkwood Tavern affair. Not only was the Brixton pub persuaded to alter its position, but the persuasion was the result of an alliance between a black group (around the *West Indian Gazette*) and white organizations – the M.C.F., the N.C.C.L. and the Lambeth Trades Council. At that time, a black militant could still write to white liberals in these terms: 'The promise of the Milkwood Tavern at the brewster sessions last week is indeed a great victory and a fillip for the furtherance of friendship between white and coloured people.'[9] Between this and the passing of the 1965 act, at least a dozen attempts were made with varying success to force changes of policy on publicans alleged to discriminate against blacks, though not all of them were taken to the sessions. Latterly the tactics were intensified: there were sit-ins and pickets at a few pubs, which usually ended in the arrest of the protesters.

The more militant methods put the police in an awkward position. In December 1964, a West Indian was refused service in the saloon bar of the Dartmouth Arms in Forest Hill (South London); he sat down with some white friends and refused to move. The landlord called the police, who convinced the demon-

albeit more for reasons of international diplomacy than humanitarianism. See Rose, op. cit., p. 210 ff.

strators that the law of trespass was on the landlord's side; and these then left. The N.C.C.L. felt perturbed that the police considered it their duty to assist the colour bar in this way, and unsuccessfully tried to raise the point with the Metropolitan Police Commissioner. One of the Home Office ministers, George Thomas, was however so concerned by the case that he took it up himself. The passing of the 1965 act soon removed this kind of burden from the police*.

Despite the Constantine case of 1943, hotels proved less amenable to direct action in the pre-1965 situation. On two occasions, campaigns were mounted against hotels found to be exercising discrimination. In 1953, the Green Park Hotel told travel agents that it would not accept bookings from coloured people. Objections were voiced in press and Parliament, and various ministers urged to use their powers against the hotel (the Minister of Food was even asked to withhold food supplies, as had happened during the war, but the Minister felt he lacked the power to do this.) The Government did however publicly support the British Travel and Holiday Association, which unsuccessfully applied discreet pressure on the hotel to change its attitude. The definition of a hotel is so vague legally[10], and the damages won by Constantine so small, that not surprisingly no-one attempted to take on the Green Park in court. This did not prevent Conservative Governments from blandly assuming the existing law provided protection for blacks. When Brockway attempted in 1960 to get the then President of the Board of Trade, Maudling, to withhold public funds from the B.T.H.A. until it ensured that none of its members practised discrimination, Maudling quoted the Hotel Proprietors Act of 1956, which re-asserted the common law principle already tested in the Constantine case, and went on: 'If anyone believes the law is not being carried out, there is recourse to the courts.'[11] Two years previously, one of Maudling's predecessors, Sir David

---

* Such neutrality in the line of duty was preferable to actually going beyond it to harass the black immigrant. In 1955, a Welsh dance hall was persuaded by a local policeman to impose a colour bar to avoid racial disturbances; he evidently felt banning blacks was preferable to protecting them. Sufficient fuss was made to get the ban withdrawn.

Eccles, had similarly resisted pressure to penalize the Goring Hotel in London, when it refused to accept three black Americans at the time of the Lambeth Conference. Though he publicly deplored such discrimination, Eccles actually urged the B.T.H.A. (of which the Goring was a member) not to revise its rules in a way that would permit the expulsion of hotels practising discrimination. Though the existing law proved so unsatisfactory, the adverse publicity both the Green Park and the Goring attracted might not have been without effect. When, early in 1961, a test was made by Stuart Hall and Mervyn Jones of racial attitudes in various London hotels for the *Observer*, both accepted Hall (a West Indian lecturer) without demur.

Dance halls, having much the same legal status as pubs, seemed no more likely to provide fruitful soil for anti-discrimination action than pubs or hotels: indeed, rather less than the latter, since there was nothing similar to the common law requirement which helped Constantine. However, thanks to the tenacity of a trade union (the Musicians' Union) racial discrimination in dance halls was challenged much more firmly than in any other area of tension before 1965.

In 1958, the union blacklisted the Scala Ballroom in Wolverhampton for operating a colour bar. The owners sued the union officials for damages, and won a temporary injunction restraining them from conspiring to make their members break their contracts. However, on the grounds that the union had a right to protect the interests of its black members, the Court of Appeal found for the union and against the ballroom. This did not of course force the ballroom to accept blacks, and since an attempt to get the local magistrates to withdraw the Scala's licence had already failed, the ballroom could conceivably have persisted in its prejudice. Economic interest won out, however, and the owners withdrew the ban in 1959.

The union was engaged in a more prolonged tussle with Mecca Ltd over the company's selective colour bar policy. Though it was unable for contractual reasons to attack Mecca in the way it attacked the Scala, it used whatever tactics lay to hand*.

*In 1958, it dissuaded a South African union from allowing a then-fashionable penny whistle band to play on the Mecca circuit.

Eric Morley, the managing director of Mecca, defended the varieties of colour bar it employed from time to time (the Bradford Locarno, for instance, in 1961 obliged all black men to bring their own partners, a rule not imposed on the whites) as the only way to prevent the kind of racial fights that forced Mecca to close down a London dance hall in 1951. The company has had to give up these policies since the passing of the 1965 Race Relations Act, without any discernibly disastrous results, though occasionally one of their ballrooms slips back into something like their old ways. In 1969 the Streatham Locarno barred a group of black youths, on the grounds that they had caused persistent disturbances. The local conciliation committee investigated the case (Mecca arguing that the act eroded their right to refuse admission) and convinced the ballroom that some of those barred were unjustifiably blacklisted. The local manager apologized and promised to avoid such illegal action again[12].

Despite the occasional triumphs in odd legal corners, the only conclusion that could be derived from the efforts of the 1950s and early 1960s was the inadequacy of all proposals which eschewed legislation. This was hardly surprising. The endemic problem of anti-racist politics – that they always involved the restriction of an existing freedom (to choose with whom you dealt, drank, lived and worked) in order to create a greater freedom – manifested itself particularly awkwardly when attempts were made, as at brewster sessions, to appeal to a body of law whose characteristic was a pride in defending the very freedom which had become oppressive. The problem was even more acute as far as incitement was concerned. Gradually, the same answer was applied in both cases: make a new law. Unfortunately, the analysis proved only half correct. Racial discrimination can at least be ameliorated by legislation; incitement is a legislative bog.

Pritt, Sorensen, Little and Ungoed-Thomas had all pioneered the legislative answer, but to Fenner Brockway must belong the credit of persisting until the powerful were converted. He first attempted a bill on the subject soon after Sorensen, with a Human Rights Bill in 1951, which would have covered the United Kingdom and its colonies[13]. In 1956, he introduced a bill restricted to this country*; it proposed a £25 fine for anyone convicted of discrimination in public places and in housing and jobs, with the additional possibility of a civil action for damages if the victim wished[14]. Support for the bill came only from a minority on the Labour Left who were traditional allies of Brockway, like Silverman and Swingler. Even when the Labour Party pledged itself to some kind of race policy in the aftermath of the 1958 disturbances, the commitment was kept separate from any kind of official Labour support for Brockway; and even an organization like the N.C.C.L., which had itself made persistent demands for race legislation in the 1940s, now appeared to think that the existing law, though not naturally the existing government, had responded quite adequately to the 1958 crisis. After all, Lord Salmon had nobly declared, in gaoling some of those convicted for taking part in the Notting Hill riots, for up to four years, that 'everyone, irrespective of the colour of their skin, is entitled to walk through our streets in peace, with their heads erect, and free from fear'.[15] The N.C.C.L. argued that the Government deserved some of the blame for the rioting because it had failed to take adequate action over some highly publicized instances of discrimination that had taken place earlier in the year (the Wolverhampton dance hall and the Goring Hotel affairs). Despite the presence of the Labour M.P. for Wolverhampton N.E., John Baird, who had promoted a private member's bill outlawing discrimination as a result of the Wolverhampton situation, at a post-riot meeting organized by the N.C.C.L., the measures proposed by the Council were limited to refusing licences to pubs and dance halls and expelling hotels from the B.T.H.A.†

*Between these two bills, a Labour peer, Lord Silkin, unsuccessfully tried to add an amendment to the Defamation Act of 1952 which would have made racial defamation an actionable tort.[16]

†One important consequence of the 1958 events was that the N.C.C.L. and the M.C.F. were no longer the only political groups concerned with race. (Racial Unity seems to have disappeared by this time.) The 'middle-class Left' and the immigrants began to organize themselves; the British Caribbean Association (which supported Brockway's bills), the Indian Workers'

By the following year, however, the N.C.C.L. had decidedly shifted its position. Pressure from its membership, and the arrival of Martin Ennals in the organization, had led to the drafting of two bills, one on discrimination and on one incitement, which were launched at an important multi-racial conference attended by representatives of over 100 bodies in November 1959. The bills were predominently the work of Ennals and Neil Lawson Q.C., one of the earliest lawyer members of the N.C.C.L. (and later one of the Law Commissioners, in the classic poacher-turned-gamekeeper syndrome). Ennals, who was forced many times in the next few years to justify his efforts to restrict free expression by an incitement bill, was convinced that the 1958 disturbances were the result of inflammatory propaganda. 'The Notting Hill riots were deliberately incited by printed material,' he wrote to a correspondent in 1962. 'The people who suffered and who were caught and imprisoned were not the people responsible for the riots, but those who were subject to the inflammatory material.' Lawson drafted the texts, which called for six months' imprisonment or a £100 fine for an incitement offence, and a £5 fine for a discrimination offence. Their influence was considerable. The emphasis given to incitement was a reflection, not just of Lawson's judgment, but of contemporary political realities. For a brief moment it looked as though the new Conservative Government might itself take some action; Butler, the Home Secretary, was showing signs of interest in an incitement bill, and an attempt was made late in 1959 by the Tory M.P. and chairman of the British Caribbean Association, Nigel Fisher, together with Brockway, Lawson and Ennals, to exploit this interest, and pressurize the Government into introducing such a bill. Butler proved a blind alley; but the N.C.C.L. analysis, which argued that a discrimination bill would serve a useful educational purpose but that an incitement measure had a

---

Association and the West Indian Standing Conference were all founded within the next two years[17]. Against this, the Mosleyite Union Movement continued to work in Kensington, and the Immigration Control Association was begun in Birmingham.

real political chance, was supported by most of those active in
race relations*.

The long-term effect of that November's work proved even
more important. The most authoritative account of the political
genesis of the 1965 Race Relations act, in its delineation of the
parentage of various parts of the act, ascribes the incitement
clause to the 1961 bill, taking it over from Sir Leslie Plummer's
Racial and Religious Insults Bill of the previous year, in the drafting of which Ennals and Lawson played the crucial role. Brockway
had himself supported the 1959 incitement texts prepared by the
N.C.C.L. from the time of the November conference.

Just at the moment when the N.C.C.L. was providing this
vital intellectual muscle in the race legislation debate, a sudden
spate of swastika daubings over Christmas 1959 and the New
Year reinforced the wider public consciousness of the incitement
problems. These swung the Jewish lobbies behind the incitement
bill campaign. Plummer, the Jewish Labour M.P. who promoted
the insults bill in the spring of 1960, allied himself, as did Brockway, to the successful N.C.C.L. effort to unite all those who
opposed racial prejudice under a common banner. The memories
of the thirties were revived; at this important moment the style
was set, and the terms of the argument defined, by those whose
attitudes to these problems were forged in the anti-Fascist
struggles. From this point until almost the actual passing of
the 1965 act, incitement continuously led discrimination as
a political issue†.

Which having been said, it is as well to remember that by that
time immigration control was a more urgent racial political issue
than either. The emphasis given to provisions against incitement
must be understood in the light of the increasing clamour from

*In the M.C.F., for instance, the West Indian and Asian members felt
more strongly about incitement than discrimination, according to Lord
Brockway.

†Characteristically of 1960, the greatest attention, as far as discrimination
was concerned, was paid to the ban on Jews at certain golf clubs. And
although the all-party support for Brockway's succession of bills continued
to grow – 140 M.P.s backed the 1961 version – one of the prices paid, without
any protest, was the dropping of the clause covering employment to
sweeten the trade unions.

Cyril Osborne and his followers to keep the blacks out. Once that was urged by respectable public figures, the inhibitions fencing in the extremes of hatred were fatally undermined.

This emphasis was given a further fillip by what has been called the 'diversion into punch-up politics'[18] which happened in the summer of 1962. In July, a meeting of Colin Jordan's National Socialist movement in Trafalgar Square was broken up by his opponents; as a result of the disturbances on that occasion, the Ministry of Works banned further meetings proposed by Jordan and other far-Right groupings. Ironically enough, radicals like Ennals, who argued keenly that restrictions on incitement were essential for democracy, defended just as vigorously the right to hold meetings where such incitements were likely to occur. In May 1963, he wrote to the Home Secretary *á propos* these bans: 'The N.C.C.L. has long considered that the powers of the Ministry of Works to grant or withhold permits for meetings in Trafalgar Square were in no sense intended to be used as a form of censorship.'

A parliamentary attempt to cope with the effects of this brief revival of Fascism was made by Tom Iremonger, a Conservative M.P., in August 1962. He sought to amend the 1936 Public Order Act by adding to section 5 the inciting of 'hatred of a racial group' as an offence, rather in the way some radical M.P.s had sought to amend the act when it was originally debated. Iremonger was no more successful than they had been, though the 1965 act did eventually amend the 1936 act – with unfortunate consequences.

Iremonger's amendment was considered the minimum requirement by the radical coalition lobbying for race legislation at the time. Since it failed to cover written material, much greater hopes were attached to the Brockway bills. At a conference on race relations organized by the N.C.C.L. in November 1962, the Labour lawyer (and later M.P.) Ivor Richard argued that 'incitement is the crucial problem which has faced us recently'. He repeated the familiar and faintly dismissive description of the discrimination provisions as 'difficult to enforce . . . but probably a valuable statement of aims and intentions'. The dynamic of this analysis was the fear of extremist action rather than the apprehension of what damage the more subtle, but surely more significant, creation of second-class citizens might do to British democracy. The unbalanced nature of this analysis is demonstrated by Richard's amplification of the 'crucial problem' in the same speech – 'the revival of anti-semitism and the new factor of resentment against Commonwealth immigrants have given Fascist groups a new lease of life'. A year later Donald Soper wrote in *Tribune* of the incitement clauses, 'This is the genuine medicine, that can begin to cure racial discrimination, and without it any other medicament will be ineffective.' It is impossible to assess what setbacks to race relations were caused by the radicals' concentration on the potential threat from miniscule Right-wing groups rather than what was actually happening to the black minority and the large group of whites, who, though prejudiced, could in no way be described as Fascist.

During 1962, a Petition against Racial Incitement, sponsored by the N.C.C.L. and the Yellow Star Movement, a Jewish organization, attracted nearly half-a-million signatures. Some possible signatories, however, showed a certain foresight – and principle – in their refusals. The Committee of 100 wrote that 'free speech means very little unless it is extended to those with whom we radically disagree', and Jock Campbell (now Lord Eskan) declined because of his 'confusion about the balance between free speech and incitement'. Such rebukes spurred Ennals to his most eloquent defence of the ultimately indefensible: 'Freedom of speech,' he wrote to an objector in October 1962:

is not an absolute right, and in our opinion the damage caused by those who publicly incite people to race hatred is greater than the damage that would be caused by imposing a restriction on their utterances. It cannot be right that in a democracy, which holds up as its highest ideals liberty and equality for all citizens, a minority should suffer a loss of their rights to live and work in peace because of the lies and half-truths disseminated about them.

This attitude received some solid legal support the following year when the Court of Criminal Appeal reversed a Quarter Sessions decision that Jordan's Trafalgar Square speech had not been likely to cause a breach of the peace as defined under the Public Order Act of 1936. Lord Parker, the Lord Chief Justice, rejected Jordan's defence that the anti-Fascists in the crowd would have caused a breach of the peace whatever he had said by ruling that 'the speaker must take his audience as he finds them, and if those words to that audience, or part of that audience, are likely to provoke a breach of the peace, then the speaker is guilty of an offence'.[19] A somewhat dangerous *carte blanche* offer to any group who wished to break up any meeting, one would have thought, though no defender of civil liberties seems to have said so publicly at the time.

The 1962 disturbances forced the politicians as well as the judges to address themselves more positively to the incitement issue. Labour's National Executive repeated the party's 1958 pledge at the autumn conference, and Harold Wilson used the occasion of an anti-apartheid meeting in March 1963 to pledge a future Labour Government to something similar to Brockway's bill. The Conservative Government continued however to preserve its ultra-liberal position defending free speech: 'Perverse and erroneous opinions must be tolerated to the fullest possible extent provided that reason and truth are left free to combat them.' (The Attorney-General in 1963.[20] Dickey points out that this apparently generous attitude concealed the Tories' essential reluctance to countenance any specific legislation on race. In most other respects, the dying Conservative Government of 1962–4 was not noted for its liberalism.)

Early in 1964, three members of the Labour Shadow Cabinet, led by Sir Frank Soskice, the lawyer who as Home Secretary was to supervise the passing of the 1965 act, drafted a bill and memorandum (presented to Labour's National Executive in July) the main concern of which was incitement. (The committee regarded legislation on jobs and leases as unenforceable.) At the same time a sub-committee of the Society of Labour Lawyers, under the future Law Commissioner Professor Andrew Martin, produced a revised version of Brockway's bill.[21] Though it deliberately confined itself to the limits accepted by Brockway, the committee drew attention to the role of conciliation in American racial disputes, and the way discrimination was dealt with by administrative rather than penal methods.[22] Neither report affected the conduct of the General Election – Labour maintained its pledge to introduce a version of the Brockway bill, but offered little further amplification of its intentions, largely perhaps because race was the one major subject of the 1964 campaign in which it was on the defensive.

So at the moment when, with the election of a Labour Government committed to legislation, a race relations act became a near certainty, the thinking that would shape the act was largely dominated by a concern over incitement and a conviction that housing and jobs were outside realistic legal limits. A group of Labour lawyers led by Anthony Lester, who had served on the Martin committee and who had spent the summer of 1964 in the United States as an Amnesty International observer with the Civil Rights movement, now eagerly developed the argument for following American practice that had already been suggested by the Martin report. They sent a memorandum to both the Home Secretary and the Lord Chancellor calling for a bill which would cover the worst problems of discrimination – housing and employment – and would work through conciliation rather than criminal penalties: and which would create a special agency to administer the law. The government ignored them. Lester and his colleagues had at last, however, transformed the race debate in Britain and made sure that henceforth it would be about the central problems of discrimination rather than the essentially peripheral issue of incitement.

Intensive lobbying early in 1965 swept important groups behind the Lester proposals – the British Caribbean Association, the Institute of Race Relations, the N.C.C.L., the Society of Labour Lawyers and, most important of all, the newly formed Campaign Against Racial Discrimination. (Lester was a member of its legal sub-committee.) C.A.R.D. was founded in December 1964, in the aftermath of the anxieties aroused in radical circles by the Smethwick result and under the impact of the visit to London of Martin Luther King. It took upon itself the formidable task of shifting official Labour thinking away from the Soskice draft and towards their own proposals*.

---

*Just as it was in the forefront of the fight to get a second act. Despite its brief life and chaotic structure, C.A.R.D. was a brave – last? – stand by liberal multi-racialism.

The passage of the 1965 act through Parliament was considerably affected by the fact that, for most politicians, race (apart from its immigration aspects) was a relatively new issue. The bill published by Soskice was, in his words, basically concerned with public order. But C.A.R.D.'s lobbying had extended as far as Thorneycroft, the Opposition spokesman, who seized on the principle of conciliation and the example of fair employment practices as useful weapons with which to attack Soskice's proposed criminal sanctions. With a tiny Parliamentary majority and a restless backbench now clamouring for the bill's discrimination provisions to be extended to employment, Soskice turned about in committee; he accepted the idea of conciliation, and established a Race Relations Board, though without the powers Lester had argued for. The result was an act which 'pleased nobody'.[23] But then nobody, except for a few people around C.A.R.D., had a firmly-rooted idea of what was required. The sustained political campaign of the previous decade had been largely over incitement. (And these clauses remained untouched. Section Six made it an offence to stir up hatred against any section of the public on racial grounds, either by written material or public utterance. Section Seven amended the Public Order Act of 1936 to include written matter and increased the penalties for convictions. *The Times*[24] argued that these powers could be used for censorship, and the N.C.C.L., remembering at last Kidd's warnings in the 1930s, attacked Section Seven as the 'most dangerous clause in the bill, a serious additional limitation of freedom of expression on matters wholly unrelated to race relations'.) The whirlwind lobby mounted by C.A.R.D. had been whirling for only a few months. It decidedly unsettled the legislators, but without so positively capturing them that they would accept C.A.R.D.'s programme in its entirety.

The limitations of the act, which applied most effectively to pubs, led to an understandable feeling on the part of the brewers that the licensed trade had been singled out as the villains of the race crisis*. Still, the new Race Relations Board reported

*The woolly definition of hotel in law meant that some of these continued to escape the new provisions. (See the report of the Race Relations Board 1966–7, p. 29.)

a ninety-four per cent success rate for its voluntary machinery in the restricted area where its writ ran in 1967–8. The second Race Relations Act, in 1968, not only extended the law to cover housing, jobs and a wide range of services but removed most of the public place anomalies that had survived the first act. Most, but not all, as the Peggy Apparicio case demonstrated in 1970. Staff at the Wolverhampton telephone exchange, where Mrs Apparicio, a 21-year-old Jamaican, worked as an operator, had booked part of the Bradmore Workingmen's Club for the staff Christmas party in 1969. The club refused to admit her. When the Board subsequently brought a prosecution against the Birmingham county court the following April, the club argued, rightly, that clubs were outside the scope of the 1968 act, and that anyway all Wolverhampton clubs operated a colour bar. The Board's contention that the club, by offering part of its facilities to the G.P.O. and its guests, had exercised public discrimination, was upheld by the judge, who awarded five shillings damages to Mrs Apparicio (the cost of her ticket) and about £1,000 costs to the Board. Though the Board won the case, the *Guardian*[25] naturally questioned whether Parliament would have given clubs this protection had the extent of the discrimination they practised been anticipated. And, in its 1971 report, the Board pinpointed the continuing privileges of workingmen's clubs as one of the most critical remaining points of racial tension.

Then, late in 1971, the Appeal Court handed down a judgment which firmly brought clubs within the scope of the act. The East Ham South Conservative Club had refused admission to an Indian post-office worker, allegedly on grounds of his colour. Lord Denning ruled that club members were a 'section of the public' as the act understood them, and that therefore membership could not be denied on racial, ethnic, or similar grounds: the Conservative club had no right to refuse admission to the Indian[25a]. Unfortunately the House of Lords subsequently overturned Denning's judgment, and the absurd anomaly remained.

The campaign that developed after the passing of the 1965 act for the extension of anti-discrimination law to housing, employment and other areas is outside the scope of this book.[25b]

A second Race Relations Act was passed in 1968 covering most of the points omitted in the first one: it rapidly achieved success in countering discrimination in advertising and insurance.[25c] The 1968 act was perhaps inevitably less successful in the more difficult areas of jobs and housing. The Race Relations Board had a long tussle with Wolverhampton Council over its un-favourable treatment of foreign-born people on its housing lists, though in 1972 Wolverhampton finally adopted a fair policy. The year before the House of Lords had decided by a majority in a case brought against the Ealing council that the Race Relations Act did not cover discrimination against aliens: only Lord Kilbrandon supported the Race Relations Board's contention that the term 'national origins' in the act covered nationality[25d]. Whatever its limitations, the act was an important and positive attempt to reduce the consequences of racialism and racial prejudice in Britain, and remains a valuable safeguard covering many fundamental civil rights. The working of the incitement law since 1965 has been distinctly less encouraging.

The forebodings of those like Martin Ennals on the amended Public Order Act – 'race relations will not be improved but political freedom will be restricted' – were swiftly borne out. Twice within a year the new powers were used, not against racialists, but against radical agitators, thus proving yet again that governments will misuse any powers that lay to hand when it suits them. In June 1966, two young men demonstrating against the visit of Sir Robert Menzies to Dover (on account of the Australian involvement in the Vietnam War) were arrested and charged under the amended act, though the charge was later changed to one of using insulting behaviour. In October, the same statute was tried against Nick Walter and others protesting against the Vietnam War at the Labour Party conference at Brighton. In December, the N.C.C.L. unsuccessfully attempted to get this development debated during the Lords' discussion of Lord Brockway's proposed amendment of the Race Relations Act (to include religious insults). The most absurd case, however, occurred the following year. In May, a poster parade was held outside an Oxford hairdressers alleged to be operating a colour bar. Six of the demonstrators were arrested and charged under section seven of the very act which had been passed to combat racial discrimination. The absurdity may have been too much for the authorities, for the charges were subsequently dropped, after considerable protests. Though the amended Public Order Act has been frequently used since 1965, this has been mostly to take advantage of the increased penalties. But the seemingly irrepressible tendency of government to use whatever legislative opportunity they get to 'tidy-up' loopholes in the law has not often proved as damaging as this tacking of a public order provision onto something as new and sensitive as race relations legislation.

In the first five years after the passing of the 1965 act, fourteen people were prosecuted under section six – in a total of seven trials[26]. (The Attorney-General told the Commons in June 1969 that up until that point he had received about 106 complaints of alleged offences covered by that section.) Nine of these were white, and five coloured. The first case, against a 17-year-old boy who stuck a racialist pamphlet on a Labour M.P.'s door, was dismissed on appeal on the grounds that neither this nor the boy's other effort – throwing a bottle containing another copy of the pamphlet through the M.P.'s window – constituted 'distribution' of racialist material in the meaning of the act. It was generally conceded, even by proponents of the law, that this was an unfortunate case with which to open the incitement batting. In the following year, two more substantial figures were successfully prosecuted. In January 1967, Colin Jordan and a colleague in the National Socialist Movement were sent to gaol for eighteen months for publishing a pamphlet, entitled *The Coloured Invasion*, which purported to show that 'the presence of this Coloured million in our midst is a menace to our nation'.* Shrewder extemists than Jordan found that the more moderate language enforced on them by the act actually improved their propaganda, since more people were persuaded by the less strident and less absurd tones – a development not foreseen by

---

*The National Socialists and other far Right groups did, however, make use of the opportunity, afforded by the act, of creating special book clubs, to 'study literature dealing with the Jewish Question' and so on. In 1966 these clubs had secured less than 600 members.[27]

the Parliamentary supporters of incitement legislation and which considerably disturbed them.[28]

The following November, Michael Abdul Malik (otherwise known as Michael de Freitas or Michael X), one of the earliest and most flamboyant propagandists for Black Power in Britain, was given twelve months' imprisonment as a result of a speech at Reading. In the same month, four other black radicals were fined under the act for speeches made at Speaker's Corner. The N.C.C.L. and others commented rather bitterly that the law designed to protect the black minority was being used more vigorously against them than against their racist opponents. Why, given their knowledge of previous similar instances of authority's abuse of its powers, the N.C.C.L. should have been surprised at this is not clear.

Then in March 1968 came the unsuccessful prosecution of five members of the Racial Preservation Society, which finally convinced Smythe at least that the incitement law was a 'dead letter'. The material distributed by the R.P.S. was couched in more sophisticated language than that of some other extremist groups, and the defendants – all middle-class men – were acquitted after a three-day trial at Sussex Assizes. The setback blunted the appetite for further prosecutions. When the N.C.C.L. passed another R.P.S. pamphlet (on 'Negro Inferiority') to the Attorney-General in June 1969, to test the likelihood of further trials, Sir Elwyn Jones argued that 'there was insufficient evidence of intention to stir up race hatred', and that 'an unsuccessful prosecution would be dangerous'. In his reply, Smythe wrote:

I sometimes wonder whether advantages in having legal powers to deal with (race hatred) are not outweighed by the propaganda value they give to those who ignore the positive aspect of race relations legislation and try to give the impression that this is an intolerable restriction on freedom of speech.

In the same month protests were made to the N.C.C.L. by people involved in a demonstration at Haringey over the local authority's proposed 'banding' of immigrant children in schools two months earlier, in which a counter demonstration by National Front members carrying 'Keep Britain White' placards was allowed to continue unmolested by the police on the grounds that these did not infringe the Race Relations Act. Smythe wrote back that he regarded the incitement clause as 'unworkable, and not to be used in any circumstances', even though he sympathized with the complainents. Thus in less than four years from the enactment of the incitement law the irrelevance of that law, and therefore the nearly thirty years of political effort that had preceded it, had become sadly apparent.

There remains the argument that, since 1965, the more extreme forms of racialist invective have largely disappeared from Britain. This has a *post hoc ergo propter hoc* quality, and is incapable of satisfactory proof. But even if the act has deterred the extremists, the essential objection remains – that it was unnecessary (to say nothing of being actually dangerous) to create a whole new apparatus of repression for such an insignificant object. Racialist utterance can have either a large or small effect. If small, why bother to outlaw it? If the circumstances ever arose where speech or literature *could* contribute to a genuine racialist terror in this country, it seems unlikely the 1965 act could prevent it, simply because the monstrous mood which would permit such a disaster would find its nourishment anyway. The only effective barrier to racialism is a libertarian one: that the great mass of people would be disgusted by it.

7. Oppressed Groups and Minority Politics

Women

Although the politics of the women's movement that exploded in the late 1960s transcended civil liberty issues, the enactment and enforcement of civil rights legislation was one of their most important objectives. The demand for anti-discrimination measures was part of a tradition that had survived from the great feminist agitation of the 1900s. In the 1940s and 1950s the campaigns on women's issues were relatively subdued, and were kept going by only a handful of organizations; they concentrated on the subject of equal pay. In the late 1960s law reform proposals, pushed by a revived and aggressive liberation movement, on a wider front, culminated in the campaign around the Conservatives' anti-discrimination bill in 1972, and its Labour successor.

Radical women in the 1930s felt that the international crisis caused by Fascism was a more pressing issue than the old feminism[1] but in the new dawn of 1945 some returned to the unfinished business: in particular, the glaring inequality in employment. That the N.C.C.L. played an important part in the campaign on this issue that developed after the Second World War was due to its general secretary Elizabeth Allen, who had a keen sense of the unfulfilled aspirations of feminism. The N.C.C.L.'s first interest in the subject came at its 1944 conference, where it rather loosely proposed 'the abolition of all practices resulting in the exploitation of women'. In the same year, the Coalition Government set up a Royal Commission on Equal Pay. The feminists' best allies were the clerical unions, which naturally had a large number of women members: the first target was the discrimination against married women in the banks, insurance companies and civil service. In all these institutions, women were required to give up their jobs on marriage, though this barrier had been temporarily lifted during the war*. In 1946, the National Union of Bank Employees put down a motion at the T.U.C. conference denouncing this prohibition. A week before it was due to be debated, the Chancellor of the Exchequer, Cripps, announced that women would be able to continue in the civil service after marriage if they wished.

One of the results of the ban on married women had been what Len White of the Civil Service Clerical Association called a 'helot class' of women clerical assistants doing the lowest-paid and most routine work, an act of oppression justified by the Civil Service administration because most of the women were expected to marry and not to make a career. After Cripps's announcement, White – an executive member of the N.C.C.L. – called for the full establishment of equal pay, since the only argument for discrimination against women on pay had been that their experience was lost on marriage: this excuse, never good anyway, had now gone.

Soon after Cripps's announcement, the Royal Commission produced its report on equal pay. Not surprisingly, three of its four women members disagreed sharply with the majority's analysis of the reasons for inequality. This suggested that women were paid less because they were less in demand, which in turn was caused by 'natural' factors such as less physical strength, less adaptability, lower career value and higher absence rates. The dissenting minority – Dame Ann Loughlin, Dr Janet Vaughan and Miss L. Nettlefold – argued that women's lower wages were the result of their inferior bargaining position rather than any so-called natural causes: 'The main cause of the low earnings of women is their exclusion from a number of trades in which they would be efficient workers . . . combined with weak trade union organization.' The report recommended that there should be equal pay in the civil service and the professions, but not in industry. This distinction was bitterly attacked by trade unionists in the N.C.C.L., who rightly saw it as an attempt to

*A cruel effect of this rule had been to compel some women to conceal their marriages, and others to remain single when they wished to marry.

drive a wedge between middle-class women and working-class women.

> What can possibly distinguish the professional woman or Government clerk, on the one hand, from her sister in industry on the other, to justify paying the former the rate for the job while the latter is paid something between one-half and three-quarters the rate?

wrote J.R. Scott of the A.E.U. in a *Civil Liberty* bulletin. The answer was unfortunately obvious: the industrial employers wanted to go on employing cheap female labour, and most male trade unionists were happy to let them do so.

It was ten years before even the limited advance proposed by the Royal Commission was realized. Though the Labour Government was committed to equal pay as a policy, not even the 325,000 women civil servants benefited immediately. An Equal Pay Committee was formed (including Elizabeth Allen of the N.C.C.L.) to campaign for the implementation of the report. Simultaneously, there was an international campaign by women's organizations all over the world to push the newly-founded United Nations into a commitment to women's equality. The U.N. set up a commission to consider the status of women in 1947, and the I.L.O. was asked to report on equal pay. The Australian delegate to the U.N. commission, Jessie Street, drew the attention of British feminists to one piece of evidence uncovered by the U.N. investigators: 'the organized edifice of sex discrimination which exists in Anglo-Saxon and many Western European countries' was far greater than that in parts of the world where underdeveloped countries were extending new rights to both sexes equally.

In Britain, real progress was very slow. In 1948, the National Provincial Bank created a new section to which women would be transferred on marriage, instead of being dismissed – 'we understand this is considered to be an advance', commented the N.C.C.L. sarcastically. The other banks dropped their marriage bars within the year*. However, the wage advances achieved by

*In 1965, the banks still operated an unofficial bar against promoting married women. The N.C.C.L. discovered that in one bank, with 2,380 branches, there were only two women bank managers – both single.

the unions in industry increased rather than diminished the gap between men and women workers, which rather nullified the value of the T.U.C.'s call in 1950 for the full implementation of Labour's equal pay policy. In 1951, as the I.L.O. was finally formulating an equal pay convention to be signed by member states, an Equal Pay Committee deputation lobbied the Ministry of Labour on behalf of the new policy; but the Government refused to vote for the convention on the familiar grounds that it was 'unrealistic' at a time of economic difficulty.

The crucial breakthrough came the following year, however. Six years after the Royal Commission's report, the L.C.C. at last voted to pay its women staff the same rate as the men, and to pay equivalent increases in jobs done solely by women. In 1953, all local authorities concluded a national agreement with the unions to pay increases which would be applied equally to both sexes, as the first step towards ending pay discrimination completely. In the same year there was an upsurge in Parliamentary activity: Conservative M.P. Irene Ward led an all-woman all-party lobby, with an equal pay petition, which was followed by another petition (with 600,000 signatures) organized by the civil service and teaching unions. Labour M.P. Douglas Houghton introduced the first of what was to become an erratic succession of private members' attempts to promote equal rights bills in the next twenty years. There was sufficient public sympathy for the principle to force Imperial Tobacco to abandon its proposal, also in 1953, to revert to a marriage bar in its Wills factories when it met with hostile criticism in the press. All this agitation bore fruit in the following year: the Government finally agreed to begin implementing the equal pay proposals in the civil service (though these were not completed until 1961), and the education authorities followed suit. The N.C.C.L., while celebrating 'a great victory in a campaign that has had to be waged over many decades', regretted that retirement pensions for women would still be lower than for men until 1961. But far more regrettable was the apparent achievement of the disruptive objective alleged against the original report in 1946, the splitting off of middle-class women from their working-class sisters. The energies of the equal pay campaigners were exhausted by their success, and the battle for the rights of industrial working women was not joined again seriously for another fifteen years. Once the middle-class unions in the civil service, local government, teaching and banks* had won their victory for their large women's memberships, there was no sufficiently powerful or organized group left to continue the fight. Certainly the male-dominated manual unions showed no comparable interest in struggling for their unorganized sisters.

For the rest of the 1950s, the N.C.C.L. continued spasmodically to oppose sexual discrimination on lesser fronts. Though the British Nationality Act of 1948 had improved the status of women to some extent, it remained basically true that women who married foreigners lost many of their rights. In 1954, the N.C.C.L. successfully represented several couples (American husbands, British wives) who were having difficulty in settling permanently in Britain. Although the Aliens Department of the Home Office admitted that, normally, British wives would not be forced to leave the country, colonial women did not enjoy the same consideration. A Gibraltarian who had lived for years in Britain was not allowed a permit for her Spanish husband when she married in 1955, despite N.C.C.L. intercession. In education, the reactionary attitudes towards women students were a long time dying. In 1956, Oxford University finally abandoned its quota system limiting women undergraduates to less than a quarter of the male total, but in the following year a London University survey found that in single-sex teacher training colleges women students suffered far greater restrictions than their male contemporaries elsewhere, particularly in forming and running political organizations. Despite an appeal from the N.C.C.L., the Minister of Education was content to allow the internal affairs of the colleges to be left to them, even when clear sex discrimination was evident.

In 1961, the N.C.C.L. remembered that the British Government had still not ratified the I.L.O. convention on equal pay, and

---

*The banks continued to lag behind the other institutions, however. The N.C.C.L.'s 1965 survey found that the major banks only had equal pay scales until the age of 23: thereafter, differentials in favour of men were imposed.

observed that only in transport were industrial workers of both sexes paid the same rates. Two years later they sponsored a study of discrimination against women, which reported in 1965. They found that seven million women received lower pay than men doing the same or similar jobs: that educational inequality was prevalent at all levels: that the legal system for guardianship of children was inadequate and unfair to women, and that there were many large anomalies in the laws covering the rights of married women. In its evidence to the Royal Commission on Trade Unions in 1966, the N.C.C.L. repeated its call for ratification of the I.L.O. convention. The following year, it took up the particular cause of women postal workers. In 1967 a Midlands postwoman, Elsie Morris, was declared redundant after twenty-one years' service: she was offered either another job further away or part-time work at her present place, with a loss of pension. Mrs Morris had been employed all those years on a 'temporary' basis: inquiries showed that 450 women were working on a similar basis, sixty of them doing men's jobs on night-shifts loading trains. All were vulnerable to the Post Office's pro-male bias which would dismiss a 'temporary' female to make room for a man. After a Parliamentary question from Labour M.P. Chris Rowland, the Government conceded that it would look into the possibility of recruiting women postal workers on the same terms as men.

From the late 1960s, the new women's liberation movement (growing in part out of the student unrest[2]) attacked discrimination on a total basis – some making a critique of capitalist society even more trenchant than that of orthodox male Marxists – and this was reflected in increased agitation on a whole range of issues. Pubs excluding women from some bars were the sites of demonstrations and sit-ins, usually unsuccessful; but abortions were legalized, married women's rights to family property were strengthened, they secured equal claims to guardianship, and were no longer forced to adopt a foreign husband's country of residence. In Parliament, the Labour Government at last passed an Equal Pay Act covering industry in 1970, though it was not due to come into effect until 1975, and there were strong suspicions that employers would find it easy to evade its provisions.[2a]

From 1967, a series of anti-discrimination bills were promoted by back-benchers every year (Labour M.P. Joyce Butler sponsoring the first). In 1972 Lady Seear's bill in the Lords and, in 1973, William Hamilton's bill in the Commons both received second readings, whereupon the Government took up the issue and published its own bill late in 1973. This covered discrimination in employment, but not education – as the backbench bills had done. Nor, unlike the Race Relations Acts, did it attack discrimination in housing (women found it harder than men to get mortgages, for instance), goods, facilities and services (where H.P. companies and TV rental firms often discriminated against women). The N.C.C.L., which had recently returned to its traditional interest in the women's rights issue, criticized even the employment provisions for leaving too many loopholes, failing to cover pensions, and withdrawing the protective regulations governing women's work. They also attacked the failure to set up an effective enforcement agency: the N.C.C.L. suggested an Equal Opportunities Commission similar to the Race Relations Board, but better equipped to take legal action. Most of these points were picked up by the new Labour Government in 1974.

Though the legislation after 1967 was undoubtedly a useful advance, the best guarantee of future equality was the radical change in the consciousness that accompanied it, and the greater readiness of women to organize themselves.

Northern Ireland Catholics

From their own point of view, the Catholics of Northern Ireland are not a minority group at all: they belong to the natural Irish majority group, but have been cut off from their fellow-countrymen by the power of British imperialism. *De facto*, however, they are a minority; indeed, between 1922 and 1969, one of the most effectively subjugated minorities in the world. Civil liberty as the British understand it has never existed in Northern Ireland. One of the many inconsistencies in the political philosophy of the Protestant governments of Northern Ireland had been their need to wipe out most of the content of British civil liberty in order to maintain their own Britishness. On their side, the British, whatever their public protestations to the contrary, have implicitly accepted the non-British character of the province by tolerating injustice there on a scale that would (hopefully) be unthinkable in Britain itself. The attempts of civil libertarians in England to make the constitutional connection work in the interests of the oppressed Catholics have inevitably been therefore limited.

After 1971, internment dramatized the absence of basic rights in Ulster, but even before its re-introduction that year the state of civil liberty in the province was generally enfeebled. Freedom of association – a freedom so basic, and, in Britain, so entrenched that there has hitherto been no need to discuss it in this book – was severely restricted. Civil servants could not join trade unions, and any association could be declared (and several were) 'unlawful'. Marches and demonstrations were more strictly regulated than in Britain. The Royal Ulster Constabulary had the power to arrest without warrant and detain for up to forty-eight hours without any 'reasonable grounds' for such actions. The writ of *habeas corpus* did not run, and the police had a general power to stop and search without warrant. There were powers to impose a curfew, to flog, to deny trial by jury, to forcibly secure witnesses, to refuse those imprisoned without trial access to friends or lawyers, to compel the giving of fingerprints and photographs without court authority, and to ban inquests after a prisoner's death. Free speech did not escape restrictions. It was an arrestable offence to spread 'false reports'; newspapers could be banned, along with films and records. Just in case this panoply of repression was not enough, the authorities gave themselves *carte blanche* to arrest anyone doing anything prejudicial to peace and order which had somehow escaped punishment under the other specific provisions.[3]

All this was considered necessary because roughly a third of the population of Northern Ireland were citizens not by consent but by force. The Protestant governments between 1920 and 1970 were happy to keep it that way. Far from trying to integrate the Catholic minority into the state, they practised, and permitted others to practise, widespread discrimination against them in politics, housing and employment. Areas where the Catholics formed a local majority, such as Londonderry*, were kept safe for the Protestant supremacy by political gerrymandering. Businessmen – largely Protestant – were given extra votes (a practice abolished in Britain in 1948) while sub-tenants, lodgers and certain other classes – largely Catholic – had no votes at all. The Protestants were politically organized into the monolithic Unionist Party (affiliated to the British Conservatives) and used their total political power to keep local authority jobs for their own people. In Londonderry in 1966, 145 of the 177 salaried employees were Protestants.[4] More important, the local councils could discriminate in housing: proportionately more Protestants were given council homes, Protestants got better houses for the same rents as Catholics, and Catholics were herded into ghettoes.

Yet discrimination on the grounds of religion was illegal. The Government of Ireland Act of 1920, which created the Northern Irish state-within-a-state, specifically forbade it.[5] From the mid-1960s, the civil rights movement in Ulster made some attempts to use the law to combat discrimination, but unfortunately the effort was not sufficiently sustained, nor the results sufficiently encouraging, to do much to mitigate the gravity of the civil war that broke out in 1969. Discrimination inevitably lessened after the British Government became directly involved in running Northern Ireland that year. The franchise was reformed, the bounaries revised and, late in 1973, the Catholics temporarily achieved real power when several Social Democratic and Labour Party members of the new assembly were given ministerial posts in the Coalition Government. The allocation of housing was taken away from local authorities in 1971 and given to a central executive. Discrimination in public service jobs decreased, but private employers inevitably proved more subborn.

Against this the police state – after 1969, a state under military occupation – had grown more repressive. The draconian measures available under the Special Powers Act (abolished and immediately renewed under the Northern Ireland (Emergency Provisions) Act

*In 1966, the city had 14,000 Catholic voters and 9,000 Protestants, but there were only eight Catholic Councillors to twelve Protestants, thanks to carefully drawn ward boundaries.[6]

of 1973) were used on a greater scale than ever before as the authorities struggled with one of this century's most persistent urban guerrilla uprisings. By 1974, with over 1,000 people killed in five years of civil war, the Government seemed less likely than ever to give up these emergency powers: but it was their previous existence through many years of peace that had been the greatest affront to liberty and, arguably, one of the major causes of the emergency itself.

The Special Powers Act was first passed by the Ulster legislature in 1922, when the I.R.A. was still fighting north and south to preserve the republican ideal of a united Ireland in the face of Lloyd George's compromise solution. It was renewed every year until 1933, when the pretence that it was only temporary emergency legislation was dropped, and the Unionists fashioned it into a permanent pillar of their supremacist state. The crucial objection to these sweeping arbitrary powers was first put by the N.C.C.L. (for thirty years almost the only British political organization to undertake a sustained opposition to the oppression in Ulster) in 1936: ordinary criminal law, together with genuinely temporary emergency powers, would cope satisfactorily with the conditions in Northern Ireland. Clearly, the continued existence of the I.R.A., with its refusal to enter the normal arena of political bargaining and its periodic resort to terrorism and guerrilla warfare, would have posed unusually awkward problems even for a genuinely democratic government; but the Unionists were more like dictators than democrats. 'The provisions of the 1922 Act,' wrote Ronald Kidd, 'went far beyond anything which could be justified under any democratic government, even in the most serious civil disturbances.'[7]

In 1935, there was serious rioting in Belfast. In the wake of the intensified repression that followed, the N.C.C.L. set up a Commission of Inquiry of impeccable legal authority – it included two K.C.s – on the pattern of the Reichstag Fire Inquiry three years earlier.* The Commission's report in 1936 laid bare the quasi-dictatorial nature of the Special Powers Act

---

*Its secretary was Neil Lawson, a Left-wing lawyer and member of the N.C.C.L., who had been secretary to the Reichstag venture. Many years later he became a Law Commissioner and High Court judge.

(the Stormont legislature could not, for instance, upset any ministerial regulation made under the act), but, although it received considerable publicity in Britain, the traditional reluctance of the British to grapple with any Irish problem unless literally forced to was reinforced that year by the greater concern with the threat posed by international Fascism. Those on the Left who should naturally have taken up a campaign to repeal the act were too deeply involved elsewhere. Even the Commission's exposure of the use of the emergency powers against people engaged in normal political activity, with no connection with terrorists whatsoever, failed to generate any long-lasting concern.

A more limited civil liberty exercise was undertaken four years later, during the round-up of Republicans after the I.R.A. campaign of 1939. Early in 1940, men imprisoned without trial in Londonderry gaol rioted in protest at their detention. Pinned in a cell on the upper landing, they tried to surrender, but were hosed repeatedly and badly beaten. The N.C.C.L. asked for a public inquiry, but this was refused. In the next few months systematic raids on Republican sympathizers (and even on ordinary Labour activists) resulted in some outrageous punishments. A 17-year-old Belfast boy was imprisoned for eighteen months for possessing a Republican bulletin on prison conditions, and two Londonderry women were each gaoled for three months for possessing a Republican (but anti-terrorist) paper. On 18 March eight men were charged under the *carte blanche* section of the Special Powers Act with agreeing to publish a newspaper advertisement in a Londonderry paper condemning the showing of British newsreels in the city's cinemas. Even in Northern Ireland, however, the courts felt this was absurd, and the charges were dismissed. Commenting on all this the N.C.C.L. warned, thirty years before it was to come disastrously true, that ' by their repressive tactics the Northern Ireland government is driving perfectly constitutional Rebublicans into the terrorist camp'. It was not just the Republicans who suffered: a Marxist weekly was banned, and in October 1940 two leading Communist trade unionists, William McCullough of the N.U.R. and Betty Sinclair, the Linen Workers' representative on the Irish Congress of Trade Unions, were sentenced to two and one years' imprisonment respectively (reduced considerably on appeal) for their part in the running of a Communist paper, the *Red Hand*, which had published an article by an I.R.A. sympathizer discussing the use of German help to end the partition in Ireland. The editors had indicated strong disagreement with the article, and the writer himself was not arrested; but the paper was banned for the rest of the year.

After the war there appeared some chance that the obnoxious special powers would be abandoned. In 1949 most of the regulations were revoked, including those permitting arrest without warrant, those permitting curfews, and, most important of all, those allowing internment. But the N.C.C.L. warned that these regulations (and any number of new ones) could be re-introduced 'at the stroke of the pen', and argued that the act needed repealing entirely. However, liberals now felt able to take some initiatives. The apparatus of discrimination came under attack after a farcical election result in 1952. A Unionist won a seat by a majority of four; it was then discovered that the number of votes cast exceeded the total electorate by two, and that at least two people were known not to have voted. Despite strong hostile criticism, the Stormont Government refused an inquiry; but in the same year they were forced to modify a clause in their Summary Jurisdiction Act which would have seriously limited the right of the press to report court proceedings.

This faint liberal dawn was short-lived: in 1953, the Unionists passed the Flags and Emblems Act enabling the police to ban the display of flags. Within a year an attempt to fly the Irish tricolour in Pomeroy, and the police attempt to prevent it, led to a riot. Much more seriously, the I.R.A. opened another campaign of violence in 1956, and the authorities responded by re-introducing all the repressive powers they had given up seven years earlier. By 1958, some 200 men had been interned[8]: thereafter the I.R.A. raids, never seriously threatening, tailed off, and internment ended in 1961. This time the Stormont Home Ministry showed no intention of taking their emergency powers off the books.

In many ways, the 1956–8 I.R.A. campaign bore little relation to the fighting of the early 1970s: it was largely conducted through border raids in rural areas, rather than the urban terrorism launched from safe Catholic ghettoes inside the two major cities of the later campaign. But in one respect there was a fore-taste of the more ferocious future; the physical ill-treatment of Republican prisoners. There were allegations that statements had been obtained after physical brutality, and in 1958 the N.C.C.L. sent an observer to the trial of two men accused of murder, Kevin Mallon and Francis Talbot, who were supposed to have been interrogated in this way. Though Mallon and Talbot were acquitted, they were immediately interned under the Special Powers Act. As a result of this and similar cases the N.C.C.L. asked Home Secretary Butler to include the R.U.C. in the terms of reference of the 1959 Royal Commission on the Police, but Butler refused on the traditional ground that 'responsibility for such matters rests with the Northern Ireland Government'.

After the failure of the I.R.A. campaign, the leaders of the Catholic community made a serious effort to achieve peaceful political and social reforms. The refusal of the Stormont Government to meet their legitimate demands, and the failure of the Labour Government at Westminster to put real pressure on Stormont until too late, were the twin causes of the subsequent disaster. Throughout these years in the 1960s, the N.C.C.L. worked hard to assist the growth of the Ulster civil rights move-ment, and to influence British politicians on their behalf. Perhaps unfortunately, they were the more successful in their first objective: without adequate support from Westminster, the civil rights movement could only match the stubbornness of the Ulster authorities with increased aggression on their own part.

An autonomous Council for Civil Liberties, based on the London model, was set up in 1959, but proved short-lived. A more substantial advance came in 1964, when a middle-class Catholic couple, the McCluskeys, founded the Campaign for Social Justice, a pressure group to oppose discrimination.[9] At the same time a delegation of non-Unionist (and therefore largely Catholic) Stormont M.P.s went to Westminster to win attention for the minority's grievances. True to the Commons' lackadaisical tradition on Ulster matters, only the Liberal leader, Grimond, received them. After these initiatives, the N.C.C.L. organized a London conference (chaired by Liberal M.P. Eric

Lubbock) early in 1965, which achieved a historic breakthrough. For the first time, representatives from all the Stormont parties agreed to discuss the problem of discrimination. The majority of those attending felt that the Westminster government had the ultimate responsibility for what was happening in Northern Ireland, and should exercise it. In particular, the failure to apply the new Race Relations Act to Ulster was seen by the non-Unionists as an evasion of the crucial problem.* The conference's call for a Royal Commission to look into all forms of discrimination – political gerrymandering as well as housing and employment – was fobbed off by the Home Office with the irrelevant point that the coming revision of Parliamentary constituency boundaries would include the Ulster seats. These of course had nothing to do with the Stormont and local election boundaries through which the crucial rigging was done. In the same year, an N.C.C.L. complaint about R.U.C. behaviour led, to the surprise of many liberals, to a lengthy investigation, which the N.C.C.L. compared to the Challenor Inquiry in London. It was moved to comment, unhappily not quite accurately, that 'the Ulster constabulary will never be the same again'.

While the British Parliament was passing up the chance to bring about peaceful reform, the Ulster courts were showing a caution which convinced the reformers they would gain little by straightforward legal action. In 1966, the Campaign for Social Justice tried to bring a case against Dungannon Council for discrimination in their housing allocations. Their application for legal aid (which had just been made available in Northern Ireland, seventeen years after the rest of Britain had obtained it) was turned down, a rejection which the N.C.C.L. understandably saw as 'a new form of discrimination, designed to prevent a frontal attack on the power to discriminate'. And the C.S.J. itself decided there was therefore no future in redress through the courts. In 1967, the Republican Clubs were declared 'unlawful associations' under the Special Powers regulations.

*Like the M.P.s, the British press missed this opportunity to alert the public while there was still a chance for peaceful change: many papers sent reporters to cover the conference, but none felt it was worth publishing anything.

Little was done to enforce the powers against the clubs, and the designation was regarded as simply a political gesture, but in 1968 a test case was brought, which for the second time offered the chance of winning a basic reform through the working of the law. A Slaughtneil Republican called McEldowney was prosecuted under the new regulation. The magistrates dismissed the charge, on the grounds the club did not constitute a threat to peace and order, but this was reversed on appeal by the Northern Ireland Appeal Court, which decided that the Home Minister had the power on his own to decide if an association was unlawful. The case went to the Lords, which by a 3–2 majority supported the appeal decision. It was another unfortunate example of the ultimate London power failing to help the Catholic reformers.

In the meantime, the situation on the streets had deteriorated. The ultra-Protestant followers of Ian Paisley rioted in June 1966, and a few weeks later Protestant gunmen murdered a Catholic barman. Both showed how the extremists were convinced the Catholics were getting too assertive.[10] At last the British Parliament and press began to show an interest. In response to this, the Ulster Premier, the liberally-inclined Terence O'Neill, offered reforms – the abolition of the University seats and of the business vote in Stormont elections. It was, of course, nowhere near enough.

The reformers then took a crucial step. On 29 January 1967, in Belfast, eighty delegates from a variety of organizations, including Smythe of the N.C.C.L. and representatives from two N.C.C.L. affiliates, the C.S.J. and the Belfast Trades Council*, founded the Northern Ireland Civil Rights Association. (The new organization immediately affiliated itself to the N.C.C.L.) The movement's first objective was to concentrate on electoral and judicial reform, and much of their early efforts went into individual casework. In June 1968, N.I.C.R.A. organized its first protest march, from Coalisland to Dungannon, to challenge the eviction of a Catholic family from a council house so that it could be taken over by the 19-year-old secretary of a Unionist politician.[11] Such an elementary demonstration of democratic

---

*The latter's representative was veteran Communist Betty Sinclair, gaoled in 1940.

grievances in a just cause was too much for the Protestant supremacists. Thereafter, the situation moved inexorably to civil war. The civil rights movement refused to be cowed by the violence of the police or the Protestant bully boys; the 'liberal' Unionists could neither satisfy the reformers nor their own followers, and were consistently outflanked from the Right; while the Labour Government just as consistently did too little too late. The British Army was sent in, August 1969 to prevent a pogrom of Catholics in the vulnerable Belfast ghettoes;[11a] the I.R.A., long defunct, began to revive in the face of military short-sightedness and political ineptitude, to the point where they were fighting an urban guerrilla campaign of such tenacity that the despised dictatorial powers of internment were again found necessary (in August 1971): eventually the logic of the situation, so long resisted, became irresistible, and in 1972 Westminster finally abandoned the 50-year-old policy of non-intervention and imposed direct rule.

For the N.C.C.L., the success of N.I.C.R.A. as a mass movement reduced the need for direct involvement, and for the first three years of the struggle (1968–71) the London organization restricted itself to a supporting role in the Westminster lobbies. In September 1969, it sponsored another London conference, bringing together the Ulster civil rights leaders and their British sympathizers, which called for the disbanding of the B–Specials (the para-military police reserve which was almost the armed wing of the Unionist Party) and for the reorganization of the R.U.C. In the following year, Smythe and Grant went as N.C.C.L. observers during the traditional July Orange parades, which passed off peacfully enough after the violence of June, though only because 17,000 troops and police were deployed through Belfast, and the Catholic areas were sealed off. From N.I.C.R.A. the N.C.C.L. learned that the lull in the violence during the previous year had not been exploited with sufficient urgency by the Stormont Government. Implementation of the reform programme was going slowly, and, after the return of the Conservatives in the June election, British troops had begun to adopt a tougher attitude in the Catholic areas. In particular, the July curfew and search of the Falls had created bitter resentment. It was subsequently clear that this had marked a turning point in Catholic attitudes towards the British Army.[12]

In the spring of 1971, the Provisionals intensified their bombing campaign, and, as the violence increased and the situation deteriorated, the N.C.C.L. had to re-think its strategy. In July 1971, after four days of rioting, British soldiers in Londonderry killed two men, Seamus Cusack and Desmond Beattie, in circumstances which infuriated the Catholics of the Bogside, who did not believe them to be gunmen. The S.D.L.P. demanded an independent public inquiry, which was refused. They then walked out of Stormont.[12a] The N.C.C.L., which had an executive member in Londonderry who was able to carry out his own enquiries, supported the S.D.L.P. demand on the grounds that only an official investigation would show the disillusioned Catholics that the Conservatives would listen to their grievances. A month later Faulkner, the Northern Ireland Premier, introduced internment without trial. Operating from inadequate intelligence lists, in one night the Army and the police lifted 342 people. For the N.C.C.L., this marked the final collapse of civil liberty in Ulster.

Just before Parliament debated the new measures in September, Smythe wrote to Edward Heath, pointing out that the civil liberty issue was at the heart of the Ulster crisis, and proposing a number of measures that would restore fundamental rights and at the same time remove the cause of the violence. Heath replied the following month, reiterating the Government's short-term tactics of trying to persuade the Catholics to join political talks, and evading the central civil rights questions.

The internment policy, disastrous enough in its own right, was made worse by the use of torture during the interrogation of the detainees. The allegations of ill-treatment made at the time were subsequently confirmed by the special inquiry undertaken by Sir Edmund Compton, the former Ombudsman.[12b] The Army's record before internment had not been particularly encouraging: accusations of physical brutality were not surprisingly frequent, but many were confirmed by independent medical reports.[13] But the sensory deprivation techniques (hooded detainees kept standing against the wall with a persistent 'white noise' in their

ears) adopted by Army and R.U.C. interrogators after internment were more subtle; and, in the long term, these were probably
even more damaging than simple brutality. The Irish Government took nearly 100 cases* of alleged torture by the British
authorities during the internment operation before the European
Commission for Human Rights in 1972 (and N.I.C.R.A.
later added several more individual petitions).

There was a second inquiry, under Lord Parker, the former
Lord Chief Justice, into the suitability of these interrogation
methods. In their evidence to the Parker committee early in
1972, the N.C.C.L. argued that these were in breach of U.N.
agreements, the Geneva convention and the European convention on human rights and that apart from all these international
codes they were of dubious legality under English common and
civil law. The Parker report justified the methods used after
internment because the information obtained saved innocent
lives; but a dissenting note by Lord Gardiner, the former Labour
Lord Chancellor, argued that the techniques were neither
morally justifiable nor indeed legal. To its credit, the Government accepted Gardiner's view and ordered the Army and the
police to stop using these methods.[13a] In 1974, one ex-internee
called Shivers, who had been subjected to 'in-depth interrogation'
in 1971 was awarded £15,000 out of court after he had brought an
action against the Northern Ireland Ministry of Home Affairs
and the Ministry of Defence.

Quite apart from these ethical and legal considerations,
however, the torture policy was disastrous in practical terms: it
hardened the support of the Catholic community for the Provisional I.R.A. This hostile attitude was scarcely lessened by the
events of 'Bloody Sunday', 30 January 1972. Thirteen unarmed
civilians on a civil rights demonstration in Londonderry were
shot and killed when the Army opened fire as the demonstrators
reached the edge of the Bogside.† Yet another inquiry had to be

---

*Much of the groundwork preparing these cases had been done by the
N.C.C.L.

†Smythe and other N.C.C.L. observers going to the demonstration were
deliberately detained by the security services; they arrived eight hours late,
and after the demonstration had been attacked.

set up, this time under Lord Chief Justice Widgery, though the Government was criticized by the International Commission of Jurists for not accepting an international inquiry, which they felt was the only way to win international acceptance for the investigation. The facts established by Widgery about the shooting did not exactly fit with the Lord Chief Justice's exoneration of the paratroopers involved. The N.C.C.L., which had put together 600 eye-witness statements in their evidence to the Inquiry, described Widgery's interpretation as 'judicial gymnastics'. The Council, in conjunction with the International League for the Rights of Man, commissioned American jurist Professor Sam Dash to analyse the tribunal's proceedings and the documentary evidence it used. His report came to radically different conclusions from Widgery's. Dash found that the Army command had, despite warnings from the Londonderry police, decided to run a high risk of civilian casualties in planning how to handle the demonstration. On the evidence considered by Widgery's tribunal, Dash concluded that the paratroopers had not been telling the truth, and that nail bombs had been planted on the victims to implicate them as I.R.A. activists; he rejected the forensic tests used to decide whether the dead men had handled guns or bombs. The Government refused to take any action on compensation claims by relatives of those killed.[14]

In the second stage of the civil war – that is, after mid-1971 – the N.C.C.L. revised its strategy. Thereafter, much greater use was made of the courts to challenge the intensified repression. The preparation of the torture cases for the European court was just one plank in this new approach; more importantly, the Northern Ireland courts were used to decide several crucial cases. There was, however, a limit to which the law could be employed, since the Army successfully avoided facing any legal action against individual soldiers on murder or manslaughter charges between 1969 and 1973. Even on lesser charges of assault, they faced very few.

The first step was to challenge the legality of the internment operations itself through *habeas corpus* applications. This ultimately failed when the House of Lords decided it had no jurisdiction in such matters as far as Ireland was concerned.

However, lesser tactical victories, particularly when incorrect arresting procedures had been used, were won in several cases in the Ulster courts, and some ex-detainees received compensation as a result. More important was the serious constitutional issue that grew out of this challenge. The Government of Ireland Act had specifically prohibited the Stormont assembly from passing legislation affecting British troops. The arrest of John Hume, the S.D.L.P. M.P., in the summer of 1971 by soldiers served as a test case when the civil rights movement decided to challenge the military powers under the Special Powers Act, which had of course been Stormont legislation. Hume's appeal against conviction was upheld by the Northern Ireland Appeal Court, which decided the British Army was not covered by the Act. (A point made thirty-six years earlier by the N.C.C.L.'s commission of inquiry.) Within twenty four hours the Westminster Parliament passed the Northern Ireland Act, legalizing all the previous illegal actions by the Army. Parliament's willingness to rubber-stamp the executive's shoddy manoeuvre on this occasion was perhaps the most serious example of the way Ulster's problems could corrupt mainland politics.

In Ulster itself, the courts began to win a new respect from the Catholic community in the way they handled lesser cases against the security forces, though the long delays, particularly in civil actions, often reduced the political value of this new attitude. Two areas of court discretion (the granting of bail and legal aid) which in England had often been unjustly exercised in political cases, oddly enough worked much more fairly in Northern Ireland. A Cobden Trust survey in 1973 found that although the police were more likely to oppose bail for Catholics than Protestants on political charges (they had some justification for this), the courts redressed the balance to some extent by a willingness to overrule police objections. As for legal aid, it was granted far more frequently than in England. Overall the Trust report found 'a small but cumulative measure of (perhaps unconscious) sympathy for Protestants or Loyalists' in the decision to prosecute, selection of charges and jury verdicts: on the other hand, the judges 'appear to have gone some way to correct the inequalities through their power to direct acquittals'.

The direct involvement of the British in Ulster after 1969 inevitably meant that the institutions of Northern Ireland would increasingly come to conform with British standards of justice, and that discrimination against the Catholics would decrease. The unresolved question, and one which intensified the paranoia of the Left, was to what extent British institutions, in particular the Army and the security forces but to some extent also Parliament and the media, had been corrupted by Northern Irish standards; to what extent the counter-guerrilla philosophies of soldiers like Brigadier Kitson, which required considerable military supervision of civilian life, might have become part of permanent government thinking in Britain itself. The long-term damage to British civil liberty from the British neglect of the oppressed Catholics of Ulster for half-a-century was literally incalculable.

Gipsies

Most ethnic or religious minorities can usually rely on the support of an outside group or country where their fellows form a majority. In the United Kingdom, the black immigrants and the Ulster Catholics could turn to their home countries or the neighbouring Irish Republic. The Jews and the gipsies of Europe suffered the near-fatal distinction of existing only as a diaspora of minorities, at least until the establishment of Israel for the Jews. But even before that the Jews had at least the advantage of living in settled and energetic communities, building power bases through their contributions to their host country's economy or culture. And with a few notorious exceptions this proved enough to protect them until liberal tolerance became a generally accepted public virtue. The gipsies, continually on the move and usually illiterate, did not even have this support – though unlike the Jews they could never be mythicized into an economic threat to the natives.

As a result, in Britain the gipsy community (estimated at about 15,000 in England and Wales in the late 1960s) did not begin to articulate their grievances until very recently, even though their history of repression and discrimination equals that of any other alien group in Britain. (They are the only group to have faced the death penalty for being a group.) The first time Parliament heard their cause sympathetically argued was in 1950, when Labour M.P. Norman Dodds spotlighted the perennial hounding of gipsies by local authorities anxious to see them move out of their particular areas. As a result of Dodds' long solitary campaign, the Government eventually, in 1962, asked the local authorities to carry out surveys of the gipsy population so that their needs could be properly assessed. (Some councils seem to have deliberately underestimated the numbers so as to reduce their own potential liability for providing sites.)

But by that time the gipsies themselves had at last begun to fight back. In 1965, there was an important legal battle. In a nasty bureaucratic manouevre, Bromley Council had evicted a group of gipsies from a tip and towed their caravans to the Orpington by-pass, where the police then prosecuted them for camping on the highway. The N.C.C.L. was asked for its help, and it advised the gipsies to appeal: since the Highways Act of 1959 specifically forbade gipsies from camping on the road, the prosecution would have to prove, so the N.C.C.L. argued, that the accused – a gipsy called George Bignall – was a gipsy and was therefore camping without lawful authority. On appeal, Bignall's counsel showed that no attempt had been made to prove he was a gipsy (a gipsy being defined in the dictionary as 'a nomad of Indian origin'), nor even that he was nomadic. Bignall won the appeal.

This soon had useful results. The Sussex police, for instance, warned Sevenoaks Council (in Kent) that towing gipsy caravans from their area over the border into Sussex left the council open to prosecution. But the value was largely lost in 1967 when the House of Lords ruled in another case that 'gipsy' need only mean someone leading a nomadic way of life. To avoid such chance semantic games with the law, the gipsies had already begun to seek surer statutory protection. The Gipsy Council was set up that year (and affiliated itself to the N.C.C.L.); on the other side, local authorities stepped up their efforts to force gipsies from their particular territories as they saw the increasing likelihood of legislation which would compel them to provide permanent sites. The methods used were not gentle. In 1968, four evictions were handled so roughly that there were official investigations into the police concerned. Even worse was the resort to strong-arm men hired from private detective agencies. Some councils were thwarted when their own employees, often members of N.U.P.E., refused to do such dirty work. When evictions did take place, the gipsies increasingly turned to well-publicized non-violent resistance.

The N.C.C.L. managed to negotiate with a few enlightened councils to arrange satisfactory solutions in their areas, and at the national level they won the support of Housing Minister Anthony Greenwood. With this support, Liberal Eric Lubbock was able in 1968 to sponsor the passage of the Caravan Sites Act. (Lubbock was M.P. for Orpington, a constituency with a sizeable gipsy population as gipsy populations went, but scarcely large in voting terms – if they had votes at all.) This act required the local authorities to provide permanent sites and facilities for those gipsies who 'normally' lived in their area. Unfortunately, the date for implementing the act was left to the discretion of the Housing Minister, who, for economic reasons, deferred it until 1970. The delay naturally encouraged several authorities to get rid of as many 'normal' residents as they could and so reduce the number of sites they would have to provide. In the intervening two years the absurd situation developed where councils were spending up to £10,000 to force evictions, more than it would have cost to build a site.

During this two-year 'war', the gipsies won sympathetic national publicity when they defied the Epsom Downs conservators who wanted to restrict their traditional right to camp on the downs during Derby Week. Arriving in large numbers on the eve of the race, they threatened to dig trenches across the course if attempts were made to remove them. But although they could organize successfully round a national event like the Derby, the gipsies were less successful in winning public support in the more mundane fight against harassment by local councils.

This continued even after the 1970 implementation date. Only a few sites had been built by then, and some councils – notably

Walsall – openly and successfully defied the new law. The Ministry, relying on 'gentle persuasion', refused to take action against them. Recalcitrant councils were supported in at least eight parts of the country (mostly the Midlands and Wales) by groups of anti-gipsy local residents: the prejudice was understandable, though not laudable, in view of the conditions in which some gipsies chose to live. To combat this, local N.C.C.L. groups, particularly those in the West Midlands, Bedfordshire and the North-West (where an alliance of local government trade unionists was formed to refuse to implement evictions), carried out campaigns against authorities using force against the gipsies and trying to evade their statutory responsibilities to provide sites. Not that all local councils were as bad as Walsall: Redbridge in London not only built a site but set up a 'head start' scheme to educate pre-school gipsy children, while, even in the West Midlands, West Bromwich and Cannock responded decently to the demands made on them. Eventually even Walsall was forced into line late in 1971, after the N.C.C.L. threatened to start proceedings against them under the 1968 act. A local gipsy had with their help obtained the legal aid necessary to bring a case: Walsall chose to change its policy rather than fight a court action.

But overall the N.C.C.L. was disappointed with the impact of the act in its first few years of operation. They felt it failed both to improve in any radical way the conditions of the gipsies and to reduce the active discrimination against them. By the beginning of 1973, only 824 pitches had been provided. Another 2,469 were planned, but this was still well short of the total of 4,000 needed. And one feature of the act which the N.C.C.L. had criticized in the 1968 debates had begun to show its damaging potential. Councils that felt they had done their duty by the gipsies could apply to be 'designated', which meant no more gipsies could settle in their areas and that those not on sites could be prosecuted or removed. After the first batch of designations were made in 1972, there was increased harassment of gipsies in the designated areas by councils using their new powers to force the surplus population out of their territory. Some M.P.s felt that this brutal procedure would compel other local authorities, who received the new influx of refugees, to hasten their own site provision programme. The N.C.C.L. sarcastically attacked this point of view, asking if 'gipsies were to be forced to break the law in order to get county councils to comply with it'. They also found their other 1968 fears, about the power to fine gipsies unwilling or unable to accept sites offered them, was well-grounded. Some councils deliberately invented regulations for the sites which they knew the gipsies could not fulfil. The N.C.C.L. called the penalty 'a whip to scourge more effectively than at present those who do not conform'.

The N.C.C.L.'s campaign in 1972 against the designation orders was badly weakened by the refusal of any M.P.s from the appropriate areas to support the gipsy cause. Indeed, in the Commons only Labour M.P. Michael Meacher, and in the Lords Lord Avebury (formerly Liberal M.P. Eric Lubbock), made real efforts on their behalf: but their attempts to annul the orders were defeated. The Government did, however, recognize the N.C.C.L.'s point that even in the designated areas there were more gipsies than sites available, and it announced it was making more money available for local authorities to build extra sites: it also delayed making any more designation orders through 1973.

The history of the gipsy campaign after 1965 is a fascinating example of the limited extent to which legislation can help a civil rights cause. The easy initial publicity success, the liberal Parliamentary lobby, both leading to legislation: but equally the ease with which this liberalism from above could be thwarted when popular support for concrete action was lacking. The N.C.C.L. at least realized that as well as legal and Parliamentary action on behalf of the gipsies, there was a vital educational role to play in communities where hostility to the travellers made it too easy for local authorities to continue a policy of harassment. Like the black groups, the gipsies in the mid-1970s had won a certain statutory protection, but faced the longer and more difficult job of gaining popular acceptance.

Mental Institutions

One of the essential characteristics of institutional minorities
(in Britain, groups like prisoners, armed servicemen, the mentally
abnormal) is that they are subjected to oppressive conditions by
law, as opposed to being born into their particular oppression –
like women, Ulster Catholics, blacks or gipsies. Institutional
oppression is achieved by regulation, and is therefore much more
capable of technical or legal reform than ethnic oppression. On
the other hand, it is at least conceivable that women, the Catholics of Northern Ireland, gipsies and black immigrants in Britain
will one day have won for themselves the same human dignity
and civil rights as the rest of the population. It is far less likely
that British society will ever do without mental hospitals, prisons
or armed forces, and the various restrictions on ordinary human
rights that go with them.

The awareness of the civil liberty issues raised by the existence
of these institutional minorities came relatively late, and then
almost by accident. In 1947 the N.C.C.L. received information
that a woman was detained in a mental ward even though she
had not been certified. It began *habeas corpus* proceedings,
and the woman was promptly released. Their curiosity aroused,
the council began to inquire into the workings of the 'mental
deficiency' laws, and discovered an enclosed bureaucratic system
of injustice of almost Kafkaesque dimensions. At least 55,000
people were detained without any form of judicial or Parliamentary control, and many without any prospect of release.
Some had been held for over twenty years – more than a life
sentence for a convict. Their labour was exploited crudely: they
were forbidden any kind of sexual relations. Worst of all, many
were in no medical sense mentally deficient.

The Mental Deficiency Act, passed in 1913, created powers to
detain people 'in need of care and protection' indefinitely. Only
about fifteen per cent of those classifiable as mentally defective
were in fact detained in 1950. The yardsticks for detention were
poor family conditions, failure at school, and delinquency, moral
or criminal. For the mentally deficient, the crucial years were be-

tween 12 and 18. If consigned to the care of the Board of Control in that time, they stood a real chance of spending a lifetime in institutions, even though research had shown that many people who were in the defective category as adolescents grew out of it in their twenties. Young people could be detained on the order of a court, or on the evidence of two doctors (neither of whom need necessarily have had psychiatric training): if they were committed with the consent of their parents, their parents could not later change their minds and get them out again. The act wrote in safeguards against unnecessary detention, but these proved completely inadequate because the system was run by an autonomous Board of Control (staffed largely by Ministry of Health administrators but not responsible to the Minister) with quasi-judicial powers over individual liberty. The Board was impregnable against any Parliamentary supervision whatsoever. In the late 1940s, it was releasing 'defectives' at the rate of one per cent per year. From 1947 onwards, the N.C.C.L. fought a fierce battle against this monstrous bureaucratic creation, and eventually triumphed in its destruction.

After the 1947 case of the uncertified woman inmate, the N.C.C.L. began to discover other examples of people wrongly certified, unjustly classified as defective, and detained long after they had reached a palpably normal level of mental development. With this discovery came the problem of dealing with the Board of Control, a body which had committed the injustices in the first place and against whose decision there was no appeal to any independent tribunal.

In 1949 the N.C.C.L. found further complications: a faintly sinister misuse of cheap labour, and sexual prejudice against women inmates. One girl, who had been temporarily retarded by bombing experiences during the war, was certified by a J.P. who was also a company director of the organization running the institution where she was detained, and which was benefiting handsomely from her competent labour at the rate of a shilling a week. Her parents illegally took her home, where she showed herself perfectly well equipped to lead a normal life. Nonetheless police, acting under the institution's orders, came and took her from her bed in the middle of the night to return her to the defectives' home. After a great deal of local protest, the girl was released on licence: and after the N.C.C.L. had taken the case up, she was eventually discharged altogether.

In another case, a girl who had been originally detained at 16 because she had 'stayed out late with soldiers' during the First World War ('moral defectives' were a category all their own) was still detained thirty years later and working for 6d. a week. Twice she had been released on licence, and twice brought back: once because she wrote a note to a man, and the second time because a friend of hers had become pregnant This second revocation was justified on the grounds that 'we naturally did not want another disaster, and although May is 45 years of age she is not beyond the age of child-bearing'. The N.C.C.L. commented bitterly that it was presumably the Board's intention to detain May either until she died under institutional care or passed the child-bearing age without 'producing a disaster'.

The publicity generated by the N.C.C.L.'s exposure of these cases brought in 200 letters with other examples of injustice: wrongful certification (five out of six randomly chosen from this correspondence were found on inquiry not to be defective at all), parent's consent not obtained, widespread exploitation of cheap labour – even those on licence were being paid less than £2 a week. This last lent a particular reinforcement to the system, since the institutions and the charities which supported them had come to rely heavily on their own inexpensive work-force of intelligent 'defectives'. In 1951 the N.C.C.L. booklet *50,000 Outside the Law* won the support of the *Lancet* and even the Conservative *Glasgow Herald* for its exposure of what was wrong; under pressure some of the mental institutions adopted a few piecemeal reforms. But, as the N.C.C.L. told those attending a conference organized in the summer of that year to launch a campaign to reform the law, it was the 1913 act itself, which encouraged the misuse of inmates as cheap labour, which was most in need of reform. The newspapers naturally found the individual case histories supplied by the N.C.C.L. excellent campaign material, and the Ministry of Health became increasingly on the defensive, particularly when it was pointed out that the Assistant Secretary at the Ministry was also the Secretary of the Board of Control. By 1953, the pressure from M.P.s and the press had proved overwhelming, and in October the Government announced that a Royal Commission would look into all the mental health laws.

In its evidence to the Royal Commission in March 1955, the N.C.C.L. summarized its experience in handling over 400 cases since 1947, in many of which release had been obtained only after a long struggle. Its analysis of the damage done to civil liberty by the existing system was widely reported:

The deprivation of freedom on unsworn and unchallenged allegations deprives the individual of elementary safeguards and cannot be justified on grounds that the legislation is protective. The deprivation of education, and the exploitation of patient labour, challenges the claim that the interests of the patient are paramount. This situation has resulted in the detention for many years of men and women who would probably not have been held to be mentally deficient ... when the Act was passed or by standards acceptable to the general public at this moment. The judicial and administrative procedures are often farcical in their brevity and nominal character, and at times not even the legal requirements are carried out. The Board of Control ... refuses facilities to enable patients to exercise their legal rights, and fails to intervene even when its attention is drawn to a palpably illegal detention.

The illegalities were amply demonstrated within a few months of the N.C.C.L. giving this evidence, when the council took up the case of Kathleen Rutty. She had passed through a series of institutions since she had entered an orphanage at the age of three months. In a classic example of institutional indifference and confusion, she was transferred at 17 from a local authority hostel to a mental home under a 'place of safety' order without any examination by a magistrate, the supposedly vital safeguard which would prevent wrongful detention. Kathleen Rutty did not have that safeguard: she spent the next seven years illegally detained. In 1956 the N.C.C.L., which had earlier heard of the case through her brother, brought *habeas corpus* proceedings before the High Court. (The previous year, the threat of such an action had been sufficient to force the Board of Control to release another detainee.) Kathleen Rutty was ordered to be released by the court, on the grounds that her original detention order had no validity. Giving judgment, the Lord Chief Justice, Lord Goddard, was scathing about the readiness of psychiatrists to commit people whom no-one else would regard as anything but normal, and commented:

There are plenty of idle, naughty and mischievous children and young persons who are not mental defectives within the meaning of the Act ... it is of first importance that the judicial authority should not think he is merely to act as a rubber stamp ... persons of whatever age are not intended to be deprived of their liberty and confined to an institution merely because doctors and officials think it would be good for them.

The majesty of the law had at last bestirred itself to stand up for the liberty of the subject and put the bureaucrats in their place.

The first result of this decision was that the Ministry of Health ordered that people out on licence (as Kathleen Rutty had been) should be completely discharged after one year.* The second was that another batch of cases – about 350 altogether – arrived in the N.C.C.L.'s letter box because of the publicity the Rutty case had received. The third was a Parliamentary campaign: the Government was forced to admit that there were nearly 6,000 people in the Rutty category who were clearly detained in illegal circumstances.

One of them was Peter Whitehead. Like Kathleen Rutty, he had spent his life since infancy being passed from one institution to another, eventually being transferred with similar indifference (and illegality) to Rampton at 18. After action on his behalf, including the start of a High Court case, by the N.C.C.L. and Labour M.P. Tom Williams, in which the inaccuracy and illegality of Whitehead's detention documents were evident, he was released. Not fancying a succession of such cases clogging up the courts, the Government released 800 people late in 1957, though this still left over 4,000 detained. 'Never before,' wrote the N.C.C.L., 'has the liberty of the subject been so lightly regarded: never before has so little been done by the Minister

---

*This was still occasionally ignored. In 1957, the N.C.C.L. protested over a case where a woman had been out on licence for eleven years without being discharged.

concerned when the facts have been publicized to remedy the injustice.' In 1958, another 1,000 were freed by the Government.

Throughout all these legal excitements the Royal Commission had been taking and digesting evidence (and incidentally providing the Ministry of Health with an excuse not to change even simple regulations – like those prohibiting sexual attachments – while it was doing so): it finally reported in May 1957. It completely vindicated the N.C.C.L.'s argument that people had been put away far too readily. The Commission was also highly critical of the practice of censoring patients' correspondence, of long licence periods, and of the ban on sexual association. It recommended a system of voluntary entry for defectives similar to that already existing for the mentally ill. However, one proposal brought sharp criticism from the N.C.C.L.: that two doctors alone would be enough to secure committal, without any examination by a magistrate. Instead of what the N.C.C.L. called an inadequate safeguard being strengthened, it would be abolished and not replaced at all.

After considering this and other comments, the Government finally published its Mental Health Bill on 5 January 1959. It was a major advance: the old 1913 act was repealed, and the Board of Control abolished. Voluntary admission was made possible: the concept of deficiency was re-defined as 'subnormality', and the old 'moral defective' category (which had seen teenage girls confined to care for thirty years after one sexual escapade) wiped out. More important, the subnormal had to be released at 25 unless they were recorded as dangerous. And although the Government accepted the idea of compulsory detention without examination by a magistrate, it set up a review tribunal to which appeals against detention could be taken.* The nastiest section of the bill was the part legalizing retrospectively in one go all the remaining 3,000 detentions of the Rutty type. In its passage through Parliament the N.C.C.L., through its M.P. supporters (particularly Dr Donald Johnson and Norman Dodds), managed to secure one important amendment: the review tribunals would have at least one lay member and patients would have the right to be repres-

*In Scotland, which had its own act in 1960, admissions had to be approved by a Sheriff, but there was no review tribunal.

tented by other people at the hearings. The act became law in the summer of 1959.

The legislation was one of the most impressive of the N.C.C.L.'s achievements. From its accidental discovery of the injustice in 1947, the N.C.C.L. had masterminded the campaign for reform of the law and had handled nearly a thousand individual cases, creating legal history as it did so. It had been handsomely supported in this by most of the press, though not, oddly enough, by the B.B.C. The campaign had also brought about a major change in the attitudes of those running the institutions themselves. As Frank Haskell, the N.C.C.L.'s assistant secretary who had almost single-handed run its mental health section since 1947, told a conference early in 1959: since the campaign, allegations of ill-treatment, once common, had almost stopped: solitary confinement was now rare: and the seizure of girls trying to get married even rarer.*

In the first year of the new act, many of those held under the old law were either discharged or transferred to voluntary status. There was a period of grace in 1960–61, during which those not released could appeal to the new tribunal: with N.C.C.L. help, many did, and generally cases where release was appropriate were won. Over the next few years, the N.C.C.L. built up a 100-strong team of volunteers prepared to act for patients at tribunal hearings throughout the country. Five years after the act came into force fully, nearly half the cases taken before the tribunal with N.C.C.L. help had been won.

Although mental institutions would always present problems – after all, between 1968 and 1973 there were seven separate inquiries into conditions in various hospitals, and prosecutions of some of the nursing staff – by the end of the decade the issue was no longer one of liberty but of treatment. Inmates could be compulsorily given drugs, electric shocks and psycho-surgery, without any judicial check. Another trend which worried the N.C.C.L. was the increasing use of the special hospitals, like Broadmoor and Rampton, to take difficult non-criminal patients.

*A sad irony of this campaign was that Haskell, who had worn himself out conducting it, died within a few weeks of the publication of the bill.

In 1973, the N.C.C.L. brought its criticisms together in its evidence to the Butler Committee on the Mentally Abnormal Offender. It was concerned about apparent police misuse of detention procedures: lack of legal aid for those appearing before the appeal tribunals: the Home Secretary's discretionary power to ignore tribunal recommendations: and the excessive power of doctors to treat patients in any way they chose. The fantasy of the treatment in *The Clockwork Orange* was unfortunately based on unpleasant reality.

Boy Soldiers

As with the mental institutions, the armed services created a peculiar kind of injustice by trapping people when they were young and not as well protected as adults. The N.C.C.L.'s campaign to reform the recruitment and conditions of servicemen was shorter than the long-drawn battle over mental health, but not quite as successful, even though the basic injustice was removed.

Increasingly in this century, the armed forces have required a substantial number of skilled technicians. Unlike many other Western countries, the British met this demand by recruiting boys who had just left school and imposing on them irrevocable long-term contracts*. In this way they hoped to train them in the various skills needed, and ensure that the cost of this expensive training was recouped by a guaranteed period of service. The young recruits could not, after their first six months, win a release from their twelve- or fifteen-year term except in rare circumstances. The world-view of a 15-year-old does not remain unchanged: inevitably many of these teenage recruits, as they grew up and changed their attitudes, felt they had been committed to what was the equivalent of a long prison sentence.

This policy ran into trouble even while national service conscription was providing the bulk of military manpower, since too

*The Canadians for instance required only five-year contracts: thereafter any renewal on a career basis could be terminated on six months' notice.

few conscripts stayed on to provide the skilled technicians
needed. In 1951, there was a mass breakout of dissatisfied boy
soldiers from the R.A.S.C. camp at Aldershot. The N.C.C.L.
was alerted to what was described as an issue affecting 'the
civil liberty of the youth of this country'. In their admitted naivety, the N.C.C.L. had felt it 'impossible that an undertaking
given at 14 or 15 should be legally enforceable, and that a boy
should pledge twelve years of his life'. Correspondence on a
particular case with the War Office soon enlightened them. They
discovered that even the right to purchase one's discharge had
been suspended because of wartime emergencies.

The N.C.C.L. did not pursue the issue at the time because
Parliament had shown itself unusually sensitive to the young
recruits' grievances. In 1952, a select committee delivered a
penetrating analysis of the problems, and recommended that the
length of the contract should be considerably shortened, and
that boy recruits should be given the chance to revise their conditions or obtain complete discharge at 18. In their evidence to the
committee the service ministries had shown some willingness to
alter the period of liability; but after the select committee had
reported, the Army and Air Force Councils did a complete about
turn and refused to drop the twelve-year contract at all. To mol-
lify the Parliamentarians, they offered to restore the right to
buy one's way out, which had been suspended since the Second
World War. Even Labour M.P.s were prepared to accept this as
a reasonable alternative to the committee's proposals. Michael
Stewart, the future Foreign Secretary, felt that the offer disposed
of the objection to long-term engagements. But the M.P.s had
been outmanoeuvred. The so-called right turned out in practice
to be a privilege accorded at the discretion of the military
authorities, and one, in the case of very skilled men, that was
extremely expensive.

The tragic implications of this political failure were not to be
seen in their full nastiness for another ten years, partly because
the problem was still relatively small in the 1950s. With the end
of conscription in 1958, however, a second disastrous decision
was taken. The Grigg Committee, set up to consider recruitment
policy, badly misjudged population and education trends in the

1960s.* It suggested that the Army in particular should expect to get between a third and a half of its total recruits from the 15–18 age bracket on long term contracts. Quite apart from the cool way this brushed aside the ethical problems arising from recruiting teenagers, the policy was not even in the interests of the armed forces themselves. Subsequent official reports (the Latey Committee on the Age of Majority in 1968 and the Prices and Incomes Board report in 1969) were to record the damaging effect of the long-term commitment on potential recruits. Only a deeply authoritarian cast of mind could have felt that seducing the impressionably young and then compelling them to serve for a long period was a more efficient method of staffing the armed forces with technicians than a system of voluntary persuasion of mature, trained adults. (A system used by both the United States and Sweden, for example.)

Inevitably the results of this ill-conceived policy soon began to show themselves. The N.C.C.L. renewed its interest in the subject in 1963, when two young R.A.F. men tried to form a C.N.D. group inside the air force, and were gaoled for four months each for such an outrageous idea. Not surprisingly their opinions at 19 were radically different from those they had held when recruited at 16: but the R.A.F. did not consider this grounds for discharging them from their twelve-year engagements. A year later the Government had to begin sifting the servicemen who were standing for Parliament in by-elections; several smart ones had discovered this was an easy way of getting out.

But the start of the unremitting campaign which was to change the system came by accident two years later. The mother of Stoker John Mayhew wrote to the N.C.C.L. about the Navy's refusal to release her son to study for a maths degree even though he had been offered places at two universities. Mayhew, recruited at 16 in 1957, had been trying to get out since 1959; in the mean-

*Grigg calculated that the 15-to 20 age group would continue to increase in numbers, whereas it was contracting in the late 1960s: and it assumed a static demand for higher education – in the event sixth form entry nearly doubled between 1958 and 1968. This was not just bad luck: another committee under Lord Crowther, analysing future educational trends, were operating at the same time on quite different, and more accurate, assumptions.

time, he had been studying A-levels in the ship boiler room. By 1965, when he was first offered a place by Bristol University, even his commanding officer was recommending his discharge. Thanks to the N.C.C.L., Parliament, press and TV took up Mayhew's case extensively in 1966, and eventually he was released a year early.

As with the mental deficiency campaign in the late 1940s, the publicity about one case produced a flood of letters with other similar examples.* The desperate quality of some of these could be seen from the various attempts made to win release – desertion, regular absence without leave, feigned or real mental illness or homosexuality, self-mutilation (one man had cut off his friend's trigger finger for him with an axe), ostentatious adoption of extreme Left-wing views. Even more desperate were the responses to failure; bed-wetting, broken homes, delinquency, slashed wrists and suicide attempts, 'all indications of a broken spirit', as the N.C.C.L. put it. Smythe was later to record that in his time as general secretary he had not dealt with an issue 'which produced such a terrible harvest of human misery'.

As well as supporting individual cases, the N.C.C.L. battered the Ministry of Defence with demands for reform. They asked for no long-term contract before 18; more frequent discharge opportunities; and a review of the discharge machinery. Gerry Reynolds, the Minister of Defence, (Administration) stalled blatantly through 1967. He assured an all-party delegation of M.P.s from the Parliamentary Civil Liberties group (including Tom Driberg, Eric Lubbock and Nigel Fisher) that the Government would report to Parliament on the subject after the Latey Committee had published its proposals about the age of majority. These appeared in mid-summer, scathingly suggesting that the recruitment system was as obsolescent as flogging and recommending that all boy entrants should be able to obtain their discharge at 18. Reynolds then excused his further procrastination on the grounds that he had not expected the report until November.

Frustrated by the year's delay, the N.C.C.L. sponsored four

*By 1970, the N.C.C.L. had tried to help more than 250 servicemen get out of the forces.

applications to the European Commission for Human Rights as test cases: they claimed breaches of the articles banning servitude, guaranteeing fair hearings before an independent tribunal, and guaranteeing effective remedies before national authority. These cases were declared inadmissible after a year of legal argument on the grounds that the servitude provisions were specifically not applicable to military service (which led the *New Law Journal* to question the value of an international civil rights convention which tolerated such practices in any form).

This wasted year set back the Parliamentary campaign, though late in 1968 Reynolds was forced to admit to M.P.s that 'morally, I would not defend this system, but in terms of meeting our defence needs I can see no alternative to it'. In the meantime the N.C.C.L. succeeded in winning occasional early releases in individual cases (sometimes with the help of Government ministers acting in their other rôle of constituency M.P.s); more often they failed. One particular case kept the publicity alive. In 1968 Corporal Michael Hall 'deserted' from Germany to come to Britain to give a press conference, and then surrender himself on the steps of the Ministry of Defence. He was given thirty-four days detention and was refused a discharge.

Finally, with falling recruitment figures, bad publicity and its own internal survey revealing widespread dissatisfaction among boy recruits, the Ministry of Defence gave in late in 1969. In November, Reynolds' successor Roy Hattersley met an N.C.C.L. deputation: he too expressed moral distaste for the system, but suggested it was the only alternative to re-introducing national service. But he also agreed the existing situation could not continue. Within a few weeks he announced that a committee was to be set up under Lord Donaldson to look into teenage recruitment.

The N.C.C.L., in its evidence to the committee, repeated its long-standing proposals. They asked for the abolition of long-term contracts before 18, short-term contracts thereafter with improved discharge options, the formation of an independent review body to hear discharge applications, and the abolition of discharge payments in compassionate cases. In addition it suggested the appointment of a military ombudsman, and allowing soldiers to join trade unions (as in Norway, Denmark, Germany and Austria). When the Donaldson Committee reported in 1970, it recommended that boy recruits should be allowed to leave at 21 (apprentices at 18), the abolition of discharge payments in compassionate cases, and earlier chance for discharge in certain circumstances. In December 1970 the Government accepted these proposals, though postponing the apprentice leaving age until 21 also, and insisting on a gradual implementation of the new scheme (so that in the Navy it would not come fully into effect until 1977).

It was, as the N.C.C.L. noted, the first time that the principle that the needs of the services were not absolute but had to be balanced against the needs of the servicemen had been recognized. It also destroyed the old system of total commitment to long-term contracts. The basic injustice was removed, but the military's determination to avoid such radical institutions as ombudsmen and trade unions meant that more general civil rights problems were left unresolved.

Part Four

Civil Liberty and Bureaucracy

8. Privacy and the Abuse of Information

The English have always been supposed to value the right to be left alone. It is a civil liberty that has flourished, not because it is enshrined in constitutional law, but because English society has such an ingrained respect for privacy that even the authorities have traditionally shown little inclination to threaten it. The belief that we do not need a bill of rights draws much of its strength from the quality of the English right to privacy.

Slowly, however, in the modern period, even this respected tradition has succumbed to the pressures set up by the rise of mass democracy. In certain sensitive areas – notably the Civil Service and the universities – those in power have grown so apprehensive of the disruptive influence of some ideas that they have resorted to para-legal measures to harass those who hold them. For the first time since the Nonconformists, the Catholics and the Jews were freed from their social and political restrictions in the nineteenth century, there has been organized discrimination against particular groups because of their beliefs. The victimization of the religious minorities was at least open; a Catholic always knows the consequences of holding his faith. Modern discrimination, however, has a more corrupting and secretive basis; because at least in theory, an individual's political beliefs are of no concern either to the State or his employers, information about them has to be obtained surreptitiously, recorded without his knowledge, and used against him dishonestly. Rarely has such information indicated any criminality, and therefore rarely has it been possible to invoke the law against the individual concerned. The easiest alternative penalty is to sack him from his job – which has the extra benefit of muddying the motives of those doing the sacking. The purge has become a minor, but regular, feature of post-war Britain.

This kind of persecution has been directed against specific – and usually small – minorities of either Fascist or extreme Marxist complexion. But the ordinary citizen has in the same period suffered a staggering erosion of his right to be left alone because of the increased determination of commercial and governmental organizations to learn as much as they can about his habits. The effect is the same, whether it is suffered by a Left-wing lecturer or a woman trying to get hire purchase credit: certain information is required, which will if necessary be used against the person concerned. The information explosion since 1945 has had a very sinister fall-out. This voracious need-to-know in both Government and industry has been accompanied by technological advance which for the first time has given those in power the ability to acquire and handle the information they want.

The growth of the information industry finally provoked a response from those who recognized that a valuable social and civic asset was fast disappearing. Because the English respect privacy, government and public opinion were susceptible to appeals to preserve it. In the late 1960s the N.C.C.L. and other groups and organizations developed a privacy campaign, spear-headed by legislative attempts to outlaw certain surveillance techniques and to close some yawning legal loopholes. But by 1974, after six years of effort, publicity successes had yet to yield practical victories.

*

There have been three definable purges in post-war Britain: 1948–56, when Cold War politics lead to a sustained harassment of Communists and fellow-travellers in the Civil Service: 1961–3, when an anti-Communist revival was directed against trade union negotiators and the years after 1968, when there was an attack on Marxists in the universities.

The 1948 purge was briefly foreshadowed by a flurry of political inquisitions in the civil service just before the war. The most serious incident was the prosecution of an Air Ministry civil servant, Major Vernon, under the Official Secrets Act in October 1938. A few months earlier four men, apparently Fascists, had broken into Vernon's Surrey home and taken some money and documents. At their trial, they defended themselves by attacking Vernon's 'Communist activities', and, although they were convicted, Vernon himself was suspended, and subsequently found guilty of two technical offences under the act for keeping official documents at his home. He was fined £50 and sacked from the Ministry.[1] The N.C.C.L. took up his case – Pritt defended Vernon at his trial – because, as they pointed out, thousands of conscientious civil servants committed technical offences all the time by taking home papers from work, and Vernon could only have been singled out for prosecution because of his supposed Left-wing sympathies. The campaign broadened out as other examples of political discrimination in government employment surfaced in the next few months.

In December 1937, the Union of Post Office Workers protested at inquiries carried out in Kilmarnock by the police into the background of two post office staff who had gone to fight for the International Brigade in Spain, and at the interrogation of other friends of theirs who were still working in the post office. A few months later, the Civil Service Clerical Association published details of Special Branch inquiries into the political attitudes of members of their executive. Early in 1939, these and similar developments led the N.C.C.L. to sponsor a conference on the civil rights of 'black coated workers', which attracted the support not only of the Left but of the Liberal leader, Sir Archibald Sinclair. A committee was set up to initiate action to secure the rights of civil servants, teachers and others, but the campaign naturally withered after the outbreak of war.

Not that the problem did. In 1940, Len White, the secretary of the C.S.C.A. and a leading member of the N.C.C.L., criticized the Government's refusal to allow civil servants with conscientious objections to war policy (often Communists at this early stage of the war, of course) to switch to non-military departments particularly as thousands of civil servants were being transferred the other way, from social service departments to the greatly expanded War Office. Two employees at the Ministry of Supply were dismissed without explanation. One was a Communist, the other a Fascist.

None of this harassment equalled the determined, formal

inquisition that was created as a result of the Cold War a few years later. The first skirmishes between the security services and the increasingly isolated Communists on this issue came in 1946. In May Dr Alan Nunn May was convicted for passing scientific secrets to the Russians, and sentenced to eighteen years' imprisonment. The N.C.C.L., which sympathized with the Communists (it had several Party members and fellow travellers on its executive) published an article soon afterwards written on behalf of the Association of Scientific Workers pleading for openness in scientific research: a worthy ideal, but a nonsense in view of the fast widening division in Europe. The N.C.C.L. also backed a campaign to get May's sentence reduced. At the same time and on rather better ground, they exposed the growing number of dismissals in the civil service at the request of M.I.5, without those concerned either knowing the nature of the charge against them or being given a chance to answer it.

That there was a security threat from some people in Government service is indisputable, as the trials or defections of Fuchs, Burgess, Maclean, Philby, Blake and the Portland naval team were to show in the next fifteen years; but the machinery to counter it set up by Attlee in March 1948 was an affront to natural justice, and far worse than the equivalent measures adopted in most other Western countries.[2] Though the Labour Government refused to create a 'loyalty oath' as in the U.S.A. – probably because it was too sophisticated to suppose a genuine spy would be inhibited by such an undertaking – they did create what David Williams has aptly described as a 'loyalty programme'.[3] Attlee told Parliament that the Government were going to weed out all the Communists or people associated with them from any jobs considered vital to the security of the State. The security services would present the appropriate minister with a *prima facie* case: the civil servant would then be told of the accusation against him (an improvement on previous practice at least) and, although Attlee promised as far as possible 'chapter and verse' for the accusation in each case, the overriding need to conceal the original sources of the information made this pledge almost useless. The civil servant could then take his case to a tribunal of three advisers, who could call witnesses but who would not allow any form of representation for the accused, nor any cross-examination by him. The report of this tribunal determined the action to be taken – either reinstatement, transfer to less sensitive work or dismissal.

Attlee's announcement met with a bitter response from the trade unions and professional associations in the civil service. With the help of the N.C.C.L., they organized two special conferences in 1948; the core of their campaign settled around the issue of representation (the lack of which fundamentally distinguished the British system from most others) and an adequate outline of the charges being made. The second objective was never achieved: the first, after a long struggle, was finally conceded in a limited form in 1962 when trade union officials were allowed to appear at initial tribunal hearings.[4]

Perhaps because of fierce public criticism, the actual effects of the purge were not too severe. By the end of 1955, some 17,000 civil servants (out of a total of a million) had been vetted, but less than 150 had actually been suspended. Most of these had after investigation been transferred to other work, nearly thirty had been re-instated in their old jobs, and fifty or so had either resigned or been sacked. In 1956, the first purge dried up for lack of material, though the machinery remained in existence.

Quite apart from the unjust nature of the machinery itself, the irrationality with which it was sometimes applied was horrifying where it was not farcical. In 1949, the N.C.C.L. became involved in several cases where government industrial workers had been dismissed as security risks. A Communist A.E.U. shop steward called Godber was suspended from his job at the Maltby Royal Ordnance factory under the purge regulations, despite the absurdity of supposing a shop floor armaments worker came anywhere near the Burgess and Maclean category; as his local convener wrote to the N.C.C.L., 'he was not, nor ever was, in a position to learn state secrets'. Even more absurd was the investigation of another armaments worker called Howard at Woolwich. Howard was better known in the factory as a canary-fancier than a crypto-Red, but he had in 1943 paid half-a-crown to the Communist Party as his thanks to a Communist workmate who had lent him some tools at an awkward time. Clearly this was dangerous fellow-travelling, and Howard was suspended from work for two months until the tribunal solemnly decided he could be allowed to go back to his job as a capstan operator without risk to national security.

Perhaps the most disturbing effect of Attlee's loyalty programme lay in its effect on private employers. Far too many of them picked up the purge mentality and applied it without even the extremely limited assessment machinery provided by the three-man tribunal in the civil service. The John Lewis Partnership was the first: in 1949, the firm tried to introduce political tests as a condition of employment. This met with such hostile criticism from all the political parties, from the trade unions, the press and even the Ministry of Labour (particularly when the N.C.C.L. revealed that the move was not unconnected with attempts by Lewis workers to improve their wages) that Lewis's abandoned the idea. In the autumn of 1950, the infection spread to teaching: various local authorities considered sacking Communists and Fascists from teaching posts. The L.C.C. quickly changed its mind under pressure from the N.C.C.L. and the trade unions, but the Middlesex County Council stood out for years against a sustained campaign to get it to reverse this outrageous policy. Then, in 1951, the Chairman of the Stevenage Development Corporation, Monica Felton, was sacked by the Ministry of Local Government because she had failed to attend a meeting. Mrs Felton had missed the meeting after a plane bringing her back from North Korea had been delayed: and it was generally believed that it was this visit to the Communist country rather than missing the meeting that was the cause of her dismissal. The N.C.C.L. pointed out that there was no conceivable security connection between Mrs Felton's job and her opinions on the Korean war. The following year produced two more examples of the Government's hysterical attitude towards non-civil servants as well as their own employees. The Nobel prize-winning physicist, Professor Powell, was dropped from a Foreign Office-sponsored tour of West German universities after the *Daily Express* had drawn the department's attention to his position as vice-president of the Communist-backed British Peace Council. The Foreign Office had at first told the *Express* that Powell's politics 'do not enter into it'. But within a day it had cancelled the tour. Worse was the Admiralty's unprecedented removal of Commander Edgar Young from the list of retired naval officers because they did not regard his Left-wing political activities as appropriate for a naval officer. The N.C.C.L. commented that not even officers interned for pro-Fascist sympathies during the war had been treated in this way, and there was an angry protest in Parliament from many M.P.s. The Admiralty stood firm, however, refusing even to see a deputation of military and naval personalities who wished to speak on Young's behalf.

Though the main civil service purge had run down by 1956, the backlash from the Burgess and Maclean affair left a last sediment of cold war nonsense in non-civil service jobs that year. The White Paper on the two defecting diplomats was published late in 1955, and as a result a team of Privy Councillors looked again at the purge procedures. Their main recommendation – published early in 1956 – was that the three-man tribunal had adopted far too stringent a standard of proof of Communist association, and that in future they should lean more heavily towards the official view of an individual's guilt. One example of this new standard was that marriage to a Communist or a sympathizer should be a sufficient disqualification.[5] Immediately several people outside the Civil Service found themselves jobless as a result of the new criterion. The most notorious case was the enforced resignation of J. H. A. Lang from his job as assistant solicitor at I.C.I. in June 1956. Lang's wife had belonged to the C.P., though she had left the party before her marriage. The Minister of Supply, Maudling, forced I.C.I. to honour its contractual obligation not to employ a security risk in a job with access to classified information. As an employee in private industry, Lang had no right of appeal to the three-man tribunal. Parliament discussed the matter, but the Government refused to tell Lang of the precise charge against him, and to state publicly why he should still be debarred from secret work. They did, however, concede that in future private industry employees could take their cases to the tribunal.[6]

The N.C.C.L. and various M.P.s soon discovered that Lang

was not the only such victim. A Scottish teacher with a Communist husband was refused a job by a county council even though they had a shortage of teachers. A cashier at a Cheltenham civil service club was sacked because her husband was a Young Communist. A mental nurse who had once stood as a Communist in a local election was persistently passed over for promotion despite his excellent qualifications and the efforts of his trade union on his behalf. Various other examples of official hostility to those with Communist associations in jobs without any remote security connection were raised in Parliament.[7] All this inspired the greatest public concern on the matter of privacy since the war. An all-party group of M.P.s formed a Committee 'to limit secret police powers', and the Labour Conference in October heard warnings that civil liberty was endangered by the telephone tapping and the letter-opening habits of the security services.

1956, the watershed year in so many ways, was the year the British lost their innocence about the nature of the country's internal surveillance systems. The liberal-minded suddenly became aware that the machinery they had tolerated when it was supposedly directed against a few Communist civil servants was now reaching out and harassing a much wider spectrum of victims, and without any conceivable justification. With the general revision of attitudes towards Khrushchev's Russia, the existence of a handful of domestic Communists seemed increasingly less menacing. And just as the secret police* were now seen to be sinisterly interested in what to ordinary people was legitimate political activity, so their means of monitoring it were taking a great technological leap forward.

The Lang case had alerted the public to the extent of the purge powers: a year later, the Marrinan case (see below, p. 307.) involving police telephone intercepts, revealed the widespread use of the supervisory techniques now available. Because of the alarm caused by the Marrinan revelations, a small committee under Lord Birkett looked at the whole issue of interceptions. They could find only dubious legal authority for the practice –

---

*The security services, as David Williams points out, are unrecognized by law and rely upon methods also unrecognized by law.[8]

indeed, one nineteenth-century Lord Chancellor had ruled that intercepting the mail was illegal at common law[9] – but in view of the undoubted usefulness of these methods in detecting crime, they recommended that with suitable safeguards they should be continued. Only the Home Secretary should have the power to authorize telephone tapping. Birkett found that the highest number of such permits in any one year before 1956 had been 241. The N.C.C.L. took an excessively idealistic attitude, calling for the abandonment of tapping altogether, but its basic criticism was clearly justified: 'No safeguard can be developed which would in fact confine the practice to matters genuinely concerned with the security of the state or the detection of serious crime.' There is no such safeguard, and the practice is too useful to be given up: but at least the Government could regularly admit how often such intercepts are used.* In 1957, the non-Communist Left discovered they had become just as interesting to the Special Branch as the Communists. The N.C.C.L. protested, in vain, to the Chief Constable of Hertfordshire after the local police had asked press photographers for prints of pictures taken at meetings protesting against the Suez invasion and the development of nuclear weapons.† This practice spread nationwide, though the police elsewhere excused it rather more subtly. In Middlesbrough they declared that photos of a C.N.D. poster parade were taken as a 'record of traffic problems', while Slough detectives snapping the Aldermaston marchers had apparently been doing so 'for social purposes'. Only at Salford did the local watch committee exercise vigilance and order pictures taken during a local C.N.D. rally to be destroyed.

The first chance to bring real pressure to bear on the Government on the security issue came with the establishment of yet

*Since 1956, no figures have been released, despite frequent demands for them from liberals of all colours. There is good reason to believe that the police regularly ignore the cumbersome process of getting a warrant from the Home Secretary. One estimate in 1966 put the number of intercepts at 12,000 a year, though, thanks to Harold Wilson, M.P.s were taken off the list that year. Another press report in 1966 suggested that two million names were on the files of the security services.

†The police it appeared had been too busy to take their own photos because they were all noting the car numbers of those attending the meeting.

another official committee on security procedures under Lord Radcliffe in 1961. (This followed the Blake and Kroger trials.) Radcliffe accepted evidence from non-Government bodies, including the N.C.C.L., which had by now adopted a more realistic attitude to telephone tapping and was arguing that publication of the annual returns for taps would at least have some restraining effect on their use. They also pursued the old point, about allowing those coming before the security tribunal to be represented: and this the Government accepted when the Radcliffe Report was published in the following year. The big setback was that the purge machinery as a result was extended to cover union officials negotiating with departments engaged on secret work. This led to a second wave of politically motivated dismissals. Officers in four civil service unions were singled out by name, and two were forced to resign. In May 1963, the C.S.C.A. formally accepted that it could no longer employ officers who could be classified as 'security risks', and authorized the dismissal, with compensation, of certain of its officials. The N.C.C.L. attacked this development as 'security gone mad', pointing out that most of the officials concerned were not Communist Party members, that they had all had long years of service to trade unionism and that in no case 'had there been even a suggestion of improper behaviour in relation to their work'.

The Radcliffe measures came at a time when there was already renewed official hostility to Left-wing trade unionists working in sensitive areas. In 1961, an A.E.U. shop steward in a Bristol aircraft factory was sacked at the instigation of the Ministry of Aviation for alleged – though denied – membership of the C.P. The N.C.C.L. and Liberal M.P. Eric Lubbock fought the case without success, but with sufficient vigour to attract requests for help from other similar victims. In 1962, the Ministry for Science ordered the dismissal of Peter Ware, a Communist shop steward who worked at a Southampton factory, part of which was engaged on work for the Atomic Energy Authority. This section was under strict security control: but Ware was employed in the non-security section. The only justification offered by the Ministry for their action was that Ware could meet workers from the secret plant in the firm's lavatories and canteen. The

N.C.C.L. commented sarcastically that even after dismissal he would continue to meet the same people in his social life and at union branch meetings – it was 'sheer persecution for no good end'. Elsewhere, at Royal Ordnance factories and War Office Inspectorates, the authorities vetoed several trade union representatives on security grounds. In 1964, a Communist A.E.U. steward was told by Quintin Hogg that he could not negotiate on behalf of workers at Aldermaston.[10]

Government paranoia in the early 1960s, the result partly of the discovery of the well-organized Soviet espionage rings and partly of the growth of the C.N.D. mass movement, was reminiscent of the early years of the Attlee purge. One of the saddest victims was Barbara Fell, prosecuted in 1962 under the Official Secrets Act. Miss Fell, who had a senior post at the Central Office of Information, foolishly passed official documents (with no security content whatsoever) to a Yugoslav press counsellor. The action perhaps merited dismissal; she received two years in prison.

By 1964, the second purge had spent itself. Surveillance of the Left continued – indeed it had to expand as the New Left grew and fragmented into factions as disillusionment with the second Wilson Government set in after 1966*. When the purge procedures returned, they surfaced in a new area: the universities. The effect was the same, however: individuals were losing their jobs because of their political beliefs.

The new victimization was a reaction to the student unrest after 1968. Though the troubles took many forms, and had many causes, the underlying issue was the authoritarian structure of the universities: the Marxist students in particular saw their assault on the undemocratic nature of the universities as part of the wider attack on late-capitalist Britain. The objects of the academic purges were to make sure that students who had been active in the disturbances found it difficult to get teaching jobs afterwards, and to weed out teachers who had been too sympathetic to the student cause. In the institutions where the

---

*The difficulty experienced by the Special Branch in keeping up with changing personalities of the various factions became evident at the Angry Brigade trial in 1972 when the Bomb Squad admitted they got no leads from the Branch after the Carr bombing.

student actions had been most disruptive in 1968 – the L.S.E., Hornsey and Guildford Art Schools* — teachers who had supported the students were dismissed. The Guildford case (where eight teachers had been sacked because they had 'trespassed' by defying administration instructions not to talk to students occupying the college) became a major subject of struggle between the extremely Conservative Surrey County Council and the various teaching and student unions. The N.C.C.L., alarmed at what it regarded as an 'invasion of civil liberties of a new kind in Britain', supported this campaign, which eventually secured the reinstatement of the teachers, though in different colleges. Elsewhere at the time there were attempts to get students and teachers to sign what were in effect loyalty oaths. Following the breaking-up of a meeting addressed by Duncan Sandys at Bradford University, the Vice-Chancellor gave five students and one lecturer the option of signing undertakings not to engage in such conduct again, or of facing disciplinary proceedings which might lead to dismissal. The N.C.C.L. criticized this as 'denying them the common right of political protest'. (Though the Bradford action was clearly wrong, the frequent disruption of Right-wing meetings at the universities in this period by supporters of the far Left was just as damaging to civil liberty: the N.C.C.L., perhaps unwisely, rarely commented on this aspect.) A former Vice-Chancellor of Cambridge University, Sir Eric Ashby, suggested in 1969 that university teachers should take some kind of Hippocratic oath, though this idea happily never won much support.

For those who wished to eliminate political opposition in this way it was of course essential to find out just who the potential victims were. The Special Branch regularly sought out student informers so that they could keep an eye on militants organizing protest actions: and the N.C.C.L. reported at least two instances when teaching staff had been approached by the police for information about their students in 1969. The value of this for the security services was seen in 1971 when it was the information they had obtained about Dutschke's political activities – legitimate though these appeared by liberal standards – that

*Only Essex, in the 1968 wave of revolts, escaped this action.

enabled Maudling, as Home Secretary, to argue that the German Marxist was a security risk and should not therefore be allowed to stay in Britain. (See above, Chapter 3, p. 152.) Before the Dutschke affair revealed the use to which such information could be put, most people had come to expect and almost tolerate this kind of Special Branch activity: much more shocking at the time was the discovery during an occupation of administration offices in Warwick University in February 1970 that files recording the students' political beliefs were kept, and this information was passed informally between the university and local employers like the car firm, Chryslers. A joint commission of the N.C.C.L. and the National Union of Students reported later that year that there was little evidence of political dossiers being kept on a wide scale in the universities, but it recommended that even necessary records – academic, disciplinarian, medical and psychiatric – should be kept separately. The N.C.C.L. warned, however, that even if the official recording of political opinion was prevented by liberal vigilance, this would hardly stop the discreet exchange of such information between the Special Branch, the university administrations and the employers.

In July 1970, the conflict inside the universities had become so endemic that a group of teachers formed a defensive body to protect the idea that an individual's politics were irrelevant in considering his professional abilities: The Council for Academic Freedom and Democracy. It operated under the auspices of the N.C.C.L.; its first chairman was Professor John Griffiths of the L.S.E. It was a timely birth. In 1970, the purge of Marxists in the universities got well under way. Unlike the sackings of 1968–9, this was not an instant response to a specific action, but a long-term decision to discriminate against people of awkward opinions.* Three cases immediately involved C.A.F.D.: all showed that non-academic criteria were being used to threaten individual jobs. At Manchester, Antony Arblaster held a teaching post in the university's philosophy department.

---

*Unlike the civil service purges, there was no formal or co-ordinated move against a particular party (in the civil service case, the Communists). Such action would have been strenuously resisted, of course: selective discrimination against various brands of Marxism was easier to attempt.

He had been encouraged to believe he would be given a permanent post when one became vacant. Early in 1970, he had publicly supported the students who had occupied part of the university for two weeks. In the summer, he was passed over for a permanent post for which he appeared an excellent candidate. An inquiry by C.A.F.D. concluded that the considerable public disquiet at this had been well-founded, and the Council called for an official inquiry. This was refused by the university. Arblaster subsequently found a job at Sheffield University.

Another teacher involved in the Manchester sit-in was Richard Atkinson. He was, in university circles at least, already famous for the part he had played in the L.S.E. agitation as a graduate student there in 1968, and at Birmingham as a junior teacher during their sit-in in 1969. Atkinson applied for a permanent job in Birmingham's sociology department in 1970. Though the faculty voted to appoint him, he was rejected by the University's appointments committee – the first time this had ever vetoed a candidate recommended by any faculty. The post was left unfilled, but Atkinson taught unofficially on the campus, his wages being paid out of a specially-raised fund. He applied for another sociology post at Birmingham in 1971, but again failed to get it. The controversy about this dragged on, with various teaching groups (like the British Sociological Association) entering into the conflict: eventually the matter died when Birmingham agreed to alter its appointment procedures.

The third, and perhaps most important case, ended in a qualified victory for the new civil liberty organization. Dr David Craig, a member of the Communist Party, had taught English at Lancaster University since it was founded in 1964. Craig was the most senior of a group of Lancaster teachers proposing various radical reforms for the university in 1970. In the following year he was demoted, for allegedly showing political bias in his teaching and examination marking, and some junior colleagues were sacked. He was also asked to sign what was, effectively, a loyalty oath. Craig refused; and, early in 1972, the Lancaster students went on strike in support of the threatened English teachers. In reply, the university vice-chancellor, Carter, suspended Dr Craig, while the rebellious students were threatened with loss of their grants. Prolonged negotiations between the university on the one side and the teaching unions and the C.A.F.D. on the other eventually led to the reinstatement of Craig, though the charges of political bias were not withdrawn.

In 1972–3, the problem spread to the School of Oriental and African Studies in London, where two Marxist teachers lost their jobs. Their chances of finding others were even more reduced since the S.O.A.S. had virtually a monopoly of academic work in this field. C.A.F.D. continued to fight for and publicize such cases; but it had become clear that those who ran the universities had almost unchallenged powers to discriminate in this way, and that the use of these powers against the far Left would continue for some time to come. Similarly the universities were prepared to consider much tougher measures against dissident students than hitherto. These, however, were more easily disputed, as the Stirling case showed in 1972. When the Queen visited the university she was the object of an abusive, and sometimes drunken, demonstration. The university failed to discipline any of those directly involved, but suspended student leaders who had organized a political protest against the visit. The injustice of this was criticized from several quarters, including C.A.F.D., and the authorities eventually abandoned the disciplinary proceedings.

Though the universities were the most prominent area of political discrimination in the early 1970s, the activities of the Special Branch elsewhere achieved considerable notoriety in 1973 and 1974. In the summer of 1973, the N.C.C.L. drew attention to the case of a Bournemouth teacher, David Ruddell, who was felt by the Special Branch to have the wrong political associations, a suspicion which they found it necessary to pass on to Ruddell's prospective employers. Though it was bad enough that the police discriminated in this way, what was worse was that Ruddell's period of political activity had been ten years earlier, and even then had been confined to the scarcely subversive ranks of C.N.D. and the Labour Party. The Special Branch attracted further unfavourable publicity as a result of involvement in an industrial dispute at an Eastleigh factory in 1974: but the most sensational incident, which glaringly exposed their methods, occurred in April that year.

An Irishman living in Luton, Kenneth Lennon, was found shot dead in a Surrey lane. Two days earlier he had given a long state-ment to Larry Grant of the N.C.C.L. This had outlined an unhappy involvement with the Special Branch. Lennon claimed to have been forced to spy on I.R.A. sympathizers in the Midlands, to have provided the tip-off which lead to the gaoling of three prominent Sinn Fein supporters in 1973, and then to have been the *agent provocateur* in an unsuccessful attempt to free these three from a Birmingham prison the following January. As a result another Irishman was gaoled: Lennon himself was ac-quitted and freed, but only after the police, Lennon said, had doctored the evidence against him to reduce his chance of being convicted. The N.C.C.L.'s publication of Lennon's story immediately after his murder provoked uproar. The allegations of police pressure, of incitement to commit crimes, of the bending of evidence, coupled with the political sensitivity of the circumstances and the tragic outcome, caused widespread con-cern. An immediate police inquiry was ordered by the Home Secretary, Jenkins: this cleared the Special Branch officers involved of any improper behaviour. The result scarcely satisfied the critics, who saw the episode as yet another demonstration of the impossibility of permitting the police to be the sole investigators of their own activities.

For years, the abuse of personal information to harass in-dividuals had been basically as a threat to the civil rights of small and unpopular political minorities. Communist civil servants and trade unionists, and Marxist lecturers, were not the material round which a campaign to protect the private beliefs of in-dividuals could successfully be built. But in the late 1960s, the growth of big government and big business made people aware that the same abuse and the same threat could occur in non-political contexts. Ironically enough, this new consciousness made privacy a political issue.

Even in the 1950s, there had been indications of the way things were going. In the early years of that decade, the N.C.C.L. fought running battles with local councils over the regulations they imposed on their tenants, requiring information or insisting on restrictions that lay well outside any legitimate concern of the housing authorities. In 1951, Cromer had threatened evictions for tenants with children who swore too much: in 1953, Paddington evicted two families whose men had gone to prison so that the home could be let to 'people more deserving of public assistance'. In the same year, the N.C.C.L. attacked the growing practice of housing committees making inquiries about the wages paid their tenants, but in 1954 they reluctantly accepted that with the growth of rebate schemes this kind of inquiry was inevitable. The most outrageous example of a local council invading the privacy of one of its tenants was the eviction of a prominent entomologist called Bunting (who was permanently disabled) from his home in 1954. Bunting kept insects in his house, perfectly secured, for study; his local council successfully tried to force him out on sanitary grounds, but when they found these did not apply, they accused him of running a business, which was naturally against their regulations. Despite the efforts of the Royal Society of Entomologists and the N.C.C.L. on his behalf, a county court eviction order was obtained against Bunting.

In the late 1950s came two cases in which the police passed information to outside organizations for use against particular individuals. The first was the debarring of a lawyer called Marrinan by the Bar Council in 1956. Investigating complaints of professional misconduct against Marrinan, the Bar Council obtained transcripts from the police of intercepted telephone calls between the lawyer and one of his clients, Billy Hill, a well-known underworld figure.[11] Marrinan was disqualified; but the public shock when details of the manoeuvre were exposed the following year forced the Home Secretary to set up the Birkett Committee to consider the whole issue of telephone tapping. (See above, p. 298). As far as the Marrinan case was concerned, the committee felt the Home Secretary had been wrong to allow the transcripts to be passed to the Bar Council, and recommended that in future such material should never be allowed outside the public service. Two years later another professional, Dr Kenneth Fox, was struck off the medical register for unprofessional conduct with a woman patient. The police handed over evidence of a telephone conversation between Dr Fox and the woman to the Medical Council, evidence obtained not by tapping the phone but by listening in on an extension with the agreement of the woman patient. The Government felt this did not come within the definition of phone intercepts, and therefore such action was not excluded under the Birkett prohibition. The N.C.C.L. considered such a quibbling distinction irrelevant to the principle involved.

The compilation of official information, and access to it by unauthorized outsiders, was to become the main issue in the privacy campaign of the late 1960s. Another substantial cause of grievance was the increasing extension of the official right of entry. In 1961, the Government told Conservative M.P. Sir Stephen McAdden that more than 10,000 public officials had the right to enter private homes without permission.* McAdden wanted this 10,000 at least to be subject to the same restrictions as gas and electricity meter readers, who had to obtain a magistrate's warrant to enforce entry except in emergencies. But even this safeguard could be abused, or prove insufficient. In 1965, an Acton lady complained to the N.C.C.L. that a meter reader had entered her home through a back door left open for the doctor while she was ill in bed: when she refused to let the intruder read the meter, the Gas Board sent an inspector the next day who threatened her with legal action for obstruction. One of the earliest successes in the privacy campaign launched by the N.C.C.L. in 1969 was the abandonment by the West Midlands magistrates of their practice of issuing entry warrants to the Gas and Electricity Board officials *en bloc*, after they had come under pressure from the Birmingham Trades Council. It was a useful advance, but it highlighted the previous lack of concern for individual rights shown by the magistrates.

Inevitably, perhaps, it was the increasing sophistication of police methods and technical equipment which inspired the N.C.C.L. to concentrate seriously on the privacy issue after 1966. (They sponsored a Cobden Trust survey which provided much of the material for the later pressure group campaign.) The

*The list was headed by 3,000 Inland Revenue men, 2,000 Customs Officers and 500 School Inspectors. (At the other end were five petrochemical inspectors.)

blood-sampling of 149 men by the Berkshire police in a murder inquiry; the fingerprinting of 533 schoolchildren in the search for a fire-raiser; Home Office discussion of a scheme to finger-print the entire country; the start of a £6m. police computer project – all took place in 1966. 'The area of our lives which we call private tends to narrow,' wrote the N.C.C.L. about these developments, which they saw as part of the 'bureaucratic complexity of an advanced industrial society, and the ruthless obsession with efficiency that goes with it'. But, in 1972, the improved criminal record system associated with the police computer at Hendon worried the N.C.C.L. less than its use to monitor 'illegal' immigrants and drug users, and the quasi-identity card system created by the transfer of all driving licence records to the Department of the Environment's Vehicle Licensing Centre at Swansea, with the separate 'driver number' for every driver in the country.

And by that date the N.C.C.L., and those groups like the British Computer Society with which they had formed an alliance, were well aware that the police were just one among many government and private agencies with abundant facilities to acquire and handle personal information on a massive scale. The Department of Health and Social Security was inevitably responsible for much of this information: in 1966, the N.C.C.L., computer experts and a small group of M.P.s from all three parties outlined to the Minister of Health, David Ennals, their concern at the storage of information in computerized data banks. The following year, the N.C.C.L. complained to the Department of Employment that some of the questions to employers about their workforce in the Department's survey of earnings were an invasion of privacy – notably those relating to strikes, stoppages and absence from work. In reply the Department admitted that information like this should not be personally identifiable. Outside the big Government ministries, the great gatherers of private particulars were the credit rating agencies, whose assessment of your credit status (obtained from previous credit transactions) was sought by various finance institutions before they would give you a loan. Though this was a justifiable service, what caused alarm was the persistent evidence of inaccuracies in these records. Since the victim never saw them (indeed, was often ignorant of their very existence) the errors could survive for years and prevent people getting credit they were eligible for. Both the Crowther Committee on Credit (1971) and the Younger Committee on Privacy (1972) endorsed the proposal originally put forward by the N.C.C.L. that the individual should have the right of access to his credit rating.

But almost worse than not knowing what your file contained was the possibility that someone else could find out, and then use that information for unjustifiable and even downright hostile purposes. The tradition of retired policemen going to work for security firms or as security staff in industry was doubtless a valuable one, but one of the dangers was the abuses to which the survival of old connections could be put. In 1968, a man newly employed by an engineering firm was given a complete account of his brushes with the law five years previously by the firm's security officer, who had clearly had access to official police files on the new employee. Some firms in the security business openly advertised their ability to obtain criminal records, private bank balances and ex-directory telephone numbers. In 1969, a tracing firm was fined £11,000 for dishonestly obtaining information: in the same year they claimed to have five million names on their files and announced an ambition of putting together dossiers on eighty per cent of Britain's households within the next ten years. In May 1971, the *Guardian* exposed the methods used by private detectives to get confidential information from Government ministries, much along the lines the N.C.C.L. had already publicized two years earlier. The newspaper story immediately prompted Heath to set up a full inquiry, and in 1973 Ian and Stuart Withers, two private detectives who had already achieved considerable notoriety on press and television for their use of bugs and other surveillance devices, were gaoled for conspiring to effect a public mischief. The Withers brothers' firm had developed a sophisticated system of telephoning banks, motor tax departments, Home Office Departments and the criminal record office for personal details.*

It was against this background that the 1971 census came in for

*In November 1974, the Lords quashed the convictions on the grounds that 'conspiracy to cause a public mischief' was not a criminal offence.

such unprecedented criticism. More people refused to co-operate than ever before. The N.C.C.L. suggested a voluntary census, with extra safeguards to preserve confidentiality, and a government ban on selling census information for commercial purposes. Labour M.P. Leslie Huckfield pursued this last idea in Parliament, but received only the assurance that this would be kept to the minimum. Within a few months, there were two incidents which justified this concern. One census enumerator in Camden, a council employee, was convicted for passing census information to the local rates department. Then the Registrar-General's office sent a survey on ex-nurses to the Department of Health that relied solely on census information, despite the Registrar-General's earlier promises that this information would not be passed 'outside' the census organization.

By 1971, the fight against the uncontrolled information industry had defined the main issues at stake, but despite considerable public and even official sympathy, there seemed little chance of an effective change in the law. Even in the 1930s, a few people – mainly academic lawyers – had been alert to the dangerous trends in contemporary society. In 1938 Professor Winfield urged that a new tort, the offensive invasion of privacy, should be recognized.[12] The idea was repeated by Professor Glanville Williams in 1950, just two years after the Porter Committee on defamation had dismissed the concept as 'primarily an offence against good taste'. In the 1950s the threats to privacy were largely seen as coming from the Hickey-type gossip columns of the press. In 1961, Lord Mancroft tried to create a legal protection against this particular kind of intrusion: he was supported by judicial notables like Lords Goddard and Denning (though the latter had a broader sense of privacy than Mancroft – he wanted telephone tapping and opening of mail included as well). Although Mancroft's bill passed the Lords, the Government refused to help it and it died in the Commons.

In the late 1960s, as a few people became aware of the keen constitutional argument on the issue in the United States, a much more comprehensive campaign got under way. This was built round two main proposals: the outlawing of certain surveillance methods, and the creation of legal protections against the abuse of legally-acquired information. Fortunately, the computer experts themselves were among the sharpest critics of the abuses resulting from technological advance, and the British Computer Society joined forces with the N.C.C.L. to produce a report recommending specific reforms in 1969: the most important was the establishment of a Data Bank Tribunal to control the way data was obtained, and to enable individuals to get access to information about themselves. Two private members' bills then publicized the idea, and suggested that the data banks should come under the supervision of the Registrar of Restrictive Practices. But the most important development that year was the bill, sponsored by Labour M.P. Brian Walden, to create a 'right to privacy'. Walden came sufficiently high on the private members' ballot for his bill to stand a chance of becoming law. At the same time Justice published their proposals for legislation on the subject. (Walden's bill, influenced by the N.C.C.L., differed from the Justice draft by seeking to control governmental invasion of privacy, and by providing a strong defence for the press.) Such was the pressure achieved in little under six months' well-organized agitation, that Home Secretary Callaghan agreed to set up the Younger Committee to consider the whole subject – except where it affected the Government itself.

To keep up the pressure, the N.C.C.L. organized a major international conference on the 'Data Bank Society', attended by more than 100 high-level representatives of Government, the law, industry and professions. In 1971, in its evidence to the Younger Committee, the N.C.C.L. attacked the limitation of the inquiry to the private sector only; indeed, it subsequently emerged that many on the Committee itself felt that the narrowness of their terms of reference was a nonsense. The Government's concern at its weak position on this was evident later when the Ministry of Aerospace announced that the problem of computers and confidentiality in the Civil Service was to be studied. After nearly three years, the Younger Committee finally produced its report. It was decidedly a damp squib after all the time and effort. It failed to grapple with two fundamental issues, the need to legislate for a general right to privacy, and the urgent need for the effective supervision of data banks. On this the report merely proposed a standing commission with limited powers. However, it did recommend the licensing of private detectives, the outlawing of some electronic devices and proposed the recognition of the tort of unlawfully acquired information. (The N.C.C.L. warned that this could inhibit the socially useful disclosure of information to the press: 'there should be a distinction between personal privacy and corporate secrecy'.) But even these mild reforms were not taken up with any enthusiasm by the Government.

Though the ideology of liberal democracy, espoused by all British Governments, firmly supports the idea of privacy, the increasing needs of government and its economic allies in the large corporations for comprehensive information about as many people as possible (and the chance to use it against 'dangerous' individuals) effectively prevented those in authority taking any positive steps to realize the concept in practice. And less than in any other area of British liberty, the courts and the law could provide little help against executive arrogance in this respect. Privacy is one of our rights that has undoubtedly been eroded rather than strengthened since the 1930s.

9. Conclusion

Britain's civil liberty record in the period between 1934 and 1974 does not at first sight appear very encouraging. In the thirties, they were gaoling demonstrators on riot charges: in the seventies, they have done so again. But like the news, a record of this kind is inevitably largely gloomy: most civil liberty issues only become issues when the damage has been done. Until someone hits a marcher on the head, or someone else locks him up, civil liberty is not in question.

To make a relative judgement, it is necessary not only to look at the incidents of repression, most of which have been, I hope, recorded here, but also at what was successfully said and done and this has not often been recorded here. Clearly, therefore, I cannot begin to prove that civil liberty is in most respects healthier than ever; but to attempt to place the matter in perspective, I offer the following subjective check list on the state of our civil rights.

Freedom of assembly was no more at risk in 1974 than 1934. Indeed, the right to demonstrate had been affirmed by the courts in the Hain case, while police handling of demonstrations had generally grown both more sophisticated and gentler since the thirties. Just as important, the kinds of demonstration had increased substantially: sit-ins, occupations, squats had all become common methods of political dissent, existing in a grey area of the law and achieving a quasi-legitimacy.

Freedom of expression, though subject to very much the same repressive laws as in the 1930s (official secrets, incitement to disaffection, obscenity) was successfully exercised on a far greater scale and with greater audacity than in those years. It would have been inconceivable for the film censor to interfere with a political documentary in the 1970s in the way that officials did in 1936, and equally inconceivable that de Montalk's poems would have put him in prison if he had written them in the 1970s.

The civil rights of oppressed groups and minorities have also clearly improved. The advance in women's rights since the thirties can be seen simply by remembering that a woman working in the Civil Service or the banks in those years would have lost her job automatically if she married. The discrimination encountered by the Ulster Catholics, by blacks and gipsies in this period has been positively inhibited by legal and administrative action, even though this has been insufficient to eradicate it completely. The mentally abnormal are not now liable to spend a lifetime subject to the arbitrary power of a bureaucracy. And those brought before a judge on a criminal charge (though not a magistrate) will be granted a defending advocate as of right rather than a spasmodically granted privilege, as well as for the first time in our history securing the democratic reality of trial by a jury of their peers.

There are, however, at least two, and perhaps three, important areas of civil liberty where our rights have clearly deteriorated since the 1930s. Freedom of movement, particularly the right to find refuge here, has almost disappeared. Anyone seeking political asylum would have been wise to avoid the Britain of Edward Heath. Secondly the supervision, or at least the surveillance, of private life and private opinions has increased alarmingly in these forty years: and although the opposition to this has also grown, in 1974 it was by no means clear that effective action to restore the *status quo ante* was likely or even possible.

And then there were the police. Public concern at the methods used by the police was much greater in the 1970s than in the 1930s. This did not necessarily mean that the police behaved worse than their predecessors – there is no reason to suppose that they did – but it did mean that the public were now aware of the reality of police work. It is still touch and go whether this new consciousness will lead to a greater toleration of police abuses (as has happened to some extent in the United States) or to positive action to help the police do their proper work properly and at the same time restrain them from doing anything improperly.

Overall, civil liberty has, despite many individual setbacks, continued to grow in Britain, because as a people we have continuously exercised our civil right. It is this continuous exercise, rather than legislation, which ultimately determines the quality of liberty. Whatever help would be obtained by securing a new Bill of Rights, as many have suggested in recent years, it would not alone be sufficient. One thing that clearly emerges from this period is that liberal laws, designed to improve the civil rights of all or part of the population, have a limited and usually only defensive value. On the other hand, oppressive laws do not necessarily destroy civil liberty either. The various incitement, obscenity and conspiracy laws, the laws controlling picketing, all were on occasions rendered harmless. Such laws can be used to restrict freedom, but they can also be thwarted, if the will to do so is there. After all, we get the freedoms we deserve.

The change in British democracy, particularly since the late 1950s, with political activity spreading to a myriad of small groups of ordinary people in their communities and workplaces, has inevitably increased the quantity (and, I would argue, the quality also) of our civil rights. But freedom is not infinite. For liberals it is an awkward fact that if we all agitated all the time, liberalism (and much else) would be inoperable. Only if we tacitly accept that we will exercise our civil rights intermittently and in relatively small numbers can civil liberty as we presently understand it work.

Fortunately, there is no sign that the British wish to become one hundred per cent political animals. Even with the extension of 'grass roots' democracy, most people choose to leave continuous political activity to a minority. What that minority needs to know is that the rest of us will not only stand up and be counted at the appropriate regular head-counting intervals, but that our support for the freedoms without which political activity cannot be pursued is constant if undemonstrative. It does not matter much that the system would collapse if we were all activists: it does matter that those that wish to be active can be and are.

Postscript

Late in November 1974, after nineteen people had been killed and hundreds badly injured in two Birmingham bomb explosions, Parliament rushed through emergency legislation to deal with the intensified I.R.A. terrorist campaign in mainland Britain. Under the Prevention of Terrorism (Emergency Provisions) Act, it became an offence to belong to the I.R.A., punishable with up to five years' gaol: to harbour an I.R.A. suspect: and to wear an I.R.A. uniform or carry banners proclaiming support for it. Police powers were strengthened: they could arrest an I.R.A. suspect without a warrant, and detain him for up to seven days without charging him or bringing him to court. Surveillance at the ports was increased, and the Home Secretary was able to exclude or deport anyone he felt was involved in terrorist activity. The act had a six months' life.

Roy Jenkins, who had rightly described the new powers as 'draconian' and unprecedented in peacetime, resisted demands for the introduction of identity cards and the restoration of hanging for bomb offences. He balanced the adverse impact of the legislation on civil liberty and the freely-conceded likelihood that some innocent people would suffer against the need to combat the savagery. The measures were widely supported: indeed, the Government had been obliged to act in the face of the widespread public anger, and to head off vigilante retribution against the Irish community in Britain.

Nonetheless, the limited practical value of the measures scarcely matched their dangerous civil liberty implications. The police themselves had long argued that banning the I.R.A. was a useless action. Though the proscription of I.R.A. uniforms was a reasonable extension of the Public Order Act provisions, the banning of slogans could inhibit legitimate expression of support for a united Ireland. The constitutional significance of the deportation powers, which distinguished between Ulster and the rest of the United Kingdom, alarmed the Protestants. And the formalization of the police habit of detention for questioning was an ominous, albeit temporary, precedent. The emergency was real enough, but demonstrated how mass political pressures in a democracy could conflict with traditions of liberty. Even a liberal like Jenkins could find it necessary to introduce dangerous restrictions for short-lived political objectives.

Appendix

The National Council for Civil Liberties

The National Council for Civil Liberties is a pressure group in the classic British tradition. Since 1934*, it has been run by a permanent staff responsible to an executive committee elected annually by the membership. The staff has grown from one man and a typist in 1934 to twenty full-time people in 1972. In 1972, there were 5,400 individual members and 450 affiliated organizations. Finance comes from membership fees, donations, special appeals and, most importantly, grants from charitable foundations. Because of its essentially political character it has never been able to qualify as a charity and thus gain the valuable tax exemptions. Since the early 1960s, however, a separate body, the Cobden Trust, set up by the N.C.C.L. to do research work, has had charitable status. In 1934, the N.C.C.L.'s income was £946. In 1972, the joint income with the Cobden Trust was nearly £50,000.

The crucial figure in the N.C.C.L. has always been the general secretary. Although the executive committee has some influence, civil liberty issues have inevitably been defined on a day-to-day basis by the immediate response of the general secretary: and most of the long-term initiatives have come from him as well. Between 1934 and 1975, there have been six general secretaries. The first was the Council's founder, Ronald Kidd. He had previously worked in publicity, journalism and advertising, and his public relations flair was invaluable in the early years of the young organization. After his death in 1942, he was succeeded by Elizabeth Allen, who ran the N.C.C.L. for eighteen years. Her father had been a Liberal M.P.; she herself had been President of the

*An earlier National Council for Civil Liberties, largely concerned with conscientious objection, existed in 1916–18: it may even have survived until the thirties, but I have not been able to trace records of this body.

Students' Union at the L.S.E., and came to the N.C.C.L. from work with the League of Nations on refugees. She retired in 1960 (and died nine years later), to be followed by Martin Ennals. Ennals, one of a trio of highly political brothers, had worked for U.N.E.S.C.O.: he revitalized an N.C.C.L. which had become badly stagnant. In 1966, he left to work for the National Committee for Commonwealth Immigrants (and went on to become Secretary-General of Amnesty International) and handed over to Tony Smythe. Smythe had once spent three months in prison as a conscientious objector – 'the best training ground for working in the N.C.C.L.,' in his own words. His previous work was with War Resisters International. In the six years he ran the N.C.C.L., its membership trebled and its income rose from £8,000 a year to nearly £50,000. He left in 1972 to work briefly for the American Civil Liberties Union in the U.S.A. before returning to Britain to become Director of Mind and the National Association for Mental Health. His successor at the N.C.C.L. was Martin Loney, a former president of the Canadian Students' Federation who had previously worked for the World University Service in Geneva. Loney was dismissed after eighteen months for 'failing to provide the policy initiation' that a majority of the N.C.C.L. executive felt was required from the general secretary. He was succeeded by Patricia Hewitt, the N.C.C.L.'s women's rights officer. She took over at a time of increasing financial stringency: N.C.C.L. income had declined in real terms and the Council could no longer afford the size of staff achieved under Smythe.

Outside its own staff, the N.C.C.L. has always relied on three groups for its effectiveness: lawyers, journalists and M.P.s. From the start it has always had a small but active membership of lawyers prepared to act in civil liberty cases, though this has never reached anything like the dimensions in the U.S.A. where lawyers can make careers out of civil rights work. In the 1930s and 1940s D. N. Pritt, Dingle Foot, Geoffrey Bing, Neil Lawson, Dudley Collard and John Platts Mills were prominent lawyers active in N.C.C.L. work: the tradition has been continued recently by men like Ben Birnberg. Since 1969, the N.C.C.L. has been able to afford a full-time lawyer on its staff (Larry

Grant was the first). Journalists have never played the same active role inside the N.C.C.L., with the obvious major exceptions in the 1930s of Kingsley Martin (the editor of the *New Statesman*) and Claud Cockburn, but the general secretaries from Kidd onwards (himself a former journalist) have usually had good relations with the press. Unless a newspaper ran a story the next day, many minor injustices would have disappeared unchecked into oblivion. A similar good relationship has existed with individual M.P.s since the 1930s, though it was perhaps at its lowest during the 1950s. In the 1930s, Pritt (Labour) and Dingle Foot (then Liberal) were ready to raise civil liberty issues in Parliament: and in the mid-1960s Smythe built up a powerful Parliamentary Civil Liberties Group under the chairmanship of Liberal M.P. Eric Lubbock. Several of the N.C.C.L.'s major campaigns, like that on privacy, gained considerable momentum from the readiness of individual M.P.s to bring in back bench bills on the subject.

Notes

Chapter 1

1. Ronald Kidd, *British Liberty in Danger*, Lawrence & Wishart, 1940, p. 47.
2. David Williams, *Keeping the Peace*, Hutchinson, 1967, p. 135 ff.; Harry Street, *Freedom, the Individual and the Law*, Pelican, 1972, pp. 56–8; Kidd, op. cit., pp. 26–9.
3. Ian Brownlie, *The Law Relating to Public Order*, Butterworth, 1968, p. 20; Kidd, op. cit., p. 22 ff.; Street, op. cit., pp. 53–4.
4. Williams, op. cit., p. 65.
5. ibid., p. 24.
6. For a detailed discussion of this, see Geoffrey Marshall, *Police and Government*, Methuen, 1965, p. 46 ff.
7. Kidd, op. cit., p. 131.
8. Williams, op. cit., p. 116.
9. Kidd, op. cit., p. 134.
10. Stuart Bowes, *The Police and Civil Liberties*, Lawrence & Wishart, 1966, p. 23.
11. Kidd, op. cit., p. 72.
12. Williams, op. cit., p. 218.
13. ibid., p. 222.
14. ibid., p. 58.
15. ibid., p. 14.
16. For discussions of the Public Order Act, see Kidd. op. cit., p. 68; Street, op. cit., pp. 47–61; Williams, op. cit., pp. 15, 56, 133, 216; Brownlie, op. cit., p. 94.
17. D. N. Pritt, *Brasshats and Bureaucrats*, Lawrence & Wishart, 1966, p. 140.
18. Kidd, op. cit., p. 172; Williams, op. cit., p. 242.
19. Kidd, op. cit., p. 174; Pritt, op. cit., p. 153; Williams, op. cit., p. 242.
20. Kidd, op. cit., p. 194.
21. ibid., p. 234.

22. Williams, op. cit., p. 296.

23. ibid., p. 61.

24. K. W. Wedderburn, *The Worker and the Law*, Penguin, 1970, (Revised Edition), p. 325.

25. Piddington v. Bates: see Williams, op. cit., p. 126; Wedderburn, op. cit., p. 324.

26. Wedderburn, op. cit., p. 324.

27. *Sunday Times*, 13 February 1972.

28. Harold Wilson, *The Labour Government 1964–70*, Weidenfeld & Nicolson/Michael Joseph, 1971.

29. Williams, op cit., p. 210; Marshall, op. cit., p. 117; Bowes, op. cit., p. 75; Street, op. cit., p. 53.

30. Street, op. cit., p. 59.

31. ibid., p. 58.

32. James D. Halloran, *Demonstrations and Communication: A Case Study*, Penguin, 1970, pp. 61–82.

33. Peter Laurie, *Scotland Yard*, Bodley Head, 1970, p. 104.

34. The *New Statesman* headline.

35. Halloran, op. cit., p. 57; C. Driver, *The Disarmers: A Study in Protest*, Hodder & Stoughton, 1964, p. 157.

36. Williams, op. cit., p. 215.

37. For the police perspective, see Richard Clutterbuck, *Protest and the Urban Guerrilla*, Cassell, 1973, pp. 27–9.

38. R. v. Aubrey-Fletcher *ex parte* Thompson.

39. Street, op. cit., p. 216.

40. Williams, op. cit., p. 227. A less controversial clause of the act, which is little more than a glorified version of 'obstructing the police', was used against Committee of 100 demonstrators at Marham in 1963 and Ruislip in 1964.

41. Stephen Sedley, *Listener*, 8 October 1970.

42. Judge Melford Stevenson in the Cambridge trial, quoted by Sedley.

43. Street, op. cit., p. 174.

Chapter 2

1. Michael Foot, *Aneurin Bevan: Volume 1*, MacGibbon & Kee, 1962, pp. 173, 179.

2. Kingsley Martin, *Editor: A Second Volume of Autobiography 1931–45*, Hutchinson, 1968, p. 7; Pritt, op. cit., p. 175; Kidd, op. cit., pp. 56–8; Street, op. cit., pp. 206–11; Williams, op. cit., pp. 186–91.

3. Kidd, op. cit., p. 99.
4. Maureen Turnbull, *Sunday Times*, 13 February 1972.
5. Street, op. cit., p. 68.
5a. For the origins of film censorship, see John Trevelyan, *What the Censor Saw*, Michael Joseph, pp. 23–9.
6. ibid., pp. 45–6.
6a. ibid.
7. Kidd, op. cit., pp. 81–5.
8. Pritt, op. cit., p. 169.
9. There was some press criticism as well. See C. H. Rolph, *Books in the Dock*, André Deutsch, 1969, pp. 87–9.
10. *Sunday Times*, 22 November 1970.
11. Street, op. cit., p. 83.
12. Street, op. cit., p. 71; Trevelyan, op. cit., p. 174, which reveals the Board's subsequent change of policy.
12a. Trevelyan, op. cit., p. 53.
13. Rolph, op. cit., pp. 93–104; Street, op. cit., pp. 120–23.
14. Rolph, op. cit., p. 96.
14a. The report of his committee was published in 1972, to widespread jeers. It made yet another attempt to give a legal definition to the legally indefinable – what is obscenity? According to Longford, 'that which outrages contemporary standards of decency or humanity acceptable to the public at large'.
15. Street, op. cit., p. 133.
16. Rolph, op. cit., p. 108.
17. ibid., p. 109.
18. ibid., p. 117.
19. ibid., p. 111.
20. Quoted in both Rolph, op. cit., p. 114, and Street, op. cit., p. 136.
20a. 'The laws against obscenity, while constituting a danger to the innocent private individual, provide no serious benefit to the public. The basic problem of founding a law that can be accepted on so subjective a concept as obscenity appears to be insuperable.' – John Montgomerie, *The Obscenity Laws*, Arts Council Report, 1969, p. 36.
21. *Ink*, 3 July 1971. The real reason for Conservative hostility to this book can be seen in Clutterbuck, op. cit., p. 175.
22. Street, op. cit., p. 139.
23. Street, op. cit., p. 139. For an excellent justification of pornography, see D. F. Barber's *Pornography and Society*, Charles Skilton, 1972.

23a. A witty summary of the progress of nudity in the advertising arts is provided in Richard Michael's *A.B.Z. of Pornography*, Panther, 1972, pp. 8–12.

24. Rolph, op. cit., p. 116.

25. ibid., p. 115.

26. Street, op. cit., p. 141.

27. See Trevelyan, op. cit., pp. 214–28, for the crisis between the Board and some local authorities in 1972.

27a. Rolph, op. cit., p. 38.

28. Street, op. cit., pp. 69–70, Trevelyan, op. cit., p. 113.

28a. Trevelyan, op. cit., pp. 129–32. The film censor offered some brave, and extremely valuable, public support for the Open Space Theatre.

29. For a less sanguine view of the impact of Mrs Whitehouse on the B.B.C., see Michael, op. cit., p. 141.

30. Street, op. cit., p. 81.

31. Tony Smith has a detailed analysis in *Index*, No. 2, Summer 1972.

32. Street, op. cit., pp. 95–9, summarizes its early decisions.

33. Street, op. cit., p. 221.

33a. Frank Stacey, *A New Bill of Rights for Britain*, David & Charles, 1973, p. 96.

34. Street, op. cit., p. 142.

35. Neville's summing up in his own defence is quoted in full, Michael, op. cit., pp. 97–105. See also Tony Palmer's *The Trials of Oz*, Blond & Briggs, 1971, and Stacey, op. cit., p. 103.

36. *Ink*, ibid.

37. *Inside Story*, No. 3, June 1972.

Chapter 3

1. Paul Foot, *Immigration and Race in British Politics*, Penguin, 1965, p. 83. He quoted Erskine May on the proud pre-twentieth century tradition of offering 'an inviolable asylum to men of every rank and condition, seeking refuge on her shores, from persecution and danger in their own lands . . .'

2. ibid., pp. 80–102, passim.

3. Quoted by Paul Foot, op. cit., p. 110.

4. ibid., p. 111.

5. *Manchester Guardian*, 16 February 1940.

6. See Stephen Castles and Godula Kosack, *Immigrant Workers and Class Structures in Western Europe*, Oxford University Press, 1973, for European migration.

7. Bob Hepple, *Race, Jobs and the Law in Britain*, Allen Lane, 1968, p 49.
8. Paul Foot, op. cit., p. 119; E. J. B. Rose, *Colour and Citizenship: Report on British Race Relationships*, Oxford University Press, 1969, p. 20.
9. Paul Foot, op. cit., p. 29.
10. ibid., p. 131.
11. ibid., pp. 135–8.
12. ibid., p. 135.
13. For a full analysis of Griffiths' campaign, see Paul Foot, op. cit., passim, also David Steel, *No Entry: The Background and Implications of the Commonwealth Immigrants Act, 1968*, C. Hurst, 1969, pp. 65–80.
14. Rose, op. cit., p. 612.
15. ibid., p. 536.
16. Steel, op. cit., p. 143.
17. *Venture*, May 1968, quoted in Rose, op. cit., p. 626.
18. Robert Benewick and Trevor Smith (Ed.), *Direct Action and Democratic Politics*, Allen & Unwin, 1973, p. 276.
19. *The Times*, 2 March 1968.
20. For a full account of the passage of the bill, see Steel, op. cit., pp. 132–217 and Rose, op. cit., pp. 610–12.
20a. Street, op. cit., p. 291.
21. *Race Today*, March 1973.
22. See Derek Humphry and Michael Ward, *Passports and Politics*, Penguin, 1974, passim.
23. Street, op. cit., p. 268. For the security methods used, see below, Chapter 8.
24. ibid., p. 193.
24a. ibid., p. 280.

Chapter 4

1. Quoted in Derek Humphry and Gus John, *Police Power and Black People*, Panther, 1972, p. 119. (Under *Introduction to Part Two*).
2. ibid., p. 115.
3. For arguments in favour of a national police force, see Ben Whitaker, *The Police*, Eyre and Spottiswoode, 1964, p. 89 ff; for a full discussion of the constitutional position, Marshall's *Police and Government*, op. cit.
4. Kidd, op. cit., p. 115.
5. Street, op. cit., p. 25.

6. Humphry and John, op. cit., p. 168.

7. Michael Schofield, *The Strange Case of Pot*, Penguin, 1971, p. 145.

8. ibid., p. 159.

9. R. M. Jackson, *Enforcing the Law*, Penguin, 1972, p. 38 ff.

9a. Stacey, op. cit., p. 43.

10. Kidd, op. cit., p. 111.

11. *Guilty Before Innocent*, published by Release, 1973, p. 13.

12. Street, op. cit., p. 38.

13. In a speech to the Annual Conference of Justice, quoted by the N.C.C.L. in *The Rights of Suspects*, p. 6.

14. Whitaker, op. cit., p. 179.

15. Release, op. cit., p. 13.

16. Mary Grigg, *The Challenor Case*, Penguin, 1965, p. 33.

17. ibid., p. 170.

18. Release, op. cit., p. 8.

19. Humphry and John, op. cit., p. 178.

20. Release, op. cit., p. 9.

21. Kidd, op. cit., p. 151.

22. All these are discussed in detail in the Release report, pp. 38–42.

23. Whitaker, op. cit., p. 39.

24. Street, op. cit., p. 32.

25. Grigg. op. cit., pp. 116–18.

26. Whitaker, op. cit., p. 188.

27. Grigg, op. cit., p. 123.

28. Fully documented in Humphry and John, op. cit.

29. For more detailed accounts of the Gomwalk and Quaye affairs, see Humphry and John, op. cit., pp. 54, 68.

30. Quoted in Humphry and John, op. cit., p. 18.

31. The full Challenor story is described by Mary Grigg in *The Challenor Case.*, op. cit

32. Release, op. cit., pp. 38–40.

33. Grigg, op. cit., p. 79.

34. Jackson, op. cit., pp. 114, 121.

35. Stacey, op. cit., p. 48.

Chapter 5

N.B. This chapter draws heavily on the Cobden Trust report *Legal Aid As A Social Service*.

1. *Sunday Times*, 30 November 1969.

2. Release, op. cit., p. 19.

3. ibid., p. 29.
4. Jackson, op. cit., pp. 163–71, which makes a reasoned, if slightly embarrassed, defence of the procedures.
5. Release, op. cit., p. 27.
6. Quoted in Release, op. cit., p. 20

Chapter 6

1. Hepple, op. cit., p. 91.
2. Kidd, op. cit., p. 69 ff. Kidd first made these points in the April 1937 issue of *Civil Liberty*.
3. Paul Foot, op. cit., p. 123; Steel, op. cit., p. 16; Rose, op. cit, p. 65.
4. Erroneously, it seems: Street, op. cit., p. 289.
5. For the detailed proposals, see Pritt, op. cit., p. 52 ff.
6. Street, op. cit., p. 210.
7. Antony Dickey, *English Law and Race Defamation*, New York Law Forum, Spring 1968.
8. Keith Hindell, *Genesis of the Race Relations Bill*, Political Quarterly, October-December 1965.
9. Claudia Jones, editor of *West Indian Gazette*, to Elizabeth Allen.
10. Street, op. cit., p. 290.
11. *The Times*, 11 November 1960.
12. Race Relations Board, annual report 1969–70, p. 50.
13. Hepple, op. cit., p. 129.
14. Hindell, op. cit.
15. Quoted in Hepple, op. cit., p. 94.
16. Dickey, op. cit.
17. Rose, op. cit., p. 292.
18. ibid., p. 221.
19. Quoted in Dickey, op. cit., p. 16. See also Street, op. cit., p. 50; and Williams, op. cit., pp. 169–72.
20. Dickey, op. cit., p. 11.
21. Rose, op. cit., p. 226. For a fuller account, see Anthony Lester and Geoffrey Bindman, *Race and Law*, Penguin, 1972.
22. Hindell, op. cit.; Hepple, op. cit., p. 131.
23. Hindell, op. cit.
24. 8 August 1965.
25. 10 April 1970.
25a. Stacey, op. cit., p. 129.
25b. It is fully discussed in Lester and Bindman, op. cit., pp. 122–49.
25c. Stacey, op. cit., p. 126.

25d. ibid., p. 127.

26. For a detailed analysis of all these prosecutions, see Antony Dickey, *Prosecutions Under the Race Relations Act, 1965, Section 6, 1965–70,* Criminal Law Review 1968, pp. 486–93.

27. Dickey, *English Law and Race Defamation* (op. cit.), p. 26.

28. ibid., p. 25.

Chapter 7

1. Sheila Rowbotham, *Hidden from History*, Pluto Press, 1973, p. 163.

2. Sheila Rowbotham, *Woman's Consciousness, Man's World*, Pelican, 1973, p. ix, quoting Juliet Mitchell, *Women's Estate*.

2a. ibid., p. 98 ff.

3. Anna Coote and Lawrence Grant, *Civil Liberty: The N.C.C.L. Guide*, Penguin, 1972, pp. 274–6.

4. The *Sunday Times* Insight Team, *Ulster*, Penguin, 1972, p. 36.

5. Kidd, op. cit., p. 56.

6. Insight, op. cit., p. 35.

7. Kidd, op. cit., p. 57.

8. Insight, op. cit., p. 17.

9. ibid., p. 41.

10. ibid., pp. 43–4.

11. ibid., p. 45.

11a. For a detailed account of the arrival of the British Army, see Clutterbuck, op. cit., pp. 63–77.

12. ibid., p. 220. By now N.I.C.R.A. had split into 'liberal' and 'radical' wings. Clutterbuck, op. cit., p. 62.

12a. Clutterbuck, op. cit., p. 57.

12b. Stacey, op. cit., pp. 35–7, Clutterbuck, op. cit., p. 101.

13. Clutterbuck, op. cit., p. 280 ff.

13a. Stacey, op. cit., pp. 38–40. Clutterbuck, op. cit., pp. 101–3.

14. Clutterbuck, pp. 110–23, describes the events of 'Bloody Sunday' from the Army's point of view.

Chapter 8

1. David Williams, *Not in the Public Interest*, Hutchinson, 1965, p. 62.

2. Street, op. cit., p. 236.

3. Williams, op. cit., p. 170.

4. ibid., p. 175.

5. ibid., p. 174.
6. Street, op. cit., p. 232.
7. Williams, op. cit., p. 178.
8. ibid., p. 135.
9. Street, op. cit., p. 41.
10. Williams, op. cit., p. 178.
11. ibid., p. 134. Street, op. cit., p. 40.
12. Alan F. Westin, *Privacy and Freedom*, Bodley Head, 1970, p. 9.

Bibliography

Kidd, Ronald, *British Liberty in Danger*, Lawrence & Wishart, 1940.

Williams, David, *Keeping the Peace*, Hutchinson, 1967.
 Not in the Public Interest, Hutchinson, 1965.

Brownlie, Ian, *The Law Relating to Public Order*, Butterworth, 1968.

Marshall, Geoffrey, *Police and Government*, Methuen, 1965.

Bowes, Stuart, *The Police and Civil Liberties*, Lawrence & Wishart, 1966.

Street, Harry, *Freedom, the Individual and the Law*, Penguin, 1967.

Pritt, D. N., *Brasshats and Bureaucrats* (Vol. 2, Autobiography), Lawrence & Wishart, 1966.

Wedderburn, K. W., *The Worker and the Law*, Penguin, 1970, Revised Edition.

Halloran, James D., *Demonstrations and Communication: A Case Study*, Penguin, 1970.

Laurie, Peter, *Scotland Yard*, Bodley Head, 1970.

Foot, Michael, *Aneurin Bevan: Volume 1*, MacGibbon & Kee, 1962.

Driver, C., *The Disarmers: A Study in Protest*, Hodder & Stoughton, 1964.

Foot, Paul, *Immigration and Race in British Politics*, Penguin, 1965.

Martin, Kingsley, *Editor: A Second Volume of Autobiography, 1931–45*, Hutchinson, 1968.

Rolph, C. H., *Books in the Dock*, André Deutsch, 1969.

Montgomerie, John, *The Obscenity Laws*, Arts Council Report, 1969.

Barber, D. F., *Pornography and Society*, Charles Skilton, 1972.

Michael, Richard, *The A.B.Z. of Pornography*, Panther, 1972.

Index No. 2, *On Censorship*, Summer 1972.

Palmer, Tony, *The Trials of Oz*, Blond & Briggs, 1971.

Castles, Stephen and Kosack, Godula, *Immigrant Workers and Class Structures in Western Europe*, Oxford University Press, 1973.

Hepple, Bob, *Race, Jobs and the Law in Britain*, Allen Lane, 1968.

Rose, E. J. B., *Colour and Citizenship: Report on British Race Relationships*, Oxford University Press, 1969.

Steel, David, *No Entry; The Background and Implications of the Commonwealth Immigrants Act, 1968*, C. Hurst, 1969.

Benewick, Robert and Smith, Trevor (Ed.), *Direct Action and Democratic Politics*, Allen & Unwin, 1973.

Humphry, Derek and John, Gus, *Police Power and Black People*, Panther, 1972.

Whitaker, Ben, *The Police*, Eyre & Spottiswoode, 1964.

Schofield, Michael, *The Strange Case of Pot*, Penguin, 1971.

Jackson, R. M., *Enforcing the Law*, Penguin, 1972.

Release, *Guilty Before Innocent* (Report by *Release* Lawyers), 1973.

Grigg, Mary, *The Challenor Case*, Penguin, 1965.

Hindell, Keith, *Genesis of the Race Relations Bill*, Political Quarterly, Oct–Dec. 1965.

Dickey, Antony, *English Law and Race Defamation*, New York Law Forum, Spring 1968.

Prosecutions Under the Race Relations Act, 1965, Criminal Law Review, 1968.

Lester, Anthony and Bindman, Geoffrey, *Race and Law*, Penguin, 1972.

Rowbotham, Sheila, *Hidden from History*, Pluto Press, 1973.

Woman's Consciousness, Man's World, Pelican, 1973.

Coote, Anna and Grant, Lawrence, *Civil Liberty: The N.C.C.L. Guide*, Penguin, 1972.

Insight, *Ulster* (The *Sunday Times* Insight Team), Penguin, 1972.

Westin, Alan F., *Privacy and Freedom*, Bodley Head, 1970.

Trevelyan, John, *What the Censor Saw*, Michael Joseph, 1973.

Stacey, Frank, *A New Bill of Rights for Britain*, David and Charles, 1973.

Clutterbuck, Richard, *Protest and the Urban Guerrilla*, Cassell, 1973.

Humphry, Derek and Ward, Michael, *Passports and Politics*, Penguin, 1974.